BANDITS, PROPHETS, AND MESSIAHS

NEW VOICES IN BIBLICAL STUDIES

Edited by
Adela Yarbro Collins
and
John J. Collins

BANDITS, PROPHETS, AND MESSIAHS

*Popular Movements in the Time
of Jesus*

Richard A. Horsley
and
John S. Hanson

A Seabury Book
WINSTON PRESS
Minneapolis • Chicago • New York

Cover design: Nancy MacLean

The Scripture quotations in this book are from the Revised Standard Version of the Bible, copyrighted 1946, 1952, © 1971, 1973 by the Division of Christian Education of the National Council of the Churches of Christ in the U.S.A., and are used by permission.

Library of Congress Catalog Card Number: 85-51463

ISBN: 0-86683-992-5 (hardcover)
ISBN: 0-86683-993-3 (paperback)

Printed in the United States of America

5 4 3 2 1

Winston Press, Inc.
600 First Avenue North
Minneapolis, Minnesota 55403

CONTENTS

ACKNOWLEDGMENTS

We would like to express appreciation to Professor William R. Poehlmann for his helpful comments and critical reading of the manuscript of chapter 1, and to Joseph Buschini, Mary L. Malone, and James Tracy, each of whom did a careful and critical reading of a substantial portion of an earlier draft of this manuscript. Our thanks also go to John J. Collins and Adela Yarbro Collins, who, as editors, made many valuable suggestions and comments. Finally, we would like to acknowledge partial support for this project through Faculty Development Grants from the University of Massachusetts, Boston, and the University of Kansas.

TABLE OF
ABBREVIATIONS

AB   Anchor Bible
ANRW   *Aufstieg und Niedergang der römischen Welt,*
      ed. H. Temporini and W. Haase
Bib   *Biblica*
CBQ   *Catholic Biblical Quarterly*
DSS   Dead Sea Scrolls
HSM   Harvard Semitic Monographs
HTR   *Harvard Theological Studies*
IDB   *Interpreter's Dictionary of the Bible*
IDBSup *Interpreter's Dictionary of the Bible,*
      Supplement
IEJ   *Israel Exploration Journal*
Int   *Interpretation*
JAAR *Journal of the American Academy of Religion*
JBL   *Journal of Biblical Literature*
JJS   *Journal of Jewish Studies*
JNES *Journal of Near Eastern Studies*
JR   *Journal of Religion*
JRS   *Journal of Roman Studies*
JSJ   *Journal for the Study of Judaism*
LCL   Loeb Classical Library
NovT *Novum Testamentum*
NTS   *New Testament Studies*
SNTSMS Society for New Testament Studies Monograph
      Series

TC   Theological Currents
TDNT   *Theological Dictionary of the New Testament*

BOOKS OF THE APOCRYPHA AND PSEUDEPIGRAPHA

2 Bar.	2 Baruch
1 Enoch	1 Enoch
4 Ezra	4 Ezra
1-2 Macc.	1-2 Maccabees
Ps(s). Sol.	Psalm(s) of Solomon
Sir.	Sirach (Ben Sira)
T. Issachar	Testament of Issachar
T. Levi	Testament of Levi
T. Reuben	Testament of Reuben
T. Simeon	Testament of Simeon

DEAD SEA SCROLLS

1QM	Milḥamah (War Scroll)
1QpHab	Pesher (Commentary) on Habakkuk from Qumran Cave 1
1QSa	Appendix to 1QS (Rule of the Community, or Manual of Discipline)
4QFlor	Florilegium (or *Eschatological Midrashim*) from Qumran Cave 4
4QpNah	Pesher (Commentary) on Nahum from Qumran Cave 4
4QTest	Testimonia Text from Qumran Cave 4

JOSEPHUS

Ag. Ap.	*Against Apion*
Ant.	*Jewish Antiquities*
J.W.	*Jewish War*

INTRODUCTION

RATIONALE AND PURPOSES

Two events that took place in Jewish Palestine during the mid-first century C.E. have been highly significant for subsequent history: the career and death of Jesus of Nazareth and the great Jewish revolt of 66-70. Jesus of Nazareth, a Jewish prophet from the remote district of Galilee, became the focal figure for what has developed into Christianity and become the dominant religious faith and established religious institution in the West. Little more than a generation after the crucifixion of Jesus, the Palestinian Jewish people erupted in a massive revolt against Roman domination which took more than four years to suppress. The consequent devastation of Palestine, including the destruction of the temple and much of the city of Jerusalem, became a great turning point for both the Jewish and Christian religious traditions. In reaction against the apocalyptic spirit and revolutionary impulse, sobered Pharisaic sages laid the foundation not only of a reconstructed Jewish society, but also of what became Rabbinic Judaism. As a result of the Roman suppression of the Jewish revolt, moreover, the nascent Christian movement turned its orientation away from Jerusalem and the temple as a geographic and symbolic center.

In both of these events the Jewish peasantry was the dynamic force, the original source of historical change and

its ramifications. Jesus came from the peasant village of Nazareth. To judge from the synoptic Gospel tradition, which
rarely even mentions any city other than Jerusalem, he spent
most of his career moving from village to village. In the most
distinctive form of his teaching, the parables, he draws analogies from the experiences of Galilean peasant life. Similarly,
in the Jewish revolt, except for the outbreak of the insurrection in Jerusalem itself, the peasantry produced the vast
majority of those who originally drove out the Romans and
who resisted the Roman reconquest of the country. Indeed,
in any traditional society such as Jewish Palestine in the first
century C.E., the peasantry comprise 90 percent or more of
the population.[1]

Yet until very recently, the modern Western assumption
has been that the common people have had little to do with
the making of history.[2] Insofar as any have ever been aware of
the existence of peasants, it is commonly believed that they
were simply very conservative folk pursuing their traditional
way of life and "vegetating in the teeth of time." Standard
treatments of Jewish history and of the background of Jesus
and the Gospels almost always discuss groups and figures
from the ruling class and from the literate middle stratum of
the society, e.g., the Herodians, the high priests and Sadducees, the Pharisees, the Essenes (especially prominent
since the discovery of the Dead Sea Scrolls in 1947), and
usually also the Zealots.[3] However, all of these groups taken
together constituted only a small fraction of the Jewish people at the time of Jesus. Our handbooks give us little or
nothing on the other 90 percent, many of whom, we have
reason to believe, often supplied the motive force in the
history of this period. The reasons for such a gap, such an
ignorance of the bulk of the population in an otherwise
heavily researched period, are not difficult to trace. Most
determinative has been the basic orientation of New Testament studies. As a field whose principal purpose has been to
interpret sacred literature, it has generally focused almost
exclusively on literature, with corresponding attention to the

ruling elites and other literate groups that produced or appeared in the literary records. The other obvious reason for the neglect of the common people is the paucity of sources and evidence.

The Jewish peasantry, however, were largely illiterate and produced no literature, except perhaps for the sayings of, and reports about, Jesus of Nazareth, which were remembered and developed in oral form until written down in the New Testament Gospels. Hence we moderns have almost no access to what the peasants were doing and thinking. Yet despite the fact that the ordinary people of the time did not produce any equivalent to the Dead Sea Scrolls of the Essenes, or the halakic rulings of the Pharisees, or apocalypses of certain other scribes, they did gather together in certain types of groups and movements, as we know from the Jewish historian Josephus, the Christian gospel tradition, and other fragmentary reports. Hence the *first* reason for writing this book is to analyze and present some of the movements and leaders among the common people in the late second temple period.

A second reason for this study is that Palestinian Jewish history must be critically reexamined now that the old "Zealot" concept has been shown to be a historical fiction, with no basis in historical evidence. Since at least the turn of the century, the concept of "the Zealots" has played an important role in scholarly writing on ancient Jewish history and the background of the New Testament as well as in both scholarly and popular views of Jesus. Despite the warnings of a few distinguished American scholars,[4] the view became enshrined in important handbooks and dictionaries in the field that at the time of Jesus there existed a religiopolitical movement of national liberation called "the Zealots."[5] According to the usual scholarly construct, the Zealot party was the same as the Fourth Philosophy founded by Judas of Galilee in opposition to enrollment for the tribute imposed along with direct Roman rule in 6 C.E., and its members,

called interchangeably "Sicarii" and "brigands" by
Josephus, agitated for Jewish liberation until they finally provoked the massive revolt in 66. This view has served an
important function in the concerns of many modern theolo-
gians and biblical scholars. As the supposed fanatical advo-
cates of violent revolution against the Romans, the "Zealots"
served as a convenient foil over against which to portray
Jesus of Nazareth as a sober prophet of pacifist love of one's
enemies. Especially in the last two decades, many European
and American scholars, responding to domestic protest and
Third-World movements of national liberation, attempted to
ward off any implication that Jesus had advocated active
resistance of any sort to the established order by contrasting
Jesus with the "Zealots".[6] The "Zealots", leaders of a Jewish
people united against Roman domination, served equally
well as a historical precedent for the Zionist cause or the
modern Jewish state fighting for its survival against hostile
neighboring states. The ancient fortress of Masada, where
supposedly the last remaining band of Zealots held out valiantly against the Roman siege, finally committing mass suicide rather than "surrender" to the alien conquerors,
became a rallying symbol for modern Israel: "Masada shall
not fall again!"[7]

Unfortunately for these studies (and the concerns of their
authors), "the Zealots" as a movement of rebellion against
Roman rule did not come into existence until the winter of
67-68 C.E., that is, until the middle of the great revolt.[8] There
is simply no evidence for an organized, religiously motivated
movement advocating armed revolt against Rome from 6-66
C.E. Otherwise, for the sixty years prior to the revolt there was
an assortment of separate and unconnected movements and
events. Among these diverse movements, the group called
Sicarii and the groups properly called brigands were not only
different from the Zealots proper, but were themselves distinctive social movements (as we shall explain further).[9] The
recognition that "the Zealots" is a modern scholarly construct and has little relation to actual Jewish history in the

first century will require several reformulations and open-
ness to new perceptions about first-century Jewish society.

First, most of the ideas believed to be distinctive to the
Zealots, almost all of them relatively widely attested in our
limited sources, were probably common Palestinian Jewish
ideas. Except for the high priests and Sadducees, the various
Jewish groups of the time were distinguished less by any
differences in theological-political concepts and eschatological orientation than by their actions or application of those
ideas and their particular social-economic interests. Second,
once we remove the log of "the Zealots" from our eye, it may
be possible to discern significant similarities (as well as differences) between Jesus and one or another of the distinctive movements that previously were lumped together,
artificially forming one monolithic liberation movement.
Third, the rallying symbol of Masada as the Zealots' last stand
may be left without any historical basis. Fourth, opposition to
the Roman rule of Jewish Palestine may have been far more
widespread and spontaneous, although perhaps less politically conscious, than previously imagined when opposition
was believed to be concentrated in the one organized Zealot
movement that was supposedly attempting to provoke
revolution for sixty years before it succeeded. Nearly all of
the movements and events were anti-Roman in orientation,
and especially the more organized movements led by popular prophets or messiahs were consciously seeking a particular sort of liberation. Finally, nearly all of the separate
movements were popular groups directed against the Jewish
ruling elite as well as against Roman rule.

Once "the Zealots" as a unified and decades-old liberation front is seen to be a modern fiction with no basis in
historical evidence, in what terms do we now understand the
developments in Jewish society of the first century C.E., in
particular, the background of Jesus and the resistance to
Roman rule that eventually erupted in widespread revolt?
The situation in Jewish society was clearly more complex

than imagined under the concept of a single organized resistance movement. The social unrest took a variety of concrete
social forms. More precisely stated, therefore, the second
reason for this study is to examine and to delineate these
concrete social forms of popular unrest. Of the movements
to be examined, the most politically conscious and deliberate were the Fourth Philosophy and the Sicarii, or "dagger
men," who carried out a program of symbolic assassination
against members of the priestly aristocracy in the late fifties
and sixties—a movement led by, and apparently comprised
largely of, "intelligentsia". But far more frequent and prominent were the many movements among the peasantry.
Besides the widespread banditry, which became epidemic
just prior to the revolt of 66-70, there were popular movements which appear to have been distinctive to Jewish society. These include messianic movements and prophetic
movements, as well as the occurrence of a type of popular
prophet reminiscent of the great oracular prophets of
Hebrew scriptures. A reading and analysis of the limited
evidence for these movements and leaders should help us
gain a clearer sense of what was occurring among the people
at the time of Jesus and just prior to the great revolt.

A third reason for this study also pertains to the delineation of these popular movements. New Testament studies,
already oriented to sacred *literature,* seeks to interpret the
meaning of scriptural words, prophecies, stories, symbols,
etc. As such, it is drawn to a focus on ideas and the history of
ideas, aided by its close relation with theology. Furthermore,
the interpretation of the significance of Jesus for Christian
faith and theology is of central importance for New Testament studies. Thus, even historical-critical studies of New
Testament Christology, interpreting the roles and titles
applied to Jesus, tend to concentrate on Jewish "expectations" of "the messiah" or "eschatological prophet," etc.[10]
We are now becoming aware of two ironies about this procedure. Evidence for such "expectations" is taken from literature, that is, material produced by literate groups such as the

Pharisees, who were apparently (at least initially) uninterested in, if not simply opposed to, Jesus and his movement. More importantly, in recent decades it has been realized that there is precious little textual (or other) evidence prior to the time of Jesus for those synthetically constructed "job descriptions" which Jesus was found to fulfill so nicely.[11] It may turn out that the most secure bits of evidence available, prior to the time of Jesus, for comparative material for christological interpretation of his role(s) and socioreligious significance are not "expectations" found in Jewish literature, written by intellectuals, but the actual concrete leaders and movements among the peasants, datable within two or three decades of Jesus' own activity.

There is also a fourth and more contemporary reason for the material this book presents. Every generation brings new and different questions to biblical history and other traditions of significance to us. In the northern Atlantic countries, where the peasantry had almost ceased to exist in the wake of twentieth-century industrialization and urbanization, we have only recently rediscovered the existence of peasants. The aristocratic elite or governing classes of traditional societies have almost always looked upon the peasants who made their own more luxurious life-style possible as somehow less than fully human. Many of us in the modern West have simply been oblivious to the existence of a peasantry. Marx and his early followers were aware of the reality of peasants, but they did not have much respect for, or confidence in, them (as a revolutionary force). Lenin, however, and especially Mao, realized that peasants could be mobilized to effect the overthrow of autocratic or imperialist regimes that had oppressed them. Nevertheless, even after the French experience in Vietnam and Algeria, it came as a surprise to Americans that the peasantry could be, as Barrington Moore suggests, the dynamite that destroys the old order.[12] With the recent American experience in Vietnam, the rise of liberation theology and base communities in Latin

America, and our increasing awareness that sharply repressive regimes in Latin America and elsewhere can evoke
organized resistance, particularly among the peasantry, we
are sharpening our interest in the Israelite and Jewish peasantry which figures so prominently in biblical history. Thus,
insofar as the material below helps to illuminate conditions
and events among the Jewish peasantry at the time and more
indirectly to illuminate the activity of Jesus and his movement, the book may be relevant to some of the new questions
now being brought to biblical history.

METHODS AND LIMITATIONS

This study of popular movements and leaders is limited and
simple. By means of the usual techniques of historical-critical analysis, we are attempting to delineate the social history
of selected groups. Perhaps the most distinctive—and problematic—aspect of this study is its deliberate focus on popular groups. Awareness of and interest in the peasantry are
relatively recent, but not unprecedented, in biblical studies
and Jewish history. In recent years Hebrew Bible scholars
have dealt with early Israel in terms of a peasant society.[13]
There are also indications that New Testament scholars and
historians of Jewish history are realizing that Palestinian
society in the first centuries B.C.E./C.E. consisted largely of
peasants, and are beginning to raise the appropriate sociological questions.[14] Once the importance of the peasantry in
biblical history has been recognized, however, one wants to
know far more than is in fact possible. At the outset we must
acknowledge that there are serious limitations on our study.
We are limited in certain ways both by the sources available
and by the elementary stage of development of our analytical
tools as applied to the sources.

   The Jewish peasantry left no literary remains, except, as
already mentioned, their influence on the gospel traditions.
The amount of archaeological evidence is at present
extremely limited, although archaeologists of the period are

beginning to shift more of their investigations from the remains of the urban locus of the ruling class to the remains of agricultural producers in villages and towns. The principal source of our fragmentary knowledge remains the reports of Josephus in his histories of the Jewish people and the Jewish War.[15] But even this source is complicated by the fact that he is biased against, and even hostile to, the common people. Josephus wrote from the standpoint of a former general of Jewish forces in Galilee fighting against the Romans after he duplicitously tried to check the progress of the revolt in anticipation of Roman victory. It was in Rome and for the Roman victors and their upper classes that he wrote, in their terms, of the remote and alien province of Judea. Similarly, his basic sympathies for the upper levels of Judean society are also evident. As for the peasants, who occupy so much of his narrative in *War,* they should stick, he implies, to producing crops and leave the conduct of serious affairs to the wellborn and educated, such as Josephus himself.

Certain literary features of Josephus's writings also make the use of his material more difficult. Both *Jewish War* and *Jewish Antiquities* have literary models, and each contains occasional allusions to prominent authors.[16] Both of these features, among others, serve to enhance Josephus's status as author and apologist. At the same time, however, they tend to obscure, intentionally or not, precisely what we seek to uncover. For example, as has long been noted, the sketch of John of Gischala, important to this study (see chapter 5), seems heavily affected by Sallust's characterization of Catiline, despite the fact that Josephus had firsthand dealings with John and harbored intense dislike of him. Further complicating our reading of Josephus, though not taken as a special issue in the following chapters, is the fact that a comparison of *War, Antiquities,* and the highly apologetic *Life* reveals many contradictions or differences in emphasis, some directly affecting our material. The differing motives in each of these works explain some of these tensions. In general, however, these works are self-serving, pro-Roman, defensive of the Jewish elite, certainly antirevolutionary, and, in effect, antipeasant. Thus, our primary source presents a number of complications and makes demands on our analytical tools.

A conceptual apparatus appropriate to understanding sociopolitical realities is in an elementary stage of development in the fields of biblical study and Jewish history. We are, of course, more and more seeking help from the social sciences.[17] However, we may want to maintain some critical perspective on what we borrow.

One respect in which our use of social scientific methods may be limited pertains to the type of society we may be studying. It was not until the 1950s and 1960s that the social sciences discovered "peasant societies" as a distinctive social type. As one of the leaders of this discovery wrote: "It seems to us that a societal type that has existed for from 6000 to 7000 years,—i.e., since the beginning of civilization— deserves recognition in its own right, not as 'intermediate' or 'transitional,' but as a genuine social and cultural form to which half or more of the people who have lived since time began have conformed."[18] We may be able to glean a great deal from anthropological and sociological generalizations and comparative materials on peasant societies. Yet extreme caution is necessary precisely in such extrapolations from certain ethnographic studies and general sociological models concerning peasant societies. Certainly no attempt at a complete sociology of Palestinian society is possible at present. Indeed, until more detailed archaeological, anthropological, and sociological analyses of Palestinian Jewish society are carried out, our knowledge may be so limited that such comparisons and contrasts must remain tentative and provisional.

Second, in attempting to understand the social conflicts which both underlay and came to expression in movements among the Jewish peasantry, we cannot simply adopt the approach of structural-functional sociology which has been so dominant in the United States until recently,[19] and which

provides some of the sociological method now being utilized in New Testament study.[20] What requires explanation,
especially in a "traditional" society such as Jewish Palestine
under Roman rule, is not the equilibrium of the whole system and the "function" of various groups within that system,
but the social turmoil and the frequent popular protests and
even uprisings. The salient characteristics of this period are
turmoil and revolt. The dynamic force in the situation, religiously and politically—to repeat the point—appears to have
been movements among the peasantry.

A third respect in which we can only make a qualified
acceptance and adaptation of social science pertains to the
broad comparative and often abstract character of much sociological study. In particular terms, this may be true even of
aspects of the broad comparative method of Max Weber,
even where his purpose was explanation of large-scale historical change—for example, in the use of the concept of
"charisma." The concept of "charismatic leadership" would
fit most of the popular leaders discussed in the chapters
below. They arise in times of distress. They stand over against
the established traditional institutional leaders of society.
Each holder of charisma, moreover, seizes the task that is
adequate for him and demands obedience and a following by
virtue of his mission.[21] Such a concept enables us to discern
primarily what is similar between leaders in the first century
and, in a broad cross-cultural comparison, all other "charismatic leaders" in any number of other societies in similar
circumstances. We recognize the usefulness of a comparative
approach which gathers illustrations from various historical
contexts to construct a composite or general picture of leadership and movements.

We have attempted, however, to avoid direct use of such
social scientific concepts (as well as traditional theologically
determined concepts). If we are attempting to gain a more
precise view of the social context and social history of Jewish
Palestine in the first century, then a move toward more

abstract sociological concepts may obscure rather than elucidate the material. For example, it is difficult to see what is
gained by labeling all prophets, regardless of social role or
location, with the highly abstract and general term
"*intermediaries*," if one is interested in discerning their particular relation to their social context.[22] Indeed, Worsley's
adaptation of Weber's concept of charisma to refer to social
relationships in social context encourages particularization
rather than abstraction. Charisma, far from being an attribute
of individual personality, must be understood as a social
relationship. "Followers . . . cleave to an appropriate
leader because he articulates and consolidates their aspirations."[23] Any such "aspirations," however, will be historically
specific and thus culturally determined. It would appear,
then, that precision in our understanding of the groups and
leaders at the time of Jesus can best be sought by focusing on
how particular groups of people responded to particular historical circumstances, as well as how distinctive Jewish traditions may have informed that response. This attempt to
delineate what was distinctive in the social forms of Jewish
popular movements will also entail some investigation of the
possible patterns or prototypes in the traditions from ancient
Israelite-Jewish society which may have influenced (and
which may help elucidate) those distinctive features of the
popular movements and leaders. That is, our attempt to
delineate particular social forms will require attention to
particular features of Jewish historical-cultural heritage as
well as a comparative perspective.

Because of the limitations of evidence and method, we can
attempt only to present a simple sociohistorical typology of
movements and leaders among the common people in the
late second temple period. The social analysis in the chapters to follow is of necessity fairly elementary. Basically the
procedure is to discern as precisely as possible the distinctive social forms taken by popular movements and leaders,

and to present the available material according to the particular social types or forms which appear to have been the
most prominent.

The study is also written with an attempt at sensitivity to
the concerns of the peasantry and a corresponding attempt at
a critical evaluation of the viewpoint of the ruling and literate groups, whose viewpoint is usually represented in most
extant literary sources (with the notable exception of the
Gospels). At the same time, we present wherever possible
the primary sources, despite the fact that they are primarily
from the problematic Josephus. We believe the stu-
dents/readers should have the principal sources directly
before them. Furthermore, most do not have a copy of
Josephus's histories at hand, and the appropriate references
are scattered throughout several "books" in Josephus's
accounts. They should also have the chance to make their
own judgments about historical sources and historical subject matter. All the Josephus translations, moreover, are new
and attempt to avoid the tendentious qualities of previous
renderings.

In the course of presenting this typology of Jewish groups
and leaders, several other matters are necessarily dealt with.
Thus, while the following chapters are not designed to
explain the causes of the revolt of 66-70, since this has been
done before, they in fact deal with many of those causes, but
they do so only secondarily and as a result of trying to clarify
certain movements among the peasantry in this period. Sec-
ondly, inasmuch as only a few movements are described and
analyzed, this is in no sense a complete social history of first
century C.E. Jewish Palestine. Thirdly, it is not our *goal* to
provide a context for an understanding of Jesus. Yet because
Jesus himself spoke to, and circulated primarily among, the
peasantry, our delineation of a number of features of peasant
life and experience has the consequence of providing material suitable, indeed perhaps even necessary, for interpreting
the message and activities of the historical Jesus of Nazareth

and his movement. Finally, although this is also not a revi-
sionist history of first-century Palestine, its sketches of particular forms of social unrest and resistance may serve as a
partial treatment of Palestinian Jewish history which leads up
to the revolt of 66-70. The study does, however, rely on a very
important rereading of the sources available in connection
with the "Zealots."

In the first chapter we present a sketch of the historical
background of the movements, not only for the period of
Roman domination itself, but also, however briefly, for the
prior (biblical) history of Israel and Judea. This more
extended background is important because the history and
historical traditions out of which the Jewish people of
Roman times emerged informed their memories and hopes.
The more immediate historical background in the Hellenizing reform, the Hellenistic persecution, and the popular
resistance to it formed the crucial historical watershed of the
apocalypticism which apparently permeated much of the
society then and at points thereafter. It was also a watershed
of the common people's more active involvement in the
periodic social-political turmoil of the times.

The second chapter focuses on the most rudimentary of
the groups to which social-economic turmoil gave rise,
social banditry. The frequency of social banditry in agrarian
societies has in many ways been an index of the degree of
social-economic change or disruption of the conditions of
the peasantry. Thus the examination of the social-economic
circumstances of Palestinian Jewish society at the beginning
of chapter 2 can also help ascertain why so many people were
prepared to form other, more sophisticated movements as
well as simply to flee to the hills to join a brigand band. A
sense of these social-economic conditions is important for
understanding any and all of these movements. Peasants
tend not to take such drastic action, abandoning homes and
land, unless their old life-patterns are no longer tolerable or
possible. The bulk of chapter 2 is devoted to an examination
of social banditry, both as an interesting phenomenon in

itself and as a revealing symptom of the disruption of the people's lives by factors beyond their control and comprehension.

Chapters 3 and 4 examine several movements and leaders which appear to represent particular social forms, all of which are distinctive to Palestinian Jewish society. It is important, therefore, to explore the ways in which each of them may have been informed by the historical-cultural traditions of Israel and Judea. For this reason, both of these chapters begin respectively with a portrayal of the Israelite heritage of popular messianic movements and of popular prophets of two types. Simultaneously, since the messianic and prophetic leaders will be the most attractive for comparison with Jesus of Nazareth, these sketches may serve the second purpose of background to the ways in which Jesus was, or came to be, understood. The second step in each chapter is to examine the circumstances which may have given rise to the revival of these particular forms from the cultural heritage or people's memory. These more precise sketches of social conditions, of course, presuppose both the background in chapter 1 and the discussion of social-economic conditions at the beginning of chapter 2. Finally, the balance of chapters 3 and 4 is devoted to the several concrete movements or figures which belong to the respective types: popular kings/messiahs and their followers, popular prophets and their movements, and oracular prophets.

Chapter 5 is included because of the prominence which the false concept of the Zealots has assumed in the fields of New Testament and Jewish history. Even though parts of its subject matter are not strictly peasant movements, it seems important to describe them because they have been unhistorically lumped together as "the Zealots." They are not only different from the Zealots, but emerge from very different social strata. Thus, we examine, as precisely as space allows, first the Fourth Philosophy (a group active in resistance to the census in 6 C.E.), then the Sicarii, or assassins (a terrorist group in the fifties), and finally the Zealots proper, who emerged as a group only in the middle of the Jewish revolt, no earlier than the winter of 67-68.

Throughout we have attempted to write with our students as well as our scholarly colleagues in mind. Thus we have tried to balance analytical presentation with narrative. We have also endeavored to avoid technical terms and frequent reference to secondary literature. Those who may be interested in more documented presentations with more elaborate references and engagement with the fields of New Testament studies and Jewish history may consult the notes for references to the articles which represent the first public manifestations of the research on which the chapters are based.

NOTES

1. See, for example, G. Sjoberg, *The Preindustrial City* (New York: Free, 1960/1966), 110.
2. See B. Moore, *Social Origins of Dictatorship and Democracy* (Boston: Beacon, 1966), 453-83.
3. A representative sample might include G. Bornkamm, *Jesus of Nazareth* (New York: Harper & Row, 1960), 34-44; R.A. Spivey and D. M. Smith, *Anatomy of the New Testament,* 3rd ed. (New York: Macmillan, 1982), 13-34; E. Schürer, *The History of the Jewish People in the Age of Jesus Christ (175 B.C.—A.D. 135),* vol. 2, rev. and ed. G. Vermes, F. Millar, and M. Black (Edinburgh: Clark, 1979).
4. K. Lake, "Appendix A: The Zealots," in *The Beginnings of Christianity,* 5 vols., ed. K. Lake and F. J. Foakes-Jackson (London/New York: Macmillan, 1920-1933), 1:421-25; S. Zeitlin, "Zealots and Sicarii," *JBL* 81 (1962): 395-98.
5. A representative sample: K. Kohler, "The Zealots," in *The Jewish Encyclopedia* (New York: Funk & Wagnalls, 1905); W. R. Farmer, "Zealot," *IDB* 4:936-39; H. Merkel, "Zealot," *IDBSup* 979-82; and the works cited in n. 3.
6. E.g., O. Cullmann, *Jesus and the Revolutionaries* (New York: Harper & Row, 1970), who also reprints the Kohler article (see n. 5) as an appendix; M. Hengel, *Was Jesus a Revolutionist?*

(Philadelphia: Fortress, 1971) and *Victory over Violence* (Philadelphia: Fortress, 1973), both of which draw on his earlier work, *Die Zeloten* (Leiden: Brill, 1961).

7. See, for example, Y. Yadin, *Masada: Herod's Fortress and the Zealots' Last Stand* (New York: Random House, 1966). S. Applebaum, "The Zealots: the Case for Revaluation," *JRS* 61 (1971): 156-70, was basically a restatement of the standard synthetic view.

8. See S. Zeitlin, in n. 4; esp. M. Smith, "Zealots and Sicarii: Their Origins and Relations," *HTR* 64 (1971): 1-19; M. Stern, "Sicarii and Zealots," in *World History of the Jewish People*, 1st ser., vol. 8, ed. M. Avi-Yonah (New Brunswick: Rutgers University, 1977), chap. 8, and *Encyclopedia Judaica*, ed. C. Roth et al., suppl. vol., 1972 (Jerusalem: Keter, 1974) 135-52, is aware that the historical evidence does not support a continuous unified group called the Zealots, but appears to defend the continuity of some sort of resistance movement through the concept of "zeal."

9. See R.A. Horsley, "Josephus and the Bandits," *JSJ* 10 (1979): 37-63, and "The Sicarii: Ancient Jewish Terrorists," *JR* 59 (1979): 435-58.

10. E.g., O. Cullmann, *The Christology of the New Testament*, rev. ed. (Philadelphia: Westminster, 1964); F. Hahn, *The Titles of Jesus in Christology* (New York: World, 1969).

11. See M. de Jonge, "The Use of the Word 'Anointed' in the Time of Jesus," *NovT* 8 (1966): 132-48; E. Rivkin, "Messiah, Jewish," *IDBSup* (1976): 588-91.

12. B. Moore, *Social Origins of Dictatorship and Democracy* (see n. 2.).

13. See G. Mendenhall, *The Tenth Generation* (Baltimore: Johns Hopkins, 1973); N. Gottwald, *The Tribes of Yahweh: A Sociology of the Religion of Liberated Israel, 1250-1000 B.C.* (Maryknoll: Orbis, 1979); M. Chaney, "Ancient Palestinian Peasant Movements and the Formation of Premonarchic Israel," in *Palestine in Transition: The Emergence of Ancient Israel*, ed. D. N. Freedman and D. F. Graf (Sheffield: Almond, 1983), 39-89.

14. E.g., S. Applebaum, "Judaea as a Roman Province: the Countryside as a Political and Economic Factor," in *Aufstieg und*

Niedergang der römischen Welt, 2nd ser., vol. 8, ed. H. Temporini and W. Haase (Berlin: de Gruyter, 1977), 355-96.

15. For a summary of Josephus' life and works, see E. Schürer, *History of the Jewish People,* vol. 2, 43-63, with [older] bibliography. Some recent studies include T. Rajak, *Josephus: The Historian and His Society* (Philadelphia: Fortress, 1984); S. J. D. Cohen, *Josephus in Galilee and Rome: His Vita and Development as a Historian* (Leiden: Brill, 1979), with bibliography; H. Attridge, *The Interpretation of Biblical History in the Antiquitates Judaicae of Flavius Josephus,* HDR 7 (Missoula: Scholars, 1976).

16. For *Jewish War* one finds the parallel *Gallic War* of Julius Caesar; for *Jewish Antiquities,* Dionysius of Halicarnassus' *Roman Antiquities.* Authors to whom allusions have been seen include Sophocles, Herodotus, Thucydides, Demosthenes.

17. Besides Chaney and Gottwald (see n. 13), see J. Gager, *Kingdom and Community: The Social World of Early Christianity* (Englewood Cliffs: Prentice-Hall, 1975); H.C. Kee, *Christian Origins in Sociological Perspective: Methods and Resources* (Philadelphia: Westminster, 1980); E. Schüssler-Fiorenza, *In Memory of Her: A Feminist Theological Reconstruction of Christian Origins* (New York: Crossroad, 1983).

18. G. M. Foster, "What is a Peasant?" in *Peasant Society: A Reader* (Boston: Little, Brown, 1967), 12.

19. E.g., R. Dahrendorf, "Out of Utopia: Toward a Reorientation of Social Analysis," *American Journal of Sociology* 64 (1958): 115-27, and *Class and Class Conflict in Industrial Society* (Stanford: Stanford University, 1959); A. Gouldner, *The Coming Crisis of Western Sociology* (New York: Basic, 1970); M. Harris, *The Rise of Anthropological Theory: A History of Theories of Culture* (New York: Crowell, 1968), chap. 19.

20. E.g., G. Theissen, *Sociology of Early Palestinian Christianity* (Philadelphia: Fortress, 1978).

21. See *From Max Weber,* ed. H. H. Gerth and C. W. Mills (New York: Oxford, 1958), 245-52; H. C. Kee, *Christian Origins,* 54-56.

22. R. R. Wilson, *Prophecy and Society in Ancient Israel* (Philadelphia: Fortress, 1980), with bibliography.

23. P. Worsley, *The Trumpet Shall Sound: A Study of Cargo Cults in Melanesia,* 2nd ed. (New York: Schocken, 1968), xii-xiv.

CHAPTER ONE

Historical Background

Until the final climactic events in Jerusalem, Jesus of Nazareth had circulated primarily among the Jewish peasantry in Galilean villages. The Gospel narratives which recount his activity have always struck those familiar with the literature of the Greek and Roman world as markedly different. One gets a picture of life far removed from the urbane and cosmopolitan world. As one distinguished scholar writes, "The narrative presents a world of two classes, the very rich and the poor. There is the Rich Man, or Prince, with his steward, and the peasantry who owe debts of a hundred measures of oil or wheat" (see Lk. 16:1-6).[1] There is a similar contrast in the parable of the king and the two debtors in Mt. 18:23-35. The story of the prodigal son (Lk. 15:11-32) "reflects a small peasant economy—a few hired servants and a single beast kept for a special feast."[2]

The fact that the Gospel narratives about Jesus' actions and sayings are so different from the "classical" literature of Greece and Rome has clear implications for us as readers, even if we are interested only in the Bible as literature, but especially if our interests extend to the concrete lives of the people portrayed in the Gospels. As our distinguished classics scholar explains,

> It is a principle of modern literary criticism to consider the poet or author in relation to his audience. Christ primarily addresses the crowds, and his illustrations must have been

1

chosen with their preoccupations in mind. . . . If the scale
of wealth and the proportion seems different in the Galilean
scene from the pattern of organized wealth in the more developed areas of the Hellenistic world, that is as likely to reflect
the actual situation in Galilee as the bias of the writer or
speaker.[3]

These comments, however, would appear to hold not simply
for the Gospels, Jesus, and Galilee, but for Palestinian Jewish
society in general in the first century C.E. Jewish Palestine as
a whole was clearly a peasant society. As Josephus explains in
his *Against Apion,*

> We are not a sea-going people, and take no pleasure in trade
> or in the dealings with others that result from it. Our cities are
> built far from the sea, and we cultivate intensively the fertile
> land we share. (1.60)

Josephus simply takes it for granted that those who actually
cultivate the "fertile land" are Jewish peasants living in the
"thickly distributed towns" and "densely populated villages" he speaks of elsewhere (see *J.W.* 3.43).

A peasant society, however, is not simply a matter of two
static classes, wealthy and poor. For the poor produce "surpluses" which are controlled by the wealthy, with the result
that conflicts between the two groups are almost unavoida-
ble. The wealthy and powerful tend to use and abuse their
power in ways that are detrimental and unfair to the peasants,
and the peasant-producers build up hostilities and resent-
ments which make the powerful anxious lest the poor strike
back at them. Besides the repeated appearance of such in
Josephus' histories (as we shall see in subsequent chapters),
they are vividly illustrated in the Gospels as well. Jesus'
opening words in Luke's "Sermon on the Plain," for example, offer hope for the peasants, but sound rather ominous
for the powerful:

> Blessed are you poor, for yours is the kingdom of God. . . .
> But woe to you that are rich, for you have received your
> consolation. (Lk. 6:20, 24)

One suspects that Jesus' parable of the vineyard (Mk. 12:1-9) only too well exemplifies the tensions in such a society, with its escalation into violent confrontation between the resentful tenants and the owner of the vineyard. It is not surprising, in light of such a social structure and its potential for conflict, that when "the chief priests and the scribes and the elders" confronted Jesus face-to-face in the temple at the Passover festival, they were more than a little apprehensive in their dealings with him, "for they were afraid of the people" (Mk. 11:27-33).

Indeed, the Jewish ruling groups had good reason to be "afraid of the people," for the common people were not docile and passively resigned to their situation in life. They held *ideals* of what life *should be* like, and a *memory* which informed and buttressed those ideals. They remembered times when their forefathers had been free, and not under the control of domestic or foreign overlords; and they remembered previous conflicts in which their forebears had become subjected, but were able successfully to reassert their freedom. The Hebrew Bible is filled with just such stories of the ancient Israelite and Jewish peasants. Although the Jewish peasants could not actually read Hebrew (except for the few who might have become scribes or Pharisees), they apparently knew the stories and remembered their own history in oral form.

The difference between the Bible in its established written form and the popular memory of its contents parallels the distinction commonly made by anthropologists between the "great tradition" and the "little tradition."[4] In a society such as that of ancient Jewish Palestine, like that of ancient Israel before it, there were two levels of cultural tradition. At the official level, in the established religion and political administration, a professional group of scribes and priests reflectively systematized and codified the important memories and stories, as well as laws and official documents. At the popular level, however, memories, tales, and mores were also remembered. The two levels of tradition, moreover, were interdependent. It was long ago recognized in biblical studies, as well as in anthropology, that the fact that the ruling elite sponsors literature and gives written form to a people's memories does not mean that they originate all cultural traditions. Further, once traditions have been given fixed, even official, written form, that form does not become the only means by which those particular traditions will be further transmitted. For example, certain stories about a people's ancestors may originate among tribal storytellers, then be given epic literary form by established scribes or priests, which in turn may influence the ongoing oral narrative form of the epic among the common people. The "great" and "little" (or popular) traditions may develop different emphases and uses for given cultural materials, but there is usually continuing interaction between them. In fact, it is precisely because we can confidently posit this interaction in the case of Jewish biblical tradition that we can speak in terms of the peasants' cultural memory as a factor in their historical actions and interactions.

It is by now a truism in theological and biblical studies that, for Israelite and Jewish faith, the people's history was a major arena in which they encountered and interacted with God and God's will. Therefore, to understand the popular movements and leaders among the peasantry in the first century C.E., it may be especially important to sketch the history from which they emerged, and which formed their memories and shaped their ideals. At the same time, we should keep in mind the two-class social structure that persisted from biblical Israel to Jewish Palestine. For such a structure, when more than 90 percent are peasants dominated by a small minority, is subject to almost inevitable tensions that are a major factor in its historical development.

ISRAEL'S ORIGINS AS A FREE PEASANTRY IN COVENANT WITH GOD

As the biblical stories of origins describe leaders such as Moses, Joshua, and other liberators, it is apparent that Israel originated as a free and independent people, with no ruling class over their heads. The exodus was clearly the paradigmatic story (later celebrated each year in the Passover festival) identifying their God as the one "who brought you out of the land of Egypt, out of the house of bondage" (Ex. 20:2). In their very origins, the Israelites had escaped from servitude to foreign rulers. Under Joshua they had come into independent possession of their land, assisted by God in their overthrowing the kings and cities (e.g., "Jericho") who then ruled the land of promise. According to one of the stories, Joshua had said to the people who, typically for peasants, held their ruling class in awe, "Come near, put your feet upon the necks of these kings. . . . Do not be afraid or dismayed; be strong and of good courage" (Josh. 10:24-25).

Not only did the early Israelites, under the leadership of Yahweh (and Moses, Joshua, Deborah, etc.), establish their independence as a peasantry free of any ruling class, they also formed a covenant with Yahweh and each other to maintain that freedom. Understood to have been given originally by God on Sinai through the mediation of Moses, and renewed at Shechem through Joshua's leadership (and periodically thereafter), the "Sinaitic" or "Mosaic" covenant functioned like a constitution for early Israel. God himself was their ruler and object of exclusive loyalty: "You shall have no other gods. . . ." Because *God* was the true king, there could be no human institution of kingship, no state in early Israel. Nor was their dynamic, transcendent ruler bound to a particular space: tribal Israel had no established temple cult. Overall social organization and religiopolitical coherence were provided through the covenant, through its periodic renewal, and through cooperation in warfare to

maintain their independence. Although threatened by conquest from without and by disintegration from within, the
free and independent peasantry of Israel managed to maintain itself for over 200 years in the hill country where the
chariot forces of the remaining Canaanite kings could not
effectively bring them under subjection (Judg. 5).[5]

Through the collective memory of the people, eventually
in the form of biblical stories, these circumstances of the
peasantry (free of overlords and kings, independent of foreign domination, living under the rule of God in a just and
egalitarian social order) became a reference point for subsequent generations, a utopian ideal over against which later
subjection to kings and foreign empires was measured and
found contrary to the will of God. As later generations of
Israelites believed, to judge from those who spoke for them,
such as the biblical prophets, the God of Israel remained
concerned to keep his people free of foreign bondage and
domestic oppression.

ESTABLISHMENT OF THE MONARCHY OVER ISRAEL AND PROPHETIC PROTEST

The Iron Age (ca. 1200-1000 B.C.E.) brought a serious threat
to Israel's independence. With newly developed military
technology, the Philistine warlords could operate effectively
in the hill country. During the eleventh century they spread
their hegemony from the coastal plain over nearly the whole
of Palestine. Israel resisted successfully, but only after the
people turned to centralized religiopolitical forms: the charismatic leader David was recognized as the *messiah,* the
anointed of Yahweh. After leading a successful resistance
against the Philistines, he eventually conquered the whole of
Palestine, including the remaining Canaanite city-states.
David established a monarchic state in Israel, a kingship
which was of the imperial type characteristic of the nations
which Israel had, up to that point, considered the great

threat to its more egalitarian way of life. The monarchy now stood in a mediating position between the Israelites and their God. The previously free tribes of Israel were now ruled from the capital in Jerusalem, the "city of David." Divine legitimation of the new monarchic order was now centered in the temple, built by David's son Solomon on Zion, the sacred mountain. The monarchy itself was understood as divinely ordained through a prophetic oracle in which God promised to perpetuate the Davidic dynasty forever (see 2 Sam. 7:14). Further, the development of "Israel" into a great nation, as represented by the Davidic monarchy, was seen as the fulfillment of an ancient promise to the great ancestors of the tribes of Israel, Abraham, Isaac, and Jacob/Israel.

Yet the Israelite peasantry did not submit to the new monarchical form easily. There were two widespread revolts against the messiah David himself,[6] and at the end of Solomon's lavish rule, ten of the Israelite tribes rebelled and formed a separate, initially less absolutist kingdom in the north, *Israel.* The Davidic dynasty, however, continued to rule the small kingdom of Judah for 400 years.

In the northern kingdom, the Israelite peasantry, or at least significant parts of it, appears never to have resigned itself to monarchic subjection. There, the classical oracular prophets Amos and Hosea not only pronounced judgment on the rulers for the oppression of the people, but criticized the institution of kingship itself (e.g., Amos 5:10-11; Hos. 8:1, 4, 14). In so doing, they were harking back to the ideals of early Israel, using the original Mosaic covenantal principles as their criteria. Although the kingdom of Judah's peasantry appears to have more readily adjusted to the monarchy (see 1 Kings 11 and 21), there, too, oracular prophets condemned the rulers for unjust practices and oppressive treatment of the common people (e.g., Mic. 3:9-12; Is. 3:13-15). Again, it is clear that the criteria of judgment were the old Mosaic covenantal principles as they invoked divine judgment and imminent destruction of the monarchy for violation of the covenant.

The actual course of events bore out prophetic indictments and judgments: the northern kingdom of Israel fell to the Assyrians in 722 B.C.E.; the weakened southern kingdom of Judah was conquered by the Babylonians in 587 B.C.E., its temple destroyed, and the royal family and most of the upper class taken into exile in Babylon. While this was a tragedy for the upper classes, there is no reason to believe that the Judean peasants shared this view. If Jeremiah, who came from a common priestly family in the village of Anathoth, represents their outlook, they viewed the temple, with its elaborate staff and ceremonial apparatus, with suspicion. They may have seen the destruction of Jerusalem and the temple as a well-deserved punishment of the ruling class for their abuses and exploitation. Jeremiah himself pronounced judgment on the temple and ruling class for ignoring the Mosaic covenant (see Jer. 7 and 26). The fact that Jeremiah's prophecies and the other prophets' oracles were remembered and collected, and then much later accepted into canonical scripture, validated the popular tradition of prophetic protest.

JUDEA UNDER THE PERSIAN EMPIRE: THE ESTABLISHMENT OF THE PRIESTLY ARISTOCRACY AT THE HEAD OF THE TEMPLE-COMMUNITY

Soon after Judah's loss of independence and the exile of the ruling class to Babylon, the Babylonians themselves were conquered by the Persians, under Cyrus, in 539 B.C.E. Then, under Darius I, Persia established a control over the Middle East that was to endure for the next 200 years. The Persians reversed the Babylonian policies of large-scale deportations of native elites and enforcement of an official state religion.

They allowed exiles to return to their native lands to pursue local customs and religion. For the Judeans, this made possible a rebuilding of the walls of Jerusalem and the temple. Yet these very building projects also meant intensified labor for the peasantry, as well as the reestablishment of the old hierarchical social structure, with Jerusalem again the administrative, social, and religious center. By the time of Nehemiah (ca. 445 B.C.E.), sharp social-economic divisions had developed as the wealthy gentry took advantage of the poorer Judeans (see Neh. 5:1-5!). Nehemiah effected a reform to the benefit of the peasantry, but such relief was temporary.

Politically, the Judeans were under an officially appointed governor, initially an heir of the Davidic dynasty. But from at least the time of Nehemiah, the governor was simply a non-Davidic Jew or other imperial servant, and messianic hopes for a restoration of the Davidic kingship receded into the background. However, under direct imperial authority, the royal scribe Ezra reorganized the Jewish community around the law he had brought from Babylon (probably an early version of what we now know as the Torah or Pentateuch). It contained materials from the popular tradition which had now become officially sanctioned by, and supportive of, the "theocratic" rule of the priestly aristocracy.

Because of the demise of a Davidic leadership, as well as the fact that the religious and civic authority was now centered in the temple, the high priesthood became the administrators of the government, and the high priest himself emerged as the head of Judean society. Along with this development, political and economic power came more firmly into the hands of the chief priestly families. Indeed, their custody of the treasury in the temple, which served as a deposit bank as well as a center of worship, provided the upper priestly class with a firm financial basis for its increasing power and influence, both internally and externally. By the end of the Persian empire, the high priest was recognized as the political and economic representative as well as the ethnic and religious head of the Judeans. In fact, what began under the Persians continued during the Hellenistic empires and on into the Roman period, namely, that Judea functioned as a temple-community under the external political control of an imperial government. For the peasantry, this situation meant religiously sanctioned taxes to support the temple and its elaborate apparatus of regular worship and special occasions, all obligatory (see Sir. 7:31). They found themselves subject to an authority that became increasingly remote from their day-to-day concerns. Until the end of Persian rule, however, there was little cultural pressure, let alone political coercion, as they lived according to Mosaic traditions.

HELLENISTIC RULE: POLITICAL SUBJECTION, CULTURAL IMPERIALISM, AND POPULAR REBELLION

Domination by the Babylonians and Persians paled in comparison with the oppression that came in the wake of conquest by Alexander the Great and his Macedonian successors (the "Fourth beast," Dan. 7:19), at least for the Judean peasantry. The Hellenistic empires of Alexander's successors brought a systematic program of increased economic exploitation and a general policy of cultural imperialism that threatened the Jews' traditional ways of life. The ruling priestly elite, who maintained their privileged social position, attracted by the glories of Hellenistic civilization, began to compromise themselves culturally, religiously, and politically. The result in Judean society was a widening gulf between the priestly elite and the peasantry, one that finally provoked a popular revolt and set the tone for the next 300 years of Jewish social and religious history.

Judea was controlled during the third century by the Ptolemies, who ruled Egypt and southern Syria; it then fell under the control of the Seleucids, who ruled from Syria to Persia at the beginning of the second century. Politically, the Hellenistic emperors maintained the arrangements for Judea set up by the Persians, essentially allowing the Jews to live according to their ancestral laws and confirming the priestly aristocratic rule. Yet economically, Judea soon felt the adverse effects of Ptolemaic rule, including an increased tax burden, a load borne chiefly by the peasantry. The disruptive intrusions of Hellenistic civilization, however, compounding the adverse economic pressures, eventually created intolerable stresses in Judean society. For example, Alexander and his successors founded numerous Hellenistic cities in Palestine, with their Greek-speaking citizens and their local gentry in control of the indigenous population, who had no citizenship rights in the cities proper. Although Jerusalem was not initially transformed into a Hellenistic city, the Hellenistic emperors governed through alliance with the ruling class, the priestly aristocracy. The high priest, for example, was responsible for the collection of taxes. Thus the Judean people saw its own representative, its mediator with its true divine King (God), collaborating closely with a foreign, pagan empire. Furthermore, entrepreneurial opportunities increased the attractiveness of Hellenistic cultural forms. The rise of the Tobiad family (see Josephus, *Ant.* 12.154-236) dramatically illustrates how, alongside the traditional theocratic authority, a new kind of power based on financial influence could succeed and gain entrance into Jerusalem's ruling circles. General Hellenistic patterns of making one's way in the world were increasingly embodied by prominent Judeans, and, correspondingly, ancestral customs, the ethical teachings of the Torah, could be ignored. The compromising cultural influences which accompanied such political-economic collaboration can only have exacerbated the alienation between the Judean peasantry and the priestly aristocracy.

HELLENISTIC "REFORM" BY THE
JEWISH ARISTOCRACY

The events leading up to and including the Maccabean revolt have often been portrayed simply as matters of religious persecution by a hostile pagan empire and a subsequent rebellion by Jews to regain their freedom of religion. However, the situation was far more complex. And, since the Hellenistic reform, popular resistance, imperial decree, and war of liberation formed a crucial turning point for subsequent Jewish history, we must devote more than cursory attention to the complexity of forces and the significance of the developments.

A little more than two decades after they had taken control of Palestine, the Seleucids were in desperate need of funds and also needed to consolidate their power vis-à-vis the increasingly restless oriental peoples. They naturally looked to the Hellenized "cities," led by wealthy aristocracies, for support, and were thus ready to pursue a more active policy of Hellenization. In 175 B.C.E. Judean priestly and lay nobility, eager to enjoy the benefits of Hellenistic civilization, seized on the ascent to power of Antiochus IV Epiphanes (God-manifest) as the occasion to carry out a "reform." They first had the High Priest Onias III's brother Joshua, who assumed the Greek name Jason, depose Onias by purchasing the high priesthood for himself by offering Antiochus considerably more than the usual tribute of 300 talents. Jason then offered Antiochus another 150 talents for "permission to establish by his authority a *gymnasion* and a body of youth for it, and to enroll the men of Jerusalem as citizens of Antioch. . . . He at once shifted his countrymen over to the Greek way of life" (2 Macc. 4:9-10; see also 1 Macc. 1:13).

Thus Jason and the reform party transformed Jerusalem into a Hellenistic city named Antioch (in honor of the ostensible "founder," Antiochus IV). They organized the citizenbody, probably recruited from the upper priestly families and gentry interested in "modernizing" the society. The establishment of a *gymnasion* and an *ephebion* were essential to the city's Hellenistic constitution. These provided education appropriate for the training of young men for participation in the citizen-body, according to the usual Greek pattern. The *gymnasion* was built directly under the citadel on the temple hill itself. "The noblest of the young men" were induced "to wear the Greek hat" (the sun hat symbolic of Hermes), and "the priests were no longer intent upon their service at the altar. Despising the sanctuary and neglecting the sacrifices, they hastened to take part in the unlawful proceedings in the wrestling arena after the call to the discus, disdaining the honors prized by their fathers and putting the highest value upon the Greek forms of prestige" (2 Macc. 4:12, 14-15). Hellenizing Jews ashamed of the symbol of their traditional covenant with God, now embarrassingly evident when they participated in the games naked, sought to "remove the marks of circumcision, and abandoned the holy covenant" (1 Macc. 1:15).

Judea was no longer an *ethnos*, a people who differed from others by living according to its ancestral laws, participating neither culturally nor economically in the dominant civilization. Jerusalem (along with Judea) was now a *polis*, whose citizen-body enjoyed self-government and participated in commerce between cities and shared cultural institutions and celebrations with other cities of the empire.

POPULAR RESISTANCE AND THE PROGRAM TO SUPPRESS THE JEWISH LAW

For most of the Judean population, the Hellenistic reform did not involve merely superficial cultural activities affecting mainly the leisured class; the reform was a threat to their very existence and identity. When the Seleucids took control of Palestine, Antiochus III had granted the Judeans permission to live "according to their ancestral laws." Now, however, at least for those against the reform, Jason and the Hellenizing aristocracy had "set aside the existing royal concessions to the Jews . . . and destroyed the lawful ways of living and introduced new customs contrary to the Law" (2 Macc. 4:11). As inhabitants of the new *polis* of Antioch, the Judean noncitizens had certain economic rights, but they no longer possessed political rights. Although the law of Moses was not yet abolished, it was completely relativized, for the new *polis,* with its Greek traditions, had replaced the Torah as the operative constitution of the state. The temple, too, now belonged to the new *polis,* and while there may not have been any cultic reform (in the narrower sense), under the new constitution decisions about religious matters (as with all others) lay with the aristocratic citizen-body and its governing council.

These developments, since they left the vast majority of the Judean people without any civil rights at all, could hardly have been matters of indifference. Moreover, this radical reform was being led by the high priesthood, the sacred mediator in the special relation between God and the Jewish people, and an institution legitimated by the "ancestral laws," which had now been relativized. The traditional defenders of the law had abandoned it for alien political and cultural forms.

Pressures of resistance began to build, somewhat later, when Menelaus, leader of a radical Hellenizing faction, conspired to purchase the high priesthood for himself, outbidding Jason by more than 300 talents and sending him into exile in the Transjordan. Raising such a tribute meant that the people were taxed at a rate that had more than doubled over four years—all to underwrite a reform that severely disrupted their traditional way of life. Since there was still difficulty in raising the promised tribute, Menelaus conspired with his brother Lysimachus to embezzle the temple treasures and vessels, which had accumulated over generations and were hardly the property of the powerful men and rulers of Jerusalem, but of the people as a whole and, ultimately, of God. When reports of these acts of sacrilege spread, popular resistance finally broke out, focused on

Lysimachus. "Since the crowds were becoming aroused and filled with anger, Lysimachus armed about three thousand men ('citizens') and launched an unjust attack. . . . But the Jews . . . picked up stones, blocks of wood, and handfuls of ashes that were lying about, and threw them in wild confusion at Lysimachus and his men" (2 Macc. 4:39-41). The people thus killed the "temple robber" himself, with several others, and routed the rest of the "citizens."

The situation was exacerbated when the emperor Antiochus Epiphanes, greeted warmly by the Hellenizers on his return from his first Egyptian campaign in 169 and desperate for funds, plundered the temple himself. Resistance intensified, and during the next year the people were able both to force Menelaus and his faction to take refuge in the citadel, and to force Jason and his troop of about a thousand back across the Jordan when he tried to retake Jerusalem for himself. Antiochus was thus hardly wrong when he interpreted news of this to mean that "Judea was in revolt" (2 Macc. 5:11). When he returned from his second Egyptian campaign, in which he was humiliatingly checked by the Romans, he punitively attacked Jerusalem, killing thousands in hand-to-hand fighting, selling many Judeans into slavery, and leaving Phrygian mercenaries in control of the city. Successful resistance continued, however, and it became necessary for Mysian mercenaries, under the Seleucid general Apollonius, to retake the city—by trickery on the Sabbath, when the Jews, in religious observance, had set down their arms. Apollonius heavily fortified the city and, both to punish the Jews and to secure the city from further rebellion, established a military colony as part of the *polis* of Antioch-at-Jerusalem.

The establishment of a military colony, however, meant that the sacred precincts of the temple and other areas in the city were profaned by the religious practices of the Syrian troops. It also meant that there were new taxes and abuses of various sorts, such as the confiscation of the land and homes

of Jews to make way for the occupying forces of Syrian sol-
dier-citizens. Far from securing the city, this desecration of
Jerusalem and further oppression of the Jewish common
people only deepened resistance and perhaps led to its more
systematic organization. Our sources speak of massive flight
from the city.

> Because of them the residents of Jerusalem fled; she became
> a dwelling of strangers; . . . and her children forsook her.
> (1 Macc. 1:38)

It became increasingly apparent that the mounting resistance was rooted in the people's determination to maintain
their traditional ways and loyalty to the law. To strike at the
root of the resistance, Antiochus finally did something
highly uncharacteristic for Hellenistic rulers. He decreed the
compulsory abandonment of the traditional Jewish customs
and observance of the law. This involved the cessation of
temple worship, the desecration of things sacred to the Jews,
the burning of Torah scrolls, and the propagation of pagan-
ism by coercion.

> He directed them to follow customs strange to the land, . . .so
> that they should forget the law and change all the ordinances.
> And whoever does not obey the command of the king shall
> die. (1 Macc. 1:44, 49-50; see also 2 Macc. 6:1-2)

THE RESURGENCE OF APOCALYPTICISM

Antiochus Epiphanes' violent repression of the popular
resistance to the Hellenizing reform produced an intense
crisis of faith for the Jews. Acquiescing in the reform would
have meant abandoning their faith in God and commitment
to the Torah. But resistance to the reform meant facing a
martyr's death. Either course appeared to lead to an inevitable termination of the Jewish faith. One response to this
crisis was an upsurge of *apocalypticism.* Desperate to understand their seemingly impossible situation, some faithful
Jews sought divine *revelation* (Greek: *apokalypsis,* hence

our term "apocalyptic") to explain why their life circumstances had become so intolerable and what plan God might
have to deliver them. Beginning with this time of crisis for
the Jews, there was an upsurge of revelatory (apocalyptic)
literature. Recent scholarly analyses have established with
considerable precision that apocalyptic literature such as the
Assumption of Moses, 1 Enoch 85-90 (The Animal Apocalypse), and possibly 1 Enoch 92-105 (The Epistle of Enoch),
as well as the book of Daniel were written in connection with
the reform crisis and resistance to the Hellenistic persecution. This literature yields at least a general sense of some
Jews' interpretation of the situation and their motivation in
resisting the persecution. It is of critical importance to
appreciate the distinctive character of the eschatological
(i.e., pertaining to "final things") expectation involved in
apocalypticism. It was not simply an urgent search for revelation, but also a consoling and often energizing conviction
that divine deliverance, even historical fulfillment, was close
at hand.

An important element in the motivation of Jews who persisted in their devotion to the law was probably their eager
desire for the fulfillment of God's ancient promises to Israel:
that they would be able to live unmolested in the promised
land, that they would be a great people, and even that
through them other peoples would receive divine blessings
(Is. 42:1-7; 49:1-6). They continued in the traditional view
that the fulfillment of God's promises was conditional on
their keeping the stipulations of the Mosaic covenant. They
also knew, however, that their failure to keep the covenant
could not be the *only* cause of their suffering and persecution. Throughout the crisis they had remained faithful. Yet
they were being persecuted and martyred precisely because
they adhered to the law when even their own high priestly
aristocracy, in alliance with the imperial authorities, had
abandoned it. It was therefore necessary to find some more
transcendent interpretation of their persecution. They were

acutely in need of a *revelation* of their history that was turning out so disastrously.

Although the learned and literate had no monopoly on revelation, the only sources we have are the literary products of teachers and scribes. Moreover, of course, the very fact that hopes for deliverance and receipt of revelation took literary form points to the fact that people who were knowledgeable in the ancestral traditions and who could write, i.e., sages, teachers, scribes, became involved in the resistance. It is likely that, as the gulf had widened between the assimilationist priestly aristocracy and the peasantry under the Hellenistic empires, the role of scribes and sages not attached to the temple establishment would have become increasingly important in the interpretation of the law for community life. Thus it may not be surprising that, when the crisis came, there were groups of "wise men" (*maskilim*), such as those who apparently produced the book of Daniel (see Dan. 11:33), who were ready to "make many understand." In continuity with the classical and postexilic prophets, the means of such revelation frequently lay in dreams and visions. Apocalyptic visionaries are portrayed as having had unusual dreams or ecstatic experiences, in which they received revelations from some of the prototypical wise men of bygone ages, such as Enoch or Daniel. The contents of the dreams or visions were fantastic dramas played out on a cosmic screen. However, just as modern clinical interpretation finds an individual's dreams pertinent to the person's life, they believed that their visions pertained to their own, now ominous, historical experiences. Some visionaries stated explicitly that their visions revealed the mysterious plan (Hebrew: *raz*; Greek: *mystērion*) that God had for the fulfillment of history ("what will be in the latter days," see Dan. 2:18-19, 28-29) and thus "explained" their present experiences in terms of how they fit into the overall divine scheme.

With their experiences thus placed in eschatological perspective via apocalyptic visions, Judeans could find some purpose and meaning in their suffering and death, whether in martyrdom for the faith (as with the Maskilim), or in armed resistance to the oppressive imperial decree (as with the Hasidim and Maccabees). Indeed, those martyred would not miss the glorious fulfillment of God's plan for the final kingdom of God, but would be resurrected to everlasting life (see Dan. 12:1-3; reflected also in the nonapocalyptic 2 Macc. 7). Jewish belief that one could enter the kingdom of God as a result of the resurrection of the dead was a creative apocalyptic response to the situation just before or at the time of the Antiochean persecution.

Similarly, inspired by such apocalyptic visions, the Judean visionaries and their associates could offer fierce resistance against insuperable odds because they were convinced that they were instruments of God's own battle against the intolerable heathen attack on the chosen instrument of salvation (2 Macc. 2:21; 1 Macc. 2:50; 3:16-22, 54-57, 60).[7] There was also, apparently, ongoing revelation concerning just what the divine will was in the Judean rebellion. At the beginning of the active rebellion, some Jews still maintained Sabbath observance in the midst of the fighting, with no resistance offered on that day to the Seleucid troops, who quickly learned when to attack most successfully (1 Macc. 2:29-38; 2 Macc. 6:11). However, in the struggle for preservation of the people of faith, and possibly under the influence of the strong drive toward the desired eschatological fulfillment, it was decided to give sanction to fighting on the Sabbath, whatever the traditional interpretation of Sabbath laws (1 Macc. 2:39-42).

To what degree the people generally were caught up in keen anticipation of imminent divine action to deliver a desperate people we have no certain way of knowing. Nevertheless, it is difficult to imagine how the Judean peasantry could have sustained such a prolonged struggle against the overwhelming odds of the Seleucid military might without supposing that at least significant segments of the people were fired by apocalyptic inspiration. They were fighting to

restore the rule of God which, they must have believed, was
imminent.

THE POPULAR REVOLT AND THE RISE OF THE
HASMONEAN DYNASTY

The resistance, which had begun even before the official
decree of forced Hellenization, quickly became a broad
peasant revolt once the persecution was inaugurated.
Although the rebellion is known as the Maccabean revolt
after its leader, Judas "the Hammer" (Maccabee), the Maccabees, or Hasmonean family, were not its instigators or its only
leaders. There is some uncertainty whether the term
Hasidim/Hasideans (pious or devoted ones) used in some
of our sources refers generally to those who remained
actively devoted to the law, or more precisely to a primarily
scribal or priestly group or party, who provided leadership in
the rebellion and produced apocalyptic literature.[8] According to 2 Macc. 14:6, they, like the Judeans generally, were
stirring up sedition and war. It seems unwarranted to link or
confine the Hasidim to a group of Sabbath pacificists and/or
a supposed scribal or priestly group who were ready to negotiate a peace as soon as their limited cultic or religious purposes could be attained. Their reputation as "mighty
warriors of Israel" (1 Macc. 2:42) would hardly have been
gained overnight. Even if the Hasidim should be understood
as referring to the faithful rebels generally, it is at least clear
that the Hasidim engaged in active rebellion included a considerable number of scribes (1 Macc. 7:12-13). It is also clear
that, whatever leadership may have been provided by such
scribes, the vast majority of the combatants in the prolonged
war of resistance must have been ordinary people, i.e., from
among the peasantry.

Judas "the Hammer," the third of five sons of a priestly
family, the Hasmoneans, soon emerged as the charismatic
leader of the rebel forces. He and other fugitives subsisted
for a time in the wilderness. From this base, by stealthily

working the byways to recruit from the villages, he and his henchmen eventually organized thousands of resisters into a fighting force. Using guerrilla strategy masterfully, Judas and his bands of peasant soldiers defeated ever-larger armies sent by the Seleucids to put down the rebellion. In decisive battles they twice defeated major expeditions organized by Lysias, Antiochus Epiphanes' viceroy over the western part of the empire, and led by his finest generals (1 Macc. 3:27-4:35). The Judean peasants' resistance only expanded and intensified when it became evident that the Seleucid plan was to confiscate the lands of those who persisted in living according to their traditional Mosaic law, to sell them into slavery in order to raise money for the overdue tribute to Rome, and to settle aliens in the confiscated territory (1 Macc. 3:35-36, 41). This Seleucid plan shows that what was at stake was not simply the religious freedoms of the Jews, but the very existence of traditional Judean society. The Maccabean revolt was a struggle by the Judean peasantry for their own social-economic survival.

For their part, the peasant guerrilla bands plundered the estates and expropriated the property of the Hellenizing aristocracy (many of whom had fled to the gentiles for safety), and distributed booty "to those who had been tortured and to the orphans and widows, and also to the aged, shares equal to their own" (2 Macc. 8:30). Finally, led by Judas, they recaptured Jerusalem itself. They immediately set to work purifying the temple, "chose blameless priests devoted to the law," and held a joyous festival to rededicate the sanctuary, which became the basis of the annual festival of Hanukkah (1 Macc. 4:36-59).

As a celebration of victory, the festival may have been somewhat premature. When some scribal Hasidim attempted rapprochement with Alcimus, a legitimate Aaronide appointed high priest in 162 B.C.E., Alcimus seized and killed sixty of them (1 Macc. 7:12-18). Then in 160 a sizable Seleucid army defeated the peasant army, killed Judas himself, and persecuted his followers (1 Macc. 9:23-27). Formally, the

Seleucids and the Hellenizers continued to rule. But the only way the Hellenizing Judean aristocracy could exercise even a modicum of actual control was for the Seleucids to maintain a large occupation army to defend the enclaves of Hellenizers, for the Judean peasantry continued their protracted guerrilla warfare under the leadership of Judas' brother Jonathan. Finally the Seleucids agreed to recognize Judea as a semi-independent temple-state. First Jonathan, in 152, and then Simon, another brother of Judas the Maccabee, got himself recognized as high priest as well as governor and commander of Judea, which thus transformed the rebel leader into a high imperial official. Under Simon, the Seleucid military garrison in the Jerusalem citadel was finally taken and the political independence of Judea more firmly established.

The Judean peasantry had sustained a successful war of national liberation, probably with some significant apocalyptic inspiration. The outcome, however, may not have been exactly what many were hoping for. Exploiting the continuing popularity of the Maccabees' victorious leadership, Simon arranged for a national assembly to proclaim him high priest, military commander, and leader of the nation in perpetuity, and was able to pass on the rule to his son John Hyrcanus. In so doing, he established the Hasmonean dynasty, which lasted for nearly a century. What had begun as a Judean peasant revolt, guerrilla warfare against Seleucid armies, ended not in the final establishment of the Kingdom of God, but simply in the establishment of a new dynasty of high priests.

The Hasmoneans John Hyrcanus (135-104 B.C.E.) and his successor, Alexander Jannaeus (104-76 B.C.E.), pursued a consistent policy of territorial expansion. They transformed the peasant militia bands of Judas the Maccabee and his brothers, who had been fighting for self-preservation, into a national army seeking conquest of gentile territories. Beginning with the Hellenistic cities on the Mediterranean coast, they gradually succeeded in conquering Samaria, Galilee, and many of the cities east of the Jordan River, eventually extending the Hasmonean kingdom to the former boundaries of the Davidic kingdom. Moreover, the Hasmoneans showed no mercy to these territories and their populations, destroying the cities and either forcing the inhabitants to become Jews or annihilating them.

It is ironic that the early Hasmoneans, who struggled for bare Jewish survival against forced Hellenization, were now followed by those who could force conquered peoples to become Jews, and who gradually adopted Hellenistic forms in their regime, even adding the title king to that of high priest by the time of Alexander Jannaeus. They also hired mercenary troops, thus binding the army directly to the king-high priest himself, and displacing the peasant militia. In effect, the Hasmonean regime became much like any other petty, semi-Hellenized oriental state.

ORIGINS OF THE QUMRAN COMMUNITY (ESSENES) AND THE PHARISEES

Such a mundane outcome to their life-and-death struggle must have been extremely disappointing to those who, in their suffering under Seleucid persecution, had become caught up in the apocalyptic hope of divine deliverance. Indeed, many of the rebel forces must have joined the struggle with the conviction that they were fighting in accordance with the divine *plan,* under the banner of "God's help" (2 Macc. 8:23). The outcome, however, in the establishment of the Hasmonean regime, hardly qualified as a manifestation of the "saints of the most high," i.e., the kingdom of God.

Although we have few or no sources with which to assess the reaction of the bulk of the peasantry to this mundane outcome, it is not impossible that the Essenes and Pharisees both emerged from that segment of Jewish society to which the Hasidim belonged when the Hasmoneans established their high priesthood and kingship. Moreover, yet a third group, the priestly, aristocratic Sadducees formed, possibly in reaction to the Pharisees.

It has become increasingly clear that the group known in ancient sources as the Essenes was the same as the utopian community living in the wilderness at Qumran, where their writings, the Dead Sea Scrolls, were recently found. Perhaps the most satisfactory reconstruction of the origins of the Qumran community is that, in direct reaction to the illegitimate assumption of the high priesthood by the Hasmoneans, numbers of the Hasidim withdrew into the wilderness by the Dead Sea to continue their disciplined preparation for the advent of the kingdom of God.[9]

The Hasidim had fought shoulder to shoulder with the Hasmoneans (against the Seleucid armies) to regain Jewish freedom from Seleucid oppression, apparently in the conviction that the theocracy and their sacred traditions were about to be restored. The high priesthood had always been occupied by a Zadokite, the legitimate succession having been broken only by the Hellenistic reform. The Hasmoneans were a priestly family, but not Zadokites. Thus when Jonathan accepted appointment to the high priesthood, and then when Simon had himself proclaimed high priest by a national assembly (while warning against any opposition and prohibiting public assembly in his absence), many among the Hasidim must have been disillusioned. Compounding their illegitimate assumption of the high priesthood, the despotic rule of the Hasmoneans must have appeared to be a mere return to the problematic past rather than the advent of the true kingdom of God that many may have been anticipating from the apocalyptic visions. It is likely that the castigations of the "Wicked Priest" in Qumran literature are directed against the Hasmonean Jonathan or Simon.

Thus Zadokite-oriented priests and others of the Hasidim, whose tradition-rooted convictions had been flouted and whose hopes for establishing a faithful and legitimate theocracy (kingdom of God) centered in the Jerusalem temple had just been dashed, separated themselves from the rest of Judean society. They organized an ideal priestly theocracy in exile, a "true Israel" headed by the only "legitimate" priesthood. Led by their "Righteous Teacher," they abandoned Jerusalem and established a utopian, ascetic community beside the Dead Sea. With their apocalyptic convictions intensified by new revelations to the Righteous Teacher, they believed themselves called by God, in the words of the ancient prophecy of (Second) Isaiah: "In the *wilderness* prepare the way of the Lord."

The discovery of the Dead Sea Scrolls has dramatically changed our picture of Palestinian Jewish society of the late second temple period. We now see, for example, that John the Baptist, Jesus, and the earliest Christian community were not unique in their intense eschatological orientation, in their sense that the fulfillment of promises and prophecies was imminent. Here at Qumran was a concrete eschatological community. It believed that through the new revelations imparted to the Teacher, the meaning of the scriptural prophecies had become clear. Indeed, what had been prophesied by Isaiah or Habakkuk or Moses himself applied to their own time and was now being fulfilled in their own community's experience and events related to it. Since the rest of Israel had fallen hopelessly under the sway of the Prince of Darkness, they alone remained as the righteous remnant, the true Israel. They felt that the ultimate fulfillment was virtually at hand, that they had to be in constant readiness for the final battle in which God would defeat the demonic forces currently dominating history, and that all the glories of a perfect new creation ("all the glories of Adam") would be bestowed upon them.

To fulfill their role in "preparing the way of the Lord" (Is. 40), they kept themselves in a constant state of readiness as the community of the *new* covenant (carefully patterned after the original Mosaic covenant). The life of the community was conducted with the utmost rigor according to an extremely strict interpretation of this new covenant. For this reason members of the community engaged in intense study of the Torah and other scriptures. Christian sources and (polemical) reconstructions have often portrayed the Pharisees as strict legal interpreters. It is now clear from the Dead Sea Scrolls, however, that the Essenes at Qumran were even more strict and rigorous interpreters of the covenant law. The Qumran community also rigorously observed certain key rituals in their eager anticipation of the eschatological fulfillment. They carried out a regular ritual bathing, apparently as a way of maintaining their purity as the community preparing the way of the Lord. They also regularly conducted the eschatological ritual of a messianic banquet, in anticipation that the Anointed Ones of Israel would soon be present to lead the celebration of final deliverance. The group was so rigorous and stable that it renewed itself through several generations, lasting over 200 years, an unusual longevity for utopian communities. Indeed, the life of the Essene community came to an end only because it was destroyed by Roman legions at the end of the Jewish revolt in 70 C.E.

Many of the Hasidim or like-minded Jews who did not become Essenes may well have emerged as Pharisees, in a somewhat different reaction to the consolidation of political and religious power by the Hasmoneans.[10] Instead of withdrawing into the wilderness these Jews formed a type of religiopolitical association in order to bring the Mosaic law more effectively to realization in Judean society. Those who became Pharisees probably held an eschatological orientation similar to that of the Qumranites, but they were not as intensely focused on the imminence of the final realization of the Kingdom. Although the Pharisees were less dominated by priestly elements, at least those of Zadokite lineage or concerns, they were just as fully committed to the Mosaic law as the rule for the people of Israel. But whereas the Essenes sought a radical and absolutely rigorous realization of the law of God in a utopian community constituted by only a remnant of Israel, the Pharisees sought to have the Torah rule the life of society as a whole.

In order to achieve such a goal, the law had to be interpreted and applied to the social, economic, and religious life of the people. Thus the Pharisees continued the work of the scribes. Because they attempted to update and adapt the Mosaic law, the Essenes called them "smooth interpreters." In one report Josephus indicates that when John Hyrcanus (135-104) broke with them, the kingdom was governed by "the laws which [the Pharisees] had set up for the people" (*Ant.* 13.296). In their work of interpretation and application of the Mosaic law, the Pharisaic scribes probably worked in continuity with earlier scribes. Thus, says Josephus, "the Pharisees handed down to the people certain regulations from earlier generations which are not written in the laws of Moses" (*Ant.* 13.297). This may be an early stage in the development of the "oral law" (oral traditions of earlier sages' interpretations and applications of the law of Moses).

Thus, to judge from Josephus, at least from the time of their break with John Hyrcanus, the Pharisees had probably come together as a group with some degree of cooperation, if not actually as a religiopolitical party with some form of internal organization.[11] This same event may also have given rise to the formation of the Sadducees as an association opposed to the Pharisees. The break between the Hasmoneans and the Pharisees may be seen as the predictable result of the rise of a new aristocracy. The Hasmonean conquests of previously non-Jewish Palestine furnished the opportunity for the enrichment of new leaders, as well as of some of the older powerful families. Military commanders collected booty and plunder; landowners expanded their holdings; and new families found places in the temple-state hierarchy. Thus there grew up around Hyrcanus and his successors a new aristocracy of wealth and affluence, composed of the new higher priestly families, high military officers, and large

landowners. Thus within a generation or two of the Maccabean popular rebellion against aristocratically-led Hellenization, there emerged the same old class division between
the wealthy aristocracy and the bulk of the people whom the
former dominated.

Under Hyrcanus, there eventually occurred a formal
realignment in the government, the society, and probably
the temple cult as well. According to the story repeated by
Josephus,[12] the Pharisees supposedly asked Hyrcanus to be
content with the kingship (political rule only) and to relin-
quish the high priesthood (i.e., social-religious authority),
which they believed he held illegitimately, since he was of a
non-Zadokite family. The Pharisees' ingenious suggestion,
of course, appeared to recognize the right of the Hasmoneans to rule Judea. Yet, since the true basis of Hasmonean rule
was not the royal throne (of David), but the traditional high
priesthood (i.e., a Jewish hierocratic state, in the postexilic
tradition, in which the royal title was primarily an ornament
to impress foreigners), the Pharisees' proposal would effectively have cut the ground of the Hasmoneans' authority from
under them. Instead of relinquishing the high priesthood,
Hyrcanus simply broke with the Pharisees, rescinded the
regulations which they had established for the society, and
allied himself with the newly formed aristocratic party of the
Sadducees. Yet Hellenistic legal and political forms were
not imposed, nor was the society left without any law. The
Sadducees instead established the law of Moses alone as the
basis of societal life, that is, the law without extensive interpretation and application through the oral law of the
scribes.[13] They thereby eliminated the need for the Pharisees' legal interpretation, such interpretation being the basic
function of the scribes in Judean society. There was thus a
realignment: the Hasmoneans and the Sadducees as the party
of the wealthy aristocracy on the one hand, over against the
Pharisees on the other. The latter turned to the people for
support since the daily life of the peasantry and urban com-

moners was based on the Mosaic law *as interpreted,* and interpretation had been in the hands of the Pharisees.

The Sadducees continued in favor and power with the Hasmoneans through the reign of Alexander Jannaeus (104-76 B.C.E.), with the Pharisees apparently an active force of opposition. Jannaeus fought prolonged wars of conquest against surrounding peoples, wars that drained resources from the Judean peasantry, and aroused popular opposition. One year, at the Feast of Tabernacles, the people even pelted their king-high priest with citrons when he appeared in ceremony. The Pharisees may have provided much of the leadership of the uprising that eventually broke out against Jannaeus' oppressive regime. In response, the arrogant Jannaeus took vengeance in an unprecedented way: he had some 800 of his opponents crucified, and slaughtered their wives and children before their eyes (Josephus, *Ant.* 13.372-83; 4QpNah 1). Thereafter thousands of Jannaeus' opponents (including many Pharisees) fled the country and remained in exile until his death. Under Jannaeus' widow and successor, Queen Salome Alexandra, the Pharisees returned to power, and played a role of at least some influence in the governing council (Sanhedrin). As a scribal psalmist of a generation later saw it, it was the arrogance and sinfulness of the Hasmoneans that brought down judgment upon Judea and Jerusalem—in the form of Roman conquest:

> Alien nations ascended Thine altar, they trampled it proudly with their sandals; because the sons of Jerusalem had defiled the holy things of the Lord. (Ps. Sol. 2:2-3)

ROMAN DOMINATION:
OPPRESSION AND REVOLT

Roman domination of Jewish Palestine began with a violent conquest followed by a prolonged period of devastating power struggles. Control of the area was fought for by rival Hasmonean factions, the Parthian empire to the east, and even rival factions in the Roman civil war then raging in the Eastern Mediterranean as well as in Italy. Then, after the highly oppressive rule of the Roman client kings (Herod and his sons), there followed direct rule by governors of the alien empire, something the Jews had not experienced since the initial Babylonian and Persian conquests. After the mid-first century C.E., moreover, the behavior of the Jewish priestly aristocracy became increasingly predatory. For the Jewish peasantry, the Herodian and Roman domination meant unusually heavy taxation, indeed a serious threat to their very existence, as many were cut off from their land. Significantly, the period of most interest with regard to popular movements and popular leaders such as Jesus of Nazareth is framed by large-scale peasant uprisings: the outbursts following the death of Herod in 4 B.C.E. and the massive revolt against Rome in 66-70 C.E., followed by a second major revolt against Rome in 132-135 C.E.

ROMAN CONQUEST AND HEROD'S REGIME

During the course of the second and especially the first century B.C.E., the Romans conquered or fell heir to the Hellenistic kingdoms in the Eastern Mediterranean. In the process, Rome basically took over and perpetuated the already established Hellenistic civilization and imperialism in the east. Following Pompey's conquest of Palestine in 63 B.C.E., the Jewish territories were continuously under Roman control, except for a few short years of temporarily successful rebellion. Pompey besieged Jerusalem, and, when the city and the temple fell into his hands, he violated the Holy of Holies (*Ant.* 14.105). The Romans "liberated" and restored the Hellenistic cities and other areas of Palestine that had been conquered and Judaized by the Hasmoneans. The remaining Jewish territories (Galilee, Perea, Idumea, along with Judea) were subjected to the tribute. Nearly a generation-long period of turmoil followed Pompey's conquest as rival Hasmonean factions and rival Roman armies vied for control of the area. At one point, the Parthians sent armies into Palestine in support of one of the rival Hasmonean leaders. The effects of this and similar actions in the civil war in Jewish Palestine were repeated devastation of the land, extraordinary levies of taxes, and general social turmoil.

In their initial conquest, and particularly in subsequent reconquests, the Romans treated the inhabitants brutally in order to induce the people to submit. Repeatedly, the Roman armies burned and completely destroyed towns and either slaughtered, crucified, or enslaved their entire populations. For example, when Cassius conquered Taricheae in Galilee, "he made slaves of some thirty thousand men," says Josephus, and he later (43 B.C.E.) enslaved the people of important regional towns such as Gophna, Emmaus, Lydda, and Thamna (*Ant.* 14.120, 272-75). In one case, such destruction was wrought merely for the failure to raise, or tardiness in raising, an extraordinary levy of taxes (*J. W.* 1.180, 219-20)! Several decades later Varus, the legate of Syria, after capturing Sepphoris, "sold its inhabitants as slaves and set the city on fire" (*Ant.* 17.288-89). And such rebels as were caught by the troops he ordered crucified—about 2,000 (*Ant.* 17.295).

In 40 B.C.E., amid the political chaos of the Roman civil war, the aggressive young Herod achieved recognition as king over the Jewish territories in Palestine.[14] He accomplished this feat through intrigue and maneuvering from one faction to another during the civil war, following a period of apprenticeship to his father in Palestinian and Roman *Realpolitik*. After subduing the resistant Jewish people with the help of Roman legions, he became the epitome of Hellenistic imperial rule as a Roman client king. His name stands in Jewish and Christian traditions as a symbol of oppressive tyranny. From 37 to 4 B.C.E. he maintained tight control over the people by means of foreign mercenaries personally loyal to himself, a strategically arranged series of fortresses and

military colonies around the countryside, and a secret service of informers. A great devotee of Hellenistic culture,
Herod sought and found fame as a magnanimous builder and
benefactor, both domestically and abroad. He had the Jewish
temple magnificently rebuilt (a project not actually finished
until just before the great revolt of 66-70). However, much
less to the liking of his Jewish subjects, he also built a thea-
ter, an amphitheater, and a fortified royal palace in Jerusalem, blatant signposts of Hellenism. He also built several
complete new cities, such as Caesarea Maritima and Sebaste,
in which he promoted the worship of the divine Augustus.
What is more, he donated temples and public buildings in
Athens, Sparta, Rhodes, and other Greek cities. Of course,
the cost of such massive building projects and of his additional beneficence to the imperial family and others was
enormous. Thus, in addition to his reliance on the extensive
royal lands he had amassed in gaining his kingdom, he
placed an immense burden of taxation on the Jewish peasantry. Although he occasionally took steps to relieve this
nearly impossible burden, at his death the country and its
people were virtually exhausted economically.[15]

In consolidating his power, Herod eliminated many of the
old Sadducean aristocracy and fostered a new aristocracy
loyal to himself. In particular, though he had vastly reduced
its powers, he placed into the high priesthood new non-
Zadokite families directly beholden to himself. Under
Herod's oppressive regime the Pharisees retained some prestige among the general populace, for they did not hesitate to
oppose the king. Twice they refused to take a loyalty oath to
the king, whom they considered illegitimate, as a "half-Jew"
(Idumean father, Arab mother), a Hellenizer, and a creature
of Rome (*Ant.* 15.368-71; 17.41-45). However, because
Herod effectively put an end to any real participation by the
Jewish people in the ordinary political process, the Pharisees
became less a political party and more a loose association of
religious brotherhoods. They attempted to influence social
life by precept and example, but now without any effective

political role or authority other than some representation on a Sanhedrin which itself had reduced powers. Whereas they had been closer to the peasantry under some of the Hasmoneans (*Ant.* 13.298), they now tended to turn in toward their own brotherhoods and schools of legal-religious interpretation (a tendency which likely continued in the post-Herodian period of direct Roman rule).

So that the ruthless Herod could pay for the many building projects arising out of his passionate devotion to Hellenistic civilization, he had to force maximum economic exploitation of both the land and the people he ruled. The burden, of course, weighed heavily on the peasantry, and the disaffected were many. But Herod maintained stringent political and social control, so that there was virtually no opportunity even for protest or outcry. Josephus writes,

> They resented his engaging in such pursuits since for them it amounted to the dismantling of their religion and the changing of their customs. These matters were widely discussed because they were constantly being provoked and stirred up. But Herod treated this situation very carefully, removing any occasion for unrest and ordering them to keep their nose to the grindstone. He disallowed public gatherings, groups walking about or normal community life; and all activity was watched. The punishments given to those caught were harsh, and both openly and secretly many were brought to the fortress Hyrcania and executed. Both in the city and on the open roads there were men who spied on those who met together. . . . Those who obstinately refused to adapt to such social constraints he punished in all kinds of ways . . . and those who showed some spirit and were indignant at his forcing [the loyalty oath] he got rid of in any way possible. (*Ant.* 15.365-69)

It is no surprise that we hear little of rebellion or even "unrest" under such a tightly controlled "police state." But some of the scribal or Pharisaic leaders and especially the masses of the peasantry were seething with resentment. When Herod finally died in 4 B.C.E., the deep and long-suppressed discontent burst forth, first in daring acts of defiance of the dying tyrant and then in spontaneous popular revolts in every district of the kingdom.

CLIENT KINGS, ROMAN GOVERNORS, AND POPULAR PROTESTS (4 B.C.E. - 66 C.E.)

After the Romans subdued the Jewish rebellions that broke out at Herod's death, they divided up Herod's kingdom among his sons. Herod Antipas (4 B.C.E. - 39 C.E.) was set up as tetrarch over the areas of Galilee and Perea. This is the Herod whose marriage John the Baptist condemned and the King Herod during whose reign Jesus worked. The areas given to him had been Judaized following their conquest by the Hasmoneans, so that much of the peasantry, especially in Galilee, was Jewish in its orientation and loyalty. But the population was mixed, and Antipas' realm included many Hellenistic towns. Moreover, continuing his father's patronage of Hellenistic culture—at the expense and to the dislike of his Jewish subjects—he rebuilt Sepphoris (which the Romans had destroyed in 4 B.C.E.) as a Hellenistic city, and founded the city of Tiberias on the west shore of the Lake of Galilee. Tiberias had a mixed population, and highly scrupulous Jews refused to join its citizen-body since it had been built on the site of a former Jewish cemetery. Even more than Tiberias, Sepphoris (quite near the village of Nazareth) was a center of Hellenistic culture.

The Romans placed (Herod) Archelaus in charge of Judea and Samaria, over the protests of a delegation of Jewish elders who petitioned for a Roman governor instead. Indeed, after nine years of Archelaus' unpopular rule the Romans deposed him. Thereafter, until the great rebellion in 66, except for three years of (Herod) Agrippa I (41-44), Judea and Samaria were governed directly by the Romans through a governor appointed by the emperor. Now the people were again subject to the tribute. Because of their fundamental

faith that they should be subject to no king but God, however, direct Roman rule and particularly the tribute were
offensive to the Jewish people. Indeed, some thought these
conditions tantamount to slavery.

The whole period of direct Roman rule from 6 to 66 C.E.
was marked by widespread discontent and periodic turbulence in Palestinian Jewish society. This period is of special
interest to Christians because it forms the context of the life
and career of Jesus, and to Jews because it is the immediate
prelude to the formation of Rabbinic Judaism. As noted, the
period is framed by the extensive peasant insurrections of 4
B.C.E. and the massive Jewish revolt of 66-70. In the chapters
that follow, we will examine the social forms taken by actual
movements of popular discontent. At this point, we may set
the stage for those movements by sketching briefly the more
general and spontaneous protests which the Jews made on
various occasions, and by examining the effects on the people of the response made by Roman governors and the Jewish ruling class.

The aspects of the "colonial situation" of Roman imperial
rule in Jewish Palestine that most concerned the people
were the fact and rate of taxation and their relative freedom
from outside interference in pursuing their traditional socioreligious way of life. The Romans took considerable care to
be sensitive to Jewish religious scruples in their handling of
Palestinian Jewish affairs. Nevertheless, as was virtually inevitable in a situation of imperial domination (occupying
troops, intercultural misunderstandings, etc.), they blun-
dered into occasional provocations that further inflamed the
situation.

The sequence of events under Herod's son Archelaus in 4
B.C.E. already prefigures the vacillation and ineptitude of the
later Roman governors from Pontius Pilate until the outbreak
of the great revolt, as well as the effect this had on the Jewish
people. Archelaus, claiming the throne immediately upon
his father's death, listened with apparent interest to loud

grievances from the people: appeals to lower the heavy rate
of taxation, to release political prisoners still in his father's
prisons, to replace the corrupted high priest with one who
would rule more in accordance with the law, and to restore
justice by discontinuing his father's repressive actions, such
as having popular leaders brutally executed. But Archelaus
became nervous when the crowds became considerably
larger and more vocal at the Passover festival. When he made
a show of force to silence the leaders of the protests, the
people stoned his military cohort, whereupon

> he unleashed his entire army on them, the infantry in a col-
> umn through the city and the cavalry in the fields. While
> everyone was busy sacrificing, the soldiers suddenly swooped
> down on them, killing about 3000 and scattering the rest into
> the nearby hills. (*J. W.* 2.12-13; see also 2.1-13; *Ant.* 17.200-18)

Not surprisingly, this (along with some further harrassment
by the Roman governor's "body-guards") touched off a
revolt by "the whole nation" (*J. W.* 2.39-54; *Ant.* 17.250-68).
From all districts peasants streamed together into Jerusalem
at Pentecost a few weeks later. They besieged the Roman
troops, then fought valiantly against them from the temple
porticoes. After the Romans burned and plundered the temple, the Jews all the more furiously

> pressed the siege, making assaults on the fortress and at the
> same time loudly ordering Sabinus and his followers to with-
> draw and not stand in the way of those who at long last were
> on the road to recovering their national independence. (*J. W.*
> 2.53)

A short time thereafter a popular messianic movement
formed in every major district of Jewish Palestine (discussed
further in chapter 3). What had begun simply as a peaceful
assembly to appeal to the ruler for redress of grievances
ended as a widespread peasant revolt. The people, already
frustrated at their oppression, were driven by the ruler's lack

of response—or rather, his brutally repressive response—to the more desperate measures of armed insurrections.

Such a pattern was repeated in the subsequent decades of Roman domination of Jewish Palestine, until the cycle escalated into the great revolt of 66. Roman officials rarely heeded Jewish protests and appeals. The protests were sometimes spontaneous, in response to a suddenly provocative incident, and sometimes more deliberate and even organized.

An incident from midcentury provides a good example of a spontaneous protest that, unheeded by the governor, Cumanus, turned into a riot and then brutal suppression of the protesters. The incident also reveals how tense the relations were between the Jewish people and the occupying Roman forces, particularly at Passover, the festival at which they celebrated their liberation from Egyptian slavery. As usual, the Jews were compelled to carry on their celebration under the watchful eyes of the Roman security forces stationed on the temple porticoes during such festivals.

> One of the soldiers lifted up his robe and bent over indecently, turning his backside towards the Jews and making a noise as indecent as his posture. This infuriated the whole crowd, who loudly appealed to Cumanus to punish the soldier. . . . [But] Cumanus, fearing the whole population would rush him, sent for reinforcements. When these troops poured into the colonnades, the Jews were panic-stricken and turned and fled from the temple into the city. But so violently did they jam up at the exits that they trampled each other and more than 30,000 were crushed to death. Thus the feast ended in mourning for the whole nation and bereavement for every household. (*J.W.* 2.224-27; *Ant.* 20.105-12)

Usually the Jewish appeals were more deliberate and organized demonstrations of concern. Earlier in the period, representatives of the ruling groups (and perhaps of the Pharisees) were involved in, or even leaders of, such appeals. Following the death of Herod, for example, a delegation of fifty Jewish elders journeyed to Rome to protest the tyrannical misrule of the Roman client Herod and his equally brutal son Archelaus, and to appeal for the "independence" of Jewish Palestine linked with the province of Syria and administered by governors from among themselves. Despite the objections of the elders that Archelaus had just celebrated the beginning of his rule with the massacre of 3,000 of his subjects, however, the Romans appointed more Herodian client rulers (*J.W.* 2.80-100; *Ant.* 17.299-320). Again, a decade later, it was "the leading Jews and Samaritans" who found "his cruelty and tyranny intolerable and brought charges against him before Caesar" (*Ant.* 17.342). The Romans replaced the hated Archelaus with their own direct administration and taxation.

There are simply no records for the next two decades (6-26), but Pontius Pilate's ruthlessly repressive rule (26-36) left a vivid impression on the people's memory. The first of several major incidents provoked by this arrogant and insensitive governor became one of the most dramatic moments in Jewish history of the first century. This may be a case of the whole people acting in unison, although it is surely significant that Josephus says nothing about the involvement, let alone leadership, of the elders, the notables, the chief priests, or the leading Pharisees. This is one of only two (known) cases of a successful protest, that is, where the Roman official took action to redress the grievance.

> As procurator of Judea, Tiberius sent Pilate, by night and under cover, to bring into Jerusalem the images of Caesar known as standards. At daybreak, this caused an enormous disturbance among the Jews. Those nearby were alarmed at the sight since it meant that their laws had been trampled on —for those laws do not permit any image to be set up in the city. The angry city mob was joined by a huge influx of people from the countryside. The Jews rushed off to Pilate in Caesarea and begged him to remove the standards from Jerusalem and to respect their ancestral laws. When Pilate refused, they threw themselves down on the ground around his house and stayed put for five days and nights.

The next day, Pilate took his seat on the tribunal in the great stadium and summoned the crowd, pretending to be ready to give them an answer. Instead he gave a pre-arranged signal to his armed soldiers to surround the Jews. Finding themselves in a ring of troops three deep, the Jews were dumbfounded. Then Pilate declared that he would cut them down unless they accepted the images of Caesar, and nodded to the soldiers to draw their swords. As if by arrangement, the Jews all fell to the ground, extended their necks, and proclaimed that they were ready to be killed rather than transgress the law. Astonished by the intensity of their religious fervor, Pilate ordered the immediate removal of the standards from Jerusalem. (*J.W.* 2.169-74).

A second provocation by Pilate, known from the Jewish philosopher Philo of Alexandria, appears to have been a separate if similar incident: Pilate's erection of votive shields or plaques ostensibly in honor of the emperor in Herod's palace. Another massive protest ensued, this time led apparently by a few members of the Herodian family. Again Pilate appears to have responded, reluctantly (*Leg. ad Gaium,* 299-305).

Another major provocation by Pilate also evoked a massive protest by the people. He took funds from the sacred treasury in the temple to pay for the construction of an aqueduct to bring water into Jerusalem. Thousands of indignant Jews assembled at the governor's tribunal to protest. This time, more characteristically for Pilate, he was in no mood to listen:

> Since he had foreseen the disturbance, Pilate had planted a troop of soldiers among the crowd, disguised in civilian clothes. They had orders not to use swords, but to beat any hecklers with clubs. He then gave the agreed signal from his tribunal. Many Jews were killed. . . . (*J.W.* 2.176-77; *Ant.* 18.60-62)

The potentially most explosive conflict was fostered by the emperor Gaius Caligula himself. "The Jewish war" with Rome would have occurred a quarter of a century earlier had it not been for the combination of persistence and patience on the part of the Jewish peasantry. Wishing to be hailed throughout the empire as a god, Gaius

> sent Petronius to Jerusalem with an army to set up statues of himself in the temple; if the Jews refused them, he was to execute the objectors and reduce the whole nation to slavery. (*J. W.* 2.185)

When Petronius halted his march at Ptolemais, in order to winter his army of two legions there, "many tens of thousands of Jews came to Petronius . . . with petitions not to force them to transgress and violate their ancestral law" (*Ant.* 18.263). Evidently impressed by their determination to submit to death rather than allow him to proceed, Petronius went to Tiberias to check on the situation in Galilee. Again he was beset by thousands baring their throats and declaring "we will die before we violate our laws" (*Ant.* 18.271). Members of the Herodian family and some of the aristocracy, apparently not involved in the protest from the outset, finally realized the seriousness of the people's resolve, and used their influence with Petronius in private conferences, urging him not to drive the people to desperation (*Ant.* 18.273-74; *J. W.* 2.193, 199). One of their principal concerns, according to Josephus, was a very practical and concrete one: economics. Apparently a rather persuasive aspect of the massive popular protest, by now several weeks in duration, was that it was also a peasant *strike*. If the fields remained unsown any longer, there would be no harvest, and therefore no means for the required tribute; the aristocracy and royalists as well as the Roman officials knew that meant "a harvest of banditry" (*Ant.* 18.272, 274, 287; *J. W.* 2.200; see the next chapter on banditry). The popular protests (which in Galilee at least were also a massive peasant strike), and the people's patient and firm persistence, proved effective in this case. Petronius decided to face the wrath of Gaius rather than to devastate the Jewish peasantry, thus depriving the emperor of the revenues derived from them (*Ant.* 18.287). Fortunately for the noble Petronius, news of the Emperor Gaius's death arrived before the emperor's command to commit suicide (*J.W.* 2.201-3; *Ant.* 18.303-9; see also 18.276-309).

At least from the time of Cumanus (48-52 C.E.), the Roman governors became increasingly callous and intransigent. In one case, Cumanus did heed the massive popular appeal for justice. A soldier from the troops sent out to punish and make prisoners of villagers who had been too slow in apprehending brigands tore up and burned a Torah scroll. Cumanus, alarmed that the massive protest might escalate into a fresh revolt, appeased the multitude with the execution of the soldier. Otherwise, however, Cumanus was brutally repressive, seemingly setting the tone for his successors as governor. As already noted, he had ordered his troops to attack the protesters in the temple at Passover. Then later in his term Cumanus' inaction in response to a protest by Galilean Jewish leaders about a Samaritan attack on some pilgrims was the principal factor in the escalation of the incident to a major conflict, whereupon he sent out his troops against the sizable force of Jewish peasants and their brigand leaders (*Ant.* 20.118-24; *J.W.* 2.232-40).

One can deduce from Josephus' accounts that, after the early appeals against the Herodians by delegations of Jewish elders in 4 B.C.E. and 6 C.E., nearly all of the protests were made by the common people, lower-class Jerusalemites, or peasants, or both. In one or two cases, members of the aristocracy or of the royal family became involved in an appeal to the Roman authorities over conflict with the Samaritans under Cumanus. Thereafter, if we can judge from Josephus' accounts, the Jewish ruling circles and other Jewish gentry made no attempt to play a mediating role, as tensions and even conflict between the Roman (and Jewish) rulers and the Jewish people at large steadily escalated during the fifties and sixties toward the great revolt.

Indeed, the actions of the Jewish governing groups compounded the alienation and conflict already exacerbated by the intransigence and repressive measures taken by the

Roman governors. The high priestly families, Herodians, and much of the wealthy aristocracy, of course, were engaged in mutually beneficial collaboration with the Roman imperial system in maintaining control in Jewish Palestine. As the social order began to crumble, the ruling elite not only made no attempt to represent the interests of the people, but contributed to the breakdown of the society in a violently predatory manner, yielding virtual "class warfare" (see *Ant.* 20.181). Rival high priestly factions maintained hired bands of ruffians, and occasionally came to blows. The leader of one faction, Ananias, however, managed to keep the upper hand by using his great wealth to bribe supporters (*Ant.* 20.213). As for the Herodians, they too had their gangs (see *Ant.* 20.214). A reflection of the effect this behavior had on the peasants, ordinary priests, and poor scribes is preserved in the Talmud: Abba Saul ben Bothnith repeated a lament from Abba Joseph ben Hanan (who was active in Jerusalem prior to the revolt):

> Woe is me because of the house of Boethus,
>   woe is me because of their staves.
> Woe is me because of the house of Hanan,
>   woe is me because of their whisperings.
> Woe is me because of the house of Kathros,
>   woe is me because of their pens.
> Woe is me because of the house of Ishmael ben Phiabi,
>   woe is me because of their fists.
> For they are high priests, and their sons are treasurers, and
>   their sons-in-law are temple overseers, and their servants
>   beat the people with clubs. (B. Pesaḥim 57a;
>   T. Menahoth 13:21)

Such practices by the high priestly families and Herodians clearly exacerbated the disintegration of the social order which they, supposedly, were responsible for maintaining.

The Roman governors, however, also contributed to the heightening of tensions. From Felix (52-60) to Florus (64-66), they became steadily more repressive and intransigent. Right up to the end, under the devious Florus, who dared, even forced, the Jewish people into outright rebellion, the people continued to appeal and protest their condition and treatment, while their ostensible leaders, high priests and nobility alike, sat idly by or collaborated in their oppression. When the legate of Syria visited Jerusalem at Passover in 64 C.E., they made a desperate protest that Florus was the ruin of the country (*J.W.* 2.280). The Jewish ruling circles, including the Herodians and chief priests, however, were unresponsive to the people's further appeal to them to join in the protest against Florus' misrule. Instead, the Jewish ruling class saved its energies to appeal to the Romans and King Agrippa II to send troops to put down the rebellion, once the people finally became that desperate.

THE GREAT REVOLT (66-70)

The Jewish revolt was a success at first. The Roman troops were rapidly driven from Jerusalem, and from both Judea and Galilee. It was basically a peasant revolt. The lower priests and some of the other Jerusalemites participated, intensively so at the outset. But participation by members of the lay or priestly aristocracy, such as the temple captain Eleazar, was a rare exception. As Josephus makes clear, especially in his *Life,* the chief priests, elders, and "leading Pharisees" (such as himself) secretly attempted to implement a moderating and mediating strategy. That is, by ostensibly assuming the *leadership* of the revolt (including preparation of defenses against the inevitable attack by Rome), they attempted to control and channel the rebellious energies of the people until they could negotiate with the Romans. But they could not control the situation for long, and the "Jewish War" ensued, in which it took the Romans three full years to reconquer the country. Josephus himself, who was the "general" placed in command of Galilee, simply deserted to the Romans after the initial battles, and assisted the Romans in reconquering his own people. Many another Jewish notable or chief priest did the same.

The Jewish peasantry, however, apparently caught up in apocalyptic hopes, would not be denied their freedom from oppressive foreign and domestic rule. In several waves and various, even rival, groups, they took over the holy city and attacked the illegitimate high priestly cliques and their other wealthy oppressors. One group, those actually called Zealots, conducted a proper election, by lot, of a new and legitimate high priest, who, although he happened to be a simple stonecutter, was from a genuine Zadokite family. The Jerusalemites, not surprisingly, resented the seizure of the city by the peasants, and a power struggle ensued between rival groups for control of the city. After expending much energy and blood battling each other, the principal groups were able finally to cooperate in the ultimately futile resistance to the prolonged Roman siege. The city finally fell to the might of Rome in 70, although it took the Romans three more years to smoke out all of the remaining pockets of resistance, including the Sicarii on Masada (*J.W.* 7.311).

The Jewish revolt and the devastating reconquest by the Romans was the decisive turning point for the development of Rabbinic Judaism. Except for the Pharisees, none of the Jewish parties or leadership groups survived the war. Some (e.g., chief priests, Sadducees) were eliminated by the rebel groups, and others by the reconquering Roman army. However, led initially by Yohanan ben Zakkai, who had abandoned Jerusalem during the revolt, a group gathering at Yavneh laid the foundations of what became generally known as Rabbinic Judaism. During the several decades after the revolt these early rabbis collected and organized their legal interpretations and applications (*halakot*). The *Mishnah* of Judaism was one significant product of this process.

Although the land was devastated and the holy city destroyed by the Romans, the passion for freedom did not die among the Jewish peasants. Nor was the apocalyptic spirit dead. Apocalyptic visions were still cultivated and the revelations written down, at least within intellectual circles. Visionaries such as those who produced 4 Ezra, in all probability written a few decades after the first revolt, were clearly still waiting for God's intervention on behalf of the people. But among the peasantry in particular many refused to give up the active pursuit of the ideal of a just society, free of foreign domination and oppression. In 132-135, sixty-two years after their devastating defeat by Roman legions, they again mounted a massive popular revolt, named after its leader, the messiah "Bar Kochba" (for details see end of chapter 3). By the end of the three-year war of attrition, the Romans had again ravaged Jewish Palestine. Following the Roman military suppression of the rebellious peasantry, the rabbinic leadership finally succeeded in blunting and suppressing a key spur to the revolt: apocalypticism. The second devastating defeat of the popular Jewish rebellion thus marks the termination of a highly dynamic 300-year period of Jewish history, one that also saw the birth of two major religions: Rabbinic Judaism and Christianity.

The Jewish people's historical heritage from ancient Israel was one of freedom from foreign domination and domestic oppression. Their historical experience, however, especially under the Hellenistic and Roman empires, was one of domination, exploitation, and even persecution. Although the priestly ruling class at times compromised or even abandoned the people's sacred traditions, at least a substantial portion of the Jewish peasantry, along with numbers of scribes and ordinary priests, remembering their heritage, remained loyal to the people's covenant with God, resisted repression, and reasserted their liberty. Memories from earlier, "biblical" times as well as from more recent reassertions of the people's independence, such as the rebellion against Antiochus Epiphanes and resistance to Alexander Jannaeus, likely were kept alive and informed the periodic resistance to the Romans and, at times, their own high priestly aristocracy.

We now want to explore more fully some of the principal social forms which popular unrest and resistance assumed in

Jewish society around the time of Jesus. In doing so, however, we would like to move beyond standard treatments of this period which suggest, in effect, that the only important groups in the context were those that left literary remains, e.g., the Essenes, or were otherwise literate, e.g., the Pharisees, or that Jesus can be understood principally in comparison with the "Zealots." The period was far more complex than this. And although the sources are limited, they do give us at least some access to the various types of groups and leaders active in Jewish society at the time of Jesus, especially among the peasantry.

NOTES

1. A. N. Sherwin-White, *Roman Law and Roman Society in the New Testament* (Oxford: Oxford University, 1963), 139.
2. Ibid., 140.
3. Ibid., 141.
4. See R. Redfield, *Peasant Society and Culture* (Chicago: University of Chicago, 1969), 70-72; E. R. Wolf, *Anthropology* (New York: Norton, 1974), 73-74; applied to the rise of the Davidic monarchy by J. W. Flanagan, "The Relocation of the Davidic Capital," *JAAR* 47 (1979): 225-27.
5. For a good treatment of Israel's formative history in greater detail, see J. Bright, *A History of Israel,* 3rd ed. (Philadelphia: Westminster, 1981); for a more explicitly sociological analysis of Israel's origins, see N. Gottwald, *The Tribes of Yahweh,* (Maryknoll: Orbis, 1979); and, including a literary perspective, see *The Hebrew Bible—A Socio-Literary Introduction* (Philadelphia: Fortress, 1985).
6. See 2 Sam. 13-20.
7. Such "holy war" ideology, not uncommon in apocalyptic works such as Daniel, is, interestingly, reflected even in the Hellenistic-style historiography of the Judean revolt contained in 2 Maccabees (see 2 Macc. 8:15, 23). See also P. D. Miller, *The Divine Warrior in Early Israel* HSM 5 (Cambridge: Harvard University, 1973).

8. See J. J. Collins, *The Apocalyptic Vision of the Book of Daniel,* HSM 16 (Missoula: Scholars, 1977), 201-5; G. W. E. Nickelsburg, "Social Aspects of Palestinian Jewish Apocalypticism", in *Apocalypticism in the Mediterranean World and the Near East,* ed. D. Hellholm (Tübingen: Mohr, 1983), 641-54. However common it has been to see both the Pharisees and Essenes as direct outgrowths from the Hasidim, the available evidence does not firmly establish it. It is, however, a plausible explanation of their origins.

9. See G. Vermes, *The Dead Sea Scrolls in English* (Baltimore: Penguin, 1968), 13, 30 and *The Dead Sea Scrolls: Qumran in Perspective* (Philadelphia: Fortress, 1981), 125-30; F. M. Cross, *The Ancient Library of Qumran and Modern Biblical Studies,* The Haskell Lectures 1956-57, rev. ed. (Garden City: Anchor, 1961), 51-52.

10. See the discussion in J. Neusner, *From Politics to Piety: The Emergence of Pharisaic Judaism* (Englewood Cliffs: Prentice-Hall, 1973), 45-66, and *The Rabbinic Traditions about the Pharisees before 70,* 3 vols. (Leiden: Brill, 1971); E. E. Urbach, *The Sages: Their Concepts and Beliefs,* 2 vols., 2nd ed. (New York: Humanities, 1979). For a different evaluation, see E. Rivkin, *A Hidden Revolution: The Pharisees' Search for the Kingdom Within* (Nashville: Abingdon, 1978).

11. See *J.W.* 1.107-14; *Ant.* 18.11-17; 13.288-98; 13.399-418.

12. *Ant.* 13.288-98. A parallel Talmudic story (*Qidd.* 66a) is told of Alexander Jannaeus.

13. It is usually held, following Josephus (*Ant.* 13.297; 18.16), that the Sadducees only followed what was written down in scripture. Yet the Sadducees could hardly have taken those texts literally, without some kind of interpretation. Thus the Sadducees may have differed from the Pharisees in the extent of their interpretive tradition and the authority attributed to it.

14. See A. Schalit, *König Herodes, der Mann und sein Werk,* Studia Judaica 4 (Berlin: de Gruyter, 1969).

15. See the discussion of economic conditions in this period in chap. 2.

CHAPTER TWO

Ancient Jewish Social Banditry

When Judas and the "posse" sent by the high priests apprehended Jesus in the garden of Gethsemane, he asked rhetori-
cally (according to Mk. 14:48 and par.), "Have you come out
as against a bandit, with swords and clubs to capture me?"
Then, following his trial and conviction, he was crucified
between two "bandits" (Mk. 15:27). Why would Jesus be
portrayed as arrested and crucified as if he were a bandit?
Judging from Josephus' reports, and other reports, brigands
were an important factor in Jewish society. They figured
prominently in Herod's rise to power. In the mid-first century, they provided leadership for Judean peasants seeking
justice when the Roman governor was slow to act. Then,
reaching epidemic proportions in the fifties and sixties, brigands made up a significant portion of the fighting forces who
drove the Roman troops from Judea in the summer and fall of
66. The most significant thing Josephus mentions about several Roman governors is that they dealt with the phenomenon of banditry.

THE CHARACTERISTICS AND CONDITIONS OF SOCIAL BANDITRY

Primarily through the work of Eric Hobsbawm we have come
to understand social banditry in peasant societies as a form of
prepolitical rebellion.[1] Social banditry arises in traditional

agrarian societies where peasants are exploited by governments and landowners, particularly in situations where many
peasants are economically vulnerable and governments are
administratively inefficient. Such banditry may increase in
times of economic crisis, caused by famine or high taxation,
for example, as well as in times of social disruption, perhaps
resulting from the imposition of a new political or social-
economic system. Hobsbawm finds historical credibility in
the popular legends that bandits right wrongs, often function
as champions of justice for the common people, and usually
enjoy the support of local peasants. In fact, instead of aiding
the authorities in capturing bandits, the people may actually
protect them. Brigands usually share, and often symbolize,
the common people's fundamental sense of justice and their
basic religious loyalties. At times banditry comes into con-
junction with millenarianism, and in some historical circumstances it accompanies or leads to peasant revolts.

Social bandits emerge from incidents and circumstances
in which what is dictated by the state or local rulers is felt to
be unjust or intolerable. Underlying such incidents, however, are general social economic conditions in which many
peasants are marginal and vulnerable. It is always a rural
phenomenon. Says Hobsbawm, "Social banditry is univer-
sally found wherever societies are based on agricul-
ture . . . and consist largely of peasants and landless
laborers ruled, oppressed and exploited by someone else—
lords, towns, governments. . . ."[2] Moreover, the social brig-
and appears only before the poor have reached political consciousness or acquired more effective methods of social
agitation. Sharp social-economic conditions provide
favorable circumstances. Banditry occurs regularly in areas
and periods of administrative inefficiency which allow
breathing space for those decreed to be outlaws, whereas a
highly controlled and repressive regime may be able to suppress bandits no matter how intolerable the conditions.

Economic crises are likely to increase the scale of banditry. Peasants who cannot keep pace with escalating taxes or

rents become cut off from the land and vulnerable to the exactions of landlords and rulers. Famines may spell disaster for peasants, forcing many to seek other sources of liveli- hood. Even economic developments in the broader interna- tional or imperial economy, which are utterly inexplicable as well as uncontrollable for the peasants, may cause a sudden or steady decline in their condition. The social dislocation caused by civil war, the disruption of an entire society by foreign conquest, or the rise or imposition of new ruling classes and social structures may mean a dramatic escalation of banditry. The decline in effective power of the regime can produce similar results.

The social-economic context of ancient Jewish banditry featured just these conditions. The same conditions, more- over, provided the context and preconditions for the other popular groups to be examined below. One is forced to ask why so many hundreds, even thousands, of Jewish peasants were prepared to abandon their homes to pursue some prophet into the wilderness, or to rise in rebellion against their Jewish and Roman overlords when the signal was given by some charismatic "king," or to flee to the hills to join some brigand band. Peasants generally do not take such dras- tic action unless conditions have become such that they can no longer simply pursue the traditional patterns of life. Thus, our examination of the social-economic conditions giving rise to social banditry can serve simultaneously as a consider- ation of the conditions of other Jewish popular movements around the time of Jesus.

Recent studies of conditions of the peasantry in countries which have experienced large-scale "peasant revolts" in the twentieth century have found that, because peasant life is so marginal economically, serious changes in those conditions are often a key factor affecting peasant unrest. By no means does this make the level of economic deprivation and oppression a simple index of the degree of resistance and rebellion. The expectations of a particular group, the politi- cal conditions of the society, and the political consciousness of the people, among other things, are important factors in almost any situation. Nevertheless, changes in economic conditions are of particular importance simply because of the basic structure of most peasant societies, in which peasants live at or near the subsistence level economically.

Furthermore, studies of peasant revolts and their conditions also indicate that "the peasantry" in a given society is never a homogeneous mass of people. There are differences in behavior and outlook between the well-off and the destitute, between tenants and proprietors, between craftsmen and crop farmers, between those who are only heavily in debt and those who have been forced off their land into the ranks of the wage-laborers. Similarly, there are variations in which large-scale social changes affect people, even within a particular village. However, the data available for the Palestinian Jewish peasantry under Roman domination and the correspondingly rudimentary development of scholarly study mean that it is not possible to carry out a very precise analysis of the economic conditions and changes, let alone a detailed analysis of how different strata of peasants reacted to certain changes. We can outline the general conditions of the Jewish peasants, and we can note particular broad changes in those conditions and the long-term effects of political circumstances on peasant life in general.

To understand why popular unrest took a particular form, such as the messianic or prophetic movements, it is necessary to examine more closely the distinctive traditions of Jewish society, out of which the people were responding to the crises of their lives (see chapters 3 and 4). In this chapter, we will first examine the general circumstances which were changing the conditions of Jewish peasant life. Then, partly as a way of illustrating how peasant life was being disrupted, and partly as a way of becoming more familiar with the conditions of peasant life, we will examine the occurrence and escalating frequency of social banditry in the period between the Roman conquest in 63 B.C.E. and the popular revolt against Rome.

THE SOCIOECONOMIC CONDITIONS
OF JEWISH SOCIAL BANDITRY AND OTHER
POPULAR MOVEMENTS

As part of his message of the coming of the kingdom of God,
Jesus exhorted his listeners: "Therefore, I tell you, do not be
anxious about your life, what you shall eat, nor about your
body, what you shall put on. . . . Instead, seek his kingdom,
and all these things shall be yours as well" (Lk. 12:22, 31; Mt.
6:25, 33). Apparently, Jewish peasants of Jesus' time did
worry about what they were going to eat and what they would
put on. What provided the means for having something to eat
or to put on was the land, or access to it. For many Jewish
peasants at the time, however, access to land had become
problematic.[3] In order to live, a peasant had to have land on
which he could raise not only enough food to survive until
the next harvest, but also enough extra grain for seed for the
next year's crops, enough for feed for a draft animal (if he
had any), enough to sell or barter for whatever necessities he
could not raise himself, and enough extra to provide for
whatever ceremonies might be celebrated to help explain
and regulate life. Over and above these necessities for the
sustenance of family or village life from one year to the next,
however, peasants were expected to produce more, namely,
a "surplus." The reason for this surplus was that peasants
"are rural cultivators whose surpluses are transferred to a
dominant group of rulers that uses the surpluses both to
underwrite its own standard of living and to distribute the
remainder to groups in society that do not farm but must be
fed for their specific goods and services in turn."[4] When so
many Jewish peasants in Jesus' time were worried about what
they would eat and wear, their worry was directly related to
the amount of surpluses which the rulers were demanding,
the ways in which the rulers were demanding them, and how
the peasantry perceived the character, the legitimacy, and
the behavior of the various types of ruling elite which their
surpluses were supporting. The way the Jewish peasants

responded, of course, had a great deal to do with how they thought these relations should be and how they were actually developing.

The primary obligation of the Jewish peasantry was the traditional tithes. Support of the elaborate priesthood and temple apparatus in Jerusalem was understood as an obligation to God. Almost from the very beginnings of civilization in the ancient Near East, the land was thought of as the estate of the god of that particular area or of the gods of the society generally. Temples were the houses of the gods, and human beings, as explained toward the end of the Babylonian creation myth, "Enuma Elish,"[5] had been created as servants of the gods, to enable them to tend to the business of maintaining order and stability in the cosmos and still have time for the banqueting appropriate to their important role in the universe. The responsibility of the vast majority of people, therefore, was to produce an abundance of goods to be brought to the temple storehouses, where the priests and "great ones" would then tend to the care and feeding of the gods.

In a similar way, early Israel also conceived of the land as belonging to its God, Yahweh. Because God had given them the land, they were to return a portion of its produce in gratitude for God's benevolence. Yahweh, however, in the original Mosaic covenantal order of early Israel, had specifically declined to build and maintain the elaborate apparatus of an institutionalized temple and priesthood, supported, of course, by peasant surpluses. Instead, the tithes or offerings to God in early Israel were apparently used in religious festivals in which God was seen as sharing the bounty with those who brought them, and they were also used to care for the poor, the widows, the landless, and local priests and Levites. Under the monarchy, however, the Davidic kings, as regents of God, laid claim both to the produce of the land and to the labor which the people supposedly owed to God, and thereby maintained the temple worship and priesthood.

When, in 587 B.C.E., the Babylonians destroyed the temple along with the rest of Jerusalem and its environs, they took into exile the ruling class, the monarch and temple priesthood. Later, the Persians, apparently on standard imperial policy, decided that it would be well to rebuild the "house" of the God of Israel—that is, "the god who is in Jerusalem" —and to restore to their position of dominance in Judea those who would tend to his worship. The descendants of the former ruling groups of Judah, especially of the old Jerusalem priesthood, were thus enabled to reestablish themselves at the head of Judean society, now centered in the reconstructed temple. The Judean peasantry—which had remained on the land during the exile of the ruling class— offered some initial resistance, but gradually acquiesced in the restoration. In gratitude for the restoration of the people in the land of promise, a renewed covenant was made with God, this time emphasizing less the care of the poor than the care of the house of God and its priesthood. In addition to a great variety of specialized offerings, the people obligated themselves

> to bring the first fruits of our ground and the first fruits of all fruit of every tree, year by year, to the house of the Lord; also to bring to the house of our God, to the priests who minister in the house of our God, the . . . firstlings of our herds and of our flocks; and to bring the first of our coarse meal, and our contributions, the first of every tree, the wine and the oil, to the priests, to the chambers of the house of our God; and to bring to the Levites the tithes from our ground, for it is the Levites who collect the tithes in all our rural towns. . . . For the people of Israel and the sons of Levi shall bring the contribution of grain, wine, and oil to the chambers, where are the vessels of the sanctuary and the priests that minister, and the gatekeepers and the singers. We will not neglect the house of our God. (Neh. 10:32-39)

While it is difficult to reach an accurate estimate of the extent of the obligation for each peasant family or clan in all these dues and tithes, it is clear that it amounted to a heavy

portion of their produce, all in basic religiopolitical obligations to the hierarchy and other priests and their activities.[6]
The people generally took these obligations seriously. For
example, even after the beginning of the great revolt, Jews in
Galilee willingly rendered up their taxes to priests. Shortly
after he and other emissaries from Jerusalem had arrived to
take charge of affairs in Galilee, Josephus notes, "My colleagues, having accumulated a large amount of money from
the tithes which they received as their priestly due, decided
to return home. . . ." (*Life*, 63), while he, of course,
declined to accept such tithes "which were due to me as a
priest" (*Life*, 80). The Pharisees themselves rigorously
observed the laws about tithing and taxation and apparently
urged the rest of the people to do likewise. There was
undoubtedly some popular grumbling, as well as simple
nonobservance and evasion. It is noteworthy, however, in
Jesus' harangue against the Pharisees that while he carica-
tures their fastidiousness about tithing laws—tithing even
the herbs mint, dill, and cummin—he criticizes only their
neglect of justice and mercy, not the basic obligation to tithe
(see Lk. 11:42; Mt. 23:23). Like the way in which many a
peasant society viewed its king, the common people looked
to the temple and high priesthood as highly positive symbols
of the unity of the people and their link with God, guardian
of the proper social order. If they were abused, the evil or
scheming advisers or ministers of the sovereign were to
blame, not the monarchy, high priesthood, or temple itself.
We may reasonably surmise, then, that the Jewish peasantry
accepted their primary and traditional obligation of tithes
and other dues to support the priesthood and temple
apparatus.

Under the Persian and Hellenistic empires, of course, the
whole society had to pay a certain amount of tribute to the
imperial administration. It is probable that this was raised by
taxation in addition to the basic tithes and sacrifices. Under
the Seleucids, the total tribute had been a third of the grain
and half of the wine and oil. Under the native Hasmonean

regime, however, it is likely that the overall obligations of the Jewish producers were reduced. It was thus a dramatic change of circumstances when Rome conquered Jewish Palestine and laid it under tribute. Now Roman tribute was superimposed on the tithes and other taxes owed to the temple and priesthood. In one of the official documents Josephus has preserved, we read,

> [Julius] Gaius Caesar, Imperator for the second time, commanded that they shall pay a tax for the city of Jerusalem, Joppa excluded, every year except the seventh, which they call the sabbatical year, because during this year they neither harvest fruit from the trees nor sow. [He also decreed] that in the second year they shall pay the tribute at Sidon, in the amount of one fourth of the produce sown; in addition, they shall also pay tithes to Hyrcanus [II] and his sons, just as they paid them to their forefathers. (*Ant.* 14.202-3)

The Jewish agricultural producers were now subject to a double taxation, probably amounting to well over 40 percent of their production. There were other Roman taxes as well, which further added to the burden of the people, but the tribute was the major drain.

Coming, as it did, immediately after a period of ostensible national independence under the Hasmoneans, Roman domination was regarded as wholly illegitimate. The tribute was seen as robbery. Indeed, it was called outright slavery by militant teachers such as Judas of Galilee, who organized active resistance to the census when the Romans took over direct administration of Judea in 6 C.E.[7] But virtually the whole society must have resented the tribute intensely. Even the priestly aristocracy, who otherwise collaborated in the Roman rule of Palestine, but whose own revenues stood effectively in competition with the Roman taxation, helped to organize protests against the excessive taxation. It did not occur to the high priests to reduce their own taxation, of course, even though they no longer needed to maintain military forces and a complete political administration of an

independent state. For the Romans, tribute was an extremely
serious matter. Any nonpayment was taken as tantamount to
rebellion, to which Rome usually responded with punitive
force. Thus the Jewish peasant producers remained subject
to this double taxation throughout the period, and it was a
serious and steady drain on their resources.

Roman conquest put pressures on the peasant economy
over and above the steady drain of double taxation. First, the
requirements for Roman civil war caused demands for special levies of taxes, large sums to be raised almost immediately. Second, the Roman armies often devastated both the
villages and their populaces. For example, four district centers (Gophna, Emmaus, Lydda, and Thamna) slow in raising
the special levy of taxes demanded by Cassius were simply
reduced to slavery (*J. W.* 1.219-22; *Ant.* 14.271-75). Also, in
the area of Emmaus, a Roman general, Machaeras, out of
pique at rival Jewish leaders, slaughtered all the Jews he met
on his retreat from Jerusalem to Emmaus (*J. W.* 1.317-19; *Ant.*
14.436). Third, the direct devastation caused by Roman
armies was compounded by further devastations resulting
from the struggles of rival Hasmonean factions seeking control of Judea, as well as Herod's prolonged effort to conquer
his "kingdom" with the help of Roman armies. While the
immediate impact of any of these special levies or devastations may have been limited, individually and collectively,
they surely had a lasting effect on the ability of certain families or villages to remain economically viable.

The Roman "liberation" of the Hellenistic cities which
had been subjected by the Hasmoneans in the second century B.C.E. in all probability had an enduring impact on the
Jewish peasantry. The Romans restored some of these cities'
previous territory as well, i.e., rural areas or villages subject
to them. Initially, only a limited number of Jews who suddenly found themselves subject to a restored Hellenistic city
would have fled across the border as refugees. But with time
and a situation of increased demand for surplus products
created by the Roman conquest, one likely effect was a

steady flow of refugees into areas still under Jewish authorities.[8] It is not difficult to imagine the various ways in which
the resultant overpopulation in the now-reduced Jewish territory would have placed additional demands on the land, its
productivity, and the producers: more mouths to feed,
increased demand for charity and tithes, expropriation, and
further subdivision of the land.

The regime of Herod the Great brought an end to social-
political turmoil due to its repressiveness. But Herod's elaborate administration and diplomatic munificence, along with
his ambitious building projects, intensified the burden on
peasant producers. Payment to the Romans remained. Tithes
for the priesthood and temple remained. Although Herod
sponsored some "economic development" of new areas in
the south and northeast, it could not have supported but a
fraction of the cost of his vast building projects (e.g., the
temple, whole new Hellenistic cities). Small wonder that the
representatives of the Jewish aristocracy, in delegation to
Rome at the death of Herod, complained that he had virtually
bled the country dry (see *Ant.* 17.304-8).

The effect of any one of these pressures on the productivity and subsistence of the Jewish peasantry would have been
to drive the peasants into debt. If a peasant family, after
rendering up 40 percent or more of its harvest, then had too
little left to survive until the next harvest, it would have to
borrow grain for food, or for seed for the next sowing. Family
members may already have tried to hire themselves out as
wage labor to a larger landholder. As Jesus' parable in Mt. 20
indicates, however, there were many more people looking
for work than could be hired (one of the effects of overpopulation already noted). Under such economic pressures, with
too little produced to meet the demands both for subsistence
and for surpluses, the peasants were forced to borrow. Continued borrowing would increase a family's debt significantly, with a great risk of complete loss of land. One would
then sink into the ranks of the rural proletariat, the landless

day laborers, or one could become a sharecropping tenant, perhaps on one's own former parcel of land.

Judging from the parables of Jesus (e.g., Mk. 12:1-9; Mt. 20:1-16), this was exactly what had been happening to the peasantry. The dominant pattern of land tenure in his time was probably still independent family holdings, with varying degrees of indebtedness, of course. But other patterns had become prominent, so much so that they could be used as vivid illustrations from which the listeners could easily draw the intended analogy. Large landed estates administered by stewards and farmed by tenants had become familiar. An oversupply of laborers was just waiting for any amount of work, even until the eleventh hour of the day. Even if some of the laborers were not landless, seeking only to supplement their inadequate produce with "outside income," in the case of both laborers and tenants, it is evident that peasants had lost, or were threatened with the loss of, their own land. Given the demand for surpluses (taxes), the mechanism by which the land was lost was indebtedness, another phenomenon familiar from Jesus' parables.

In ancient Israel, by contrast, under Mosaic covenantal stipulations to prevent peasant loss of land through indebtedness, provisions were made for the release of debts and debt-slaves every seventh year (see Ex. 21:2; Deut. 15:1-18; Lev. 25:35-42). Moreover, in the event that people still lost their land, despite the sabbatical release, there was (supposedly) the Jubilee Year, a proclamation of liberty in which each person should return to the original family inheritance (see Lev. 25:8-24). Although there are serious doubts that the Jubilee Year was actually observed, it was clearly an ideal in the people's minds. The sabbatical release of debts was, apparently, taken with some degree of seriousness in the late second temple period. Because of the double taxation, Jewish and Roman, compounded by Herod's demands, there was considerable pressure for peasants to obtain loans. But because the sabbatical release was taken seriously, potential creditors were reluctant to make loans in the last few years prior to the sabbatical year. Assuming the historicity of its promulgation (which has been disputed), this was the context and the purpose of the *prosbul* established by the Pharisaic sage Hillel, under Herod's reign. So that the desperate peasants could obtain the needed loans from otherwise reluctant creditors, Hillel designed a legal ruse by which the provisions of the law of sabbatical release of debts could be bypassed.

> [A loan secured by] a *prosbul* is not cancelled [by the seventh year]. This is one of the things that Hillel the Elder ordained. This is the formula of the *prosbul*: I affirm to you, such-a-one and such-a-one, the judges in such a place, that touching any debt due to me, I will collect it whensoever I will. (M. Shevuot 10.3-4)

The short-term effect of such a provision was surely relief for hungry and overtaxed peasants. The long-range effect was permanent debt.

An indebted peasantry, however, was yet another mechanism by which the wealthy and powerful could extract still more surplus from the producers. For not only did they have to deduct 40 percent or more from their total harvest for tribute and tithes, they still had loans to repay and even (the supposedly illegal) interest on the loans as well. Thus, simply by making loans, the wealthy could have their debtors out in the villages producing the goods necessary for their more leisurely life-style in Jerusalem (100 measures of oil here and a 100 measures of wheat there, as in Jesus' parable in Lk. 16:5-7).

Ironically, the wealth which thus accrued to the rich and powerful priests, Herodians, and others in Jerusalem contributed further to the spiral of peasant indebtedness, loss of land, and the growth of large landed estates. From the tithes and other dues to the priesthood and temple, through repayment and interest on loans, and even through the contributions which Diaspora Jews from around the world sent to the

temple, surplus wealth flowed into, and piled up in, Jerusalem. There were no mechanisms, however, by which these
resources could be channeled to the people most in need;
most of the contributions to the poor came from the villages
and small towns themselves. Rather, some of the surplus
wealth was used on luxury goods or simply stored in the
temple treasury, in the form of valuable metals or objects.
But much of this wealth was also apparently "invested" in
land. And the means by which this was done was high-inter-
est loans to needy peasants, many of whom eventually had to
forfeit their ancestral lands to their creditors.

Another factor which strongly contributed to popular
unrest, and is closely related to peasant indebtedness and
loss of land, was periodic drought, and the resultant famine.
There had been a serious drought and famine in 25-24 B.C.E.,
as well as a very severe one in the late forties C.E. Queen
Helena of Adiabene (a convert to Judaism), then on a pil-
grimage to Jerusalem, provided some relief for the
Jerusalemites (see *Ant.* 20.51-53, 101). But the prolonged
famine undoubtedly forced many more peasants into debt
and caused many finally to lose their holdings altogether. As
we shall see, the famine of the late forties was almost certainly an important factor contributing to the growing social
turmoil of the fifties and sixties.

A final factor contributing to the turbulence of first-century C.E. society and the readiness of Jewish peasants to join
various movements was the illegitimate character, the compromised position, and the exploitative behavior of the Jewish ruling class. Even under conditions of hardship and
exploitation, a subject peasantry might continue to acquiesce to the authority of the established rulers of the society.
However, this was not the case in Jewish society of the first
century. As Josephus notes, in connection with his report of
the high priestly servants' expropriation of the tithes right off
the threshing floors: "Hostility and violent factionalism
flared between high priests on one side, and the priests and
leaders of the Jerusalem masses on the other" (*Ant.* 20.180).

Despite the tensions between classes in Jewish society, the temple was in the main a highly positive *symbol* for most Jews in Palestine, as was, apparently, the priesthood generally. Yet precisely because of the importance of the temple as a religiopolitical symbol, the high priests of the late second temple period and the temple administration generally seemed of questionable legitimacy. The Hasmoneans, originally leaders of the popular revolt against the Hellenizing elite, were non-Zadokite usurpers of the high priestly office. The high priestly families which Herod brought in and which monopolized the chief priestly offices right up to the Jewish revolt were, some of them, not even Palestinian Jewish families, but powerful families from the Diaspora. More serious was their increasingly exploitative behavior vis-à-vis both the ordinary priests and the people generally, as Josephus indicated. One major reason for such behavior was the fact that the priestly aristocracy owed its very position of wealth and power to the Romans. As a result, and in order to stay at the head of Jewish society, it had to collaborate with the Roman imperial system. Its compromised position was vividly dramatized just prior to the outbreak of the revolt in 66. The tribute was in arrears. For the Romans, as we have noted, this was tantamount to rebellion. Thus the aristocracy itself hurriedly set about trying to collect the tribute from a populace that was hardly in a mood to "render unto Caesar. . . ." Not surprisingly, the widespread insurrection that exploded a few weeks later was directed against the priestly aristocracy as well as against the Romans. Yet, the aristocracy, if not the Romans, were well aware of the hard-pressed circumstances of the peasantry in general, and they were certainly aware of the direct connection between the people's inability to raise crops sufficient to meet the heavy demands for taxes and the existence and growth of banditry. Earlier, after a prolonged peasant strike protesting the Emperor Gaius' orders to erect a statue of himself as a god in the temple, some members of the Herodian family warned the Syrian legate Petronius that if the standoff was further extended, "bandit raids would sprout up—since the fields were not planted—and payment of the tribute would be impossible" (*Ant.* 18.274; the whole incident: *Ant.* 20.261-78; *J.W.* 2.184-203).

SOCIAL BANDITRY IN PALESTINE

With the conditions so difficult for the Jewish peasantry, it is not surprising to find upsurges of banditry. Rome's delegation of Pompey (64 B.C.E.) to "pacify" the eastern Mediterranean inaugurated a new era of foreign domination for the Jews. It also began a generation-long period of extreme political and social-economic turmoil in Palestine. Pompey's settlement of the Palestinian political situation had left the last Hasmonean king-high priest, Hyrcanus, with only the rural and mainly Jewish core of the Hasmonean kingdom. As noted earlier in this chapter, this caused an acute shortage of land for Jewish peasants, particularly in the border areas.

In 57 B.C.E. the proconsul in Syria, Gabinius, infamous for his extortions, granted the local nobility governing power in their respective districts, an arrangement which placed the peasantry under direct pressure from their gentry. Vast numbers of people thus predictably rallied to the side of Aristobulus, the rival Hasmonean, in 56-55, but Gabinius suppressed the rebellion. Nevertheless, only after Caesar's consolidation of power in Rome could Hyrcanus' prime minister, Antipater (Herod's father), acquire sufficient power to rule Palestine effectively (48-47).

It is no surprise that we find banditry thriving in the aftermath of this period of civil war and political-economic strife. "Hezekiah, a brigand-chief with a very large gang, was overrunning the district on the Syrian frontier" (*J.W.* 1.204). The Galileans who joined the brigand band led by Hezekiah were probably victims of, and fugitives from, the shifting political and economic situation as well as the newly acquired power of the local nobility (*J.W.* 1.204-11; *Ant.*

14.159-74). This "very large gang" of brigands was raiding primarily along the Syrian border area—at least until Antipater's consolidation of power ended the period of central governmental weakness. Herod, delegated by his father, Antipater, to govern Galilee, soon caught and killed Hezekiah and many of his brigands, much to the pleasure of the Syrians and consternation of the Galilean peasants, as we shall see.

A decade later we find Herod once again suppressing brigands along with other rebels in Galilee. "Brigands who lived in caves were over-running much of the countryside and inflicting injuries on the inhabitants as much as a war would have done" (*J.W.* 1.304). As in Italy and other areas of the Roman empire, so in Galilee large numbers of brigands appeared in the wake of renewed civil war. Moreover, the special Roman taxes suddenly levied by Cassius and vigorously collected by Herod had been an aggravating factor in Galilee. Just as the peasants had earlier rallied to the cause of Aristobulus against Hyrcanus and Antipater, so they took the side of his son Antigonus when the Parthians installed him in power in 40-39 B.C.E. Herod raised an army to regain control in 39-38. The Galilean brigands pursued by Herod in 38 were clearly an important part of the continuing opposition to Herod as he attempted to consolidate his own power as the Romans' client king. These brigands were not an isolated pocket of resistance, but rather one very distinctive form of the continuing and extensive popular resistance to Herod. Prior to the scholarly discovery of the social reality of banditry, it was argued that the brigands in this situation are to be identified simply with the remaining supporters of Antigonus, another rival Hasmonean. But such an explanation fails to appreciate the complexity of the situation of Galilean peasant resistance. For Josephus says quite clearly that, after "Galilee" (the gentry) joined his side, Herod first captured the strongholds and only then proceeded against the large force of brigands (*J.W.* 1.303-4).

On the basis of these circumstances it is not difficult to deduce which inhabitants were being attacked by the bandits (*J. W.* 1.304). The most unlikely candidates are the peasants, who viewed Herod and the gentry who had joined him as the enemy, not the bandits. Rather, the inhabitants attacked by the brigands were the Galilean gentry. Although the common people had drowned a number of them in the Sea of Galilee, the notables apparently had made some progress in reestablishing their control. The brigands had found it necessary to retreat to the caves in the precipitous cliffs near the village of Arbela. But they remained strong enough to harass the gentry, and they posed a threat to Herod's complete control of Galilee. Indeed, the brigands were either strong enough or bold enough to attack Herod and his whole army as he advanced on their stronghold. Herod, however, with his superior military force, was able to slaughter many of the bandits and to chase others across the Jordan River. Those who escaped retreated to their nearly inaccessible stronghold in the caves. After a while Herod finally devised a way to attack these brigands in their caves, a story that Josephus recounts with great relish (*J. W.* 1.304-13; *Ant.* 14.415-30):

> With ropes he lowered [over the cliffs] the toughest of his men in large baskets until they reached the mouths of the caves; they then slaughtered the brigands and their families, and threw firebrands at those who resisted. . . . Not a one of them voluntarily surrendered and of those brought out forcibly many preferred death to captivity [*J. W.* 1.311]. . . . An old man who had been caught inside one of the caves with his wife and seven children . . . stood at the entrance and cut down each of his sons as they came to the mouth of the cave, and then his wife. After throwing their dead bodies down the steep slope, he threw himself down too, thus submitting to death rather than slavery. (*Ant.* 14.429-30)

We possess little or no evidence of banditry for the long reign of Herod. But this does not mean there was none at all. The presence of some brigands in the popular messianic movement in Perea following the death of Herod suggests that there may occasionally have been some bandits in the outlying areas. Herod's regime, however, was indeed "efficient." He maintained strict and oppressive social control by means of a network of fortresses throughout the realm, a large army, a security police, and even a system of informers. Thus, despite the harsh economic demands made by the Herodian regime, it was extremely difficult for banditry to emerge; prolonged bandit activity was impossible, and no subversive activity of any form could long escape detection. A Pharisaic saying attributed to the Herodian period well expresses the prevailing atmosphere: "Love work and hate mastery, and make not thyself known to the government" (Pirke Abot 1.10).

Our principal source, Josephus, provides little information about the period from the Roman deposition of Herod's son and successor in Judea, Archelaus, to the end of the reign of Agrippa I (6-44 C.E.). Perhaps his own lack of sources for the period partly explains why he does not report any significant bandit activity until nearly mid-first century. Consequently, it is also difficult to determine just how typical may have been the brigand troop led by Tholomaus toward the end of this period, or what special circumstances may have surrounded such bandit activity. Besides the heavy burden of double taxation, the situation of alien rule was frequently aggravated further by offensive incidents as well. Because of the Jews' unusual religious customs and sensitivities, the general Roman policy was to handle them delicately. Unfortunately, however, there occurred periodic provocations by hostile soldiers or Samaritans and particularly by the more insensitive and ruthless Roman governors. Pontius Pilate, the most notorious, governor from 26-36 C.E., and hardly the indecisive fellow portrayed in the Christian Gospels, provoked some major incidents and immediately suppressed with ruthless military violence any suspicious activity among the populace, such as protests and prophetic movements (*Ant.* 18.55-62, 85-87; *J.W.* 2.169-77).

If the Christian gospel tradition in Mk. 15:27 is historically reliable, "and with him they crucified two bandits,"[9] it provides evidence of some banditry during the life of Jesus and the administration of Pontius Pilate. Some time later, the brigand group led by Tholomaus made raids primarily in Idumea and along the border of Arabia (*Ant.* 20.5). It must have been a band of considerable size; Josephus calls Tholomaus a "brigand-chief," a term he elsewhere applies only to Hezekiah before him and Eleazar after him, both of whom were leaders of large troops of brigands. Other groups besides that led by Tholomaus certainly existed at points around the country at the time. In addition to the capture and execution of Tholomaus, one of the things that Josephus includes regarding the administration of Fadus (44-46 C.E.) was the purge of brigand groups from "the whole of Judea" (*Ant.* 20.5). Josephus has also exaggerated Fadus' success, for he later mentions that the bandit leader Eleazar ben Dinai had been active for twenty years before finally being captured under the procurator Felix (52-60) (*Ant.* 20.160-61). Thus, although we do not know for sure just how prevalent banditry was during the whole period from Archelaus to Agrippa I, we do know that there was considerable bandit activity during the thirties and forties.

Banditry increased sharply around mid-first century. This is almost certainly due to the severe famine that occurred under the procurator Tiberius Alexander (46-48 C.E.). Famine, as has been noted, is one of the special economic circumstances almost certain to result in an upsurge of bandit activity—especially in the case of the Jewish peasantry already bearing the burden of double taxation, alien rule, and occasional provocations. By piecing together a number of Josephus' incidental comments we can reconstruct several significant features of the expanding Jewish banditry. A leader and his following could operate for a considerable period of time without being caught, as illustrated by the twenty-year career of Eleazar (*J.W.* 2.253). More than just Eleazar's band were strong enough to conduct rather bold operations. Among the disorders originating from banditry, "on the public road going to Beth-horon some brigands swooped down on a certain Stephen, a servant of Caesar, and robbed him of his baggage" (*J. W.* 2.228). The daring of such brigand groups may well have been due to their apparently substantial size. Eleazar had numerous followers ("many associates," *J. W.* 2.253) whom he had "organized into a company" (*Ant.* 20.161). And Eleazar and Alexander had a following sufficiently large to lead a massive retaliatory raiding expedition for the Judean peasantry into Samaria (*J. W.* 2.235; *Ant.* 20.121). Moreover, actions taken by the authorities to capture or punish the existing bands of brigands led to the outbreak of even further banditry. "Many of them [Jewish peasants] turned to banditry out of recklessness, and throughout the whole country there were raids, and among the more daring, revolts" (*J.W.* 2.238). Finally, the sheer number of brigands must have been considerable in the years following the famine, a period during which both Cumanus (48-52) and Felix (52-60) devoted great energy to the suppression of banditry. Although, following Cumanus' military action against the expedition of Judean peasants and brigands into Samaria, "the people were scattered and the brigands withdrew to their strongholds," [Josephus adds significantly] "from then on the whole of Judea was infested with brigands" (*Ant.* 20.124). "Felix captured the brigand-chief Eleazar, who for twenty years had plundered the country, as well as many of his associates, and sent them to Rome for trial. The number of brigands that he crucified . . . was enormous" (*J. W.* 2.253).

A few years before the revolt, Jewish banditry multiplied to epidemic proportions in spite of, if not because of, the measures taken by the Roman governors. Conditions under the administration of Albinus (62-64) were precisely those which favored widespread banditry (see *J. W.* 2.272-73; *Ant.* 20.215). In addition to general resentment of Roman domination, rich and poor were sharply polarized (see *Ant.* 20.180, cited above). Albinus further aggravated the situation with an extraordinary levy of taxes. His predecessor, Festus (60-62), had established a repressive policy and had imprisoned many, even for trivial offenses. Albinus reversed this policy and accepted ransoms from the relatives of many prisoners. The direct effect of this inconsistent administrative policy did not escape Josephus: "Thus the prison was cleared of inmates, but the land then became infested with brigands" (*Ant.* 20.215). The next procurator, Gessius Florus, displayed similar behavior, only more publicly and outrageously. To Josephus and other well-to-do Jews, Florus' administration seemed a partnership with the brigands. Josephus claims that now "the majority of people" (*hoi polloi*) practiced banditry, and that whole towns were ruined (*Ant.* 20.255). The banditry evidently took its toll on the gentry, for many wealthy Jews left their estates in search of safer surroundings among the Gentiles. With little to lose from increasing disorder, a sizable portion of the population had become outlaws. Expanding banditry became a major factor leading to the outbreak of the massive revolt against the Romans. For example, large groups of brigands already held sway as a dominant force in Galilee when Josephus arrived to take charge of organizing the defenses in 66-67.

RELATIONS BETWEEN BRIGANDS AND PEASANTS

Social bandits usually have the support and even the protection of their village or of the people in general. They may even periodically rejoin their community with no difficulty. Although the authorities demand local assistance in capturing brigands, the people do not often cooperate, and may actually protect the outlaws. Often it is possible to apprehend or kill brigands only through special means such as betrayal or trickery. The local common people will tend to regard a fugitive from the alien justice of the rich and powerful as honorable, as a victim of injustice, or even as a noble hero. A successful brigand may even be a symbol of hope for the peasants that their oppression is not inevitable.

Moreover, as Hobsbawm points out, there is historical substance behind the legends that brigands right wrongs. Among the rich from whom the brigand takes—for the poor have little worth taking—are the usual enemies of the poor: wealthy landowners and overlords, church prelates and genteel clerics who live in leisurely style off the labor and tithes of the peasants, and foreign rulers and others who have upset the traditional order of life. Some magnanimous Robin Hoods, such as Pancho Villa, actually also give to the poor. But beyond this simple redistribution of goods there are numerous ways in which brigands serve as defenders and champions of the common people.

Social bandits also generally share the fundamental values and religion of the peasant society of which they remain at least a marginal part. They may be defenders of the faith as well as of what is right. They are not enemies of the king or pope, unless of course the king is a foreign despot or otherwise illegitimate according to the peasants' traditional orientation. The bandit himself is viewed as just and cannot be in conflict with justice or its divine source. In fact, the bandit himself may represent a divine justice that the peasants have rarely experienced, but for which they may continue to hold out hope in a manner not unrelated to biblical fantasies:

> I the scriptures have fulfilled,
> Though a wicked life I led.
> When the naked I beheld
> I've clothed them and fed;
> Sometime in a coat of winter's pride,
> Sometime in russet grey,
> The naked I've clothed and hungry I've fed,
> And the rich I've sent empty away.[10]

In brief, over against the unjust and oppressive regime of local gentry or a distant government, the common people stand to protect their kin and friends who have run afoul of the official law and order through intransigence or misfortune. The social brigand is viewed as a hero of righteousness and a symbol of the people's hope for a restoration of a more just order.

The length of the career of Eleazar ben Dinai and the manner of his eventual capture illustrate Hobsbawm's point that brigands usually enjoy the support of the peasants.[11] It was only by trickery, by offering false assurances, that the procurator Felix was able to capture the elusive brigand-chief. To be sure, the inaccessible terrain of the Judean mountains which he used as his base of operations provided good protection. But Eleazar was unafraid to operate openly in the Judean and Samaritan countryside. For him to have sustained a twenty-year career obviously required the protection of the peasantry.

Hezekiah and his followers, nearly a century earlier, provide the clearest example of brigands as innocent heroes, victims of the tyrannical law and order imposed by the young Herod. Numerous relatives of the brigands made the long journey from Galilee to Jerusalem, where "daily in the temple the mothers of the men who had been killed by Herod kept begging the king-high priest and the elders to have Herod brought to judgment in the Sanhedrin for what he had done" (*Ant.* 14.168). One would expect bereaved mothers to bewail their dead sons, even if they had been heinous criminals executed by legitimate political authorities. But the popular response in this case went considerably beyond bereavement to an extensive demonstration, three days' journey from home, of righteous indignation at Herod's exercise of tyrannical power. The common people regarded the brigands as honorable men, unjustly murdered. From Hobsbawm's material one is reminded of the prayer of the women of San Stefano for the safety of the Calabrian bandit: "Musolino is innocent/ They have condemned him unjustly;/ Oh, Madonna, oh Saint Joseph,/ Let him always be under your protection . . . / Oh Jesus, oh my Madonna. . ."[12]

However, the Jewish peasants not only supported bandits and viewed them as heroic victims of injustice, but also protected them and were willing to suffer the consequences. In Palestine as elsewhere in the Empire, Roman governors expected local native officials to capture brigands and criminals. The Jewish village leaders did not oblige the imperial expectations. When bandits robbed Caesar's servant Stephen near Beth-horon, the local villagers, far from pursuing and apprehending the outlaws, protected them instead. The procurator, Cumanus, accordingly ordered the inhabitants (at least the village elders) brought up to Jerusalem in chains and took vengeance by having their villages plundered. On the plundering expedition a Roman soldier burned a copy of the Torah, a famous incident that provoked a great protest by the whole Jewish populace. Even before the protest of the Torah burning, however, it is evident that the local peasants around Beth-horon were willing to suffer the consequences of sheltering the brigands (*Ant.* 20.113-17; *J. W.* 2.228-31). Josephus indicates the relationship clearly, if briefly, in a summary statement: "The number of brigands that he crucified, as well as the number of common people who were found to be their accomplices and punished by him, was enormous" (*J. W.* 2.253).

Those robbed or attacked by Jewish brigands were indeed the wealthy Jewish landowners and representatives of foreign domination. Josephus wrote that the Galilean "brigands who lived in caves [in 38 B.C.E.] were over-running much of the countryside and inflicting injuries on the inhabitants as much as a war would have done" (*J. W.* 1.304). Through analysis of the social-historical circumstances, we determined that the "inhabitants" in this case were the wealthy Galilean gentry who had joined forces with Herod in order to reassert their control over the country. It is clear that the Galilean peasantry also viewed their gentry as enemies. The brigands in these circumstances were part of a widespread popular opposition to the Galilean notables and Herod, in his campaign to take full control in Palestine. Following

Herod's defeat of the remaining supporters of the last rival Hasmonean, Antigonus, and his destruction of the cave-dwelling brigands, there were two further popular uprisings within the same year (38 B.C.E.). In the second of these the people drowned their nobles in the Sea of Galilee (*J.W.* 1.314-16, 326; *Ant.* 14.431-33).

The wealthy gentry were still the object of brigand attacks a century later as banditry escalated to epidemic proportions just prior to the outbreak of the great revolt in 66 C.E. In this case, it is noteworthy how Josephus distinguishes "the Jews," i.e., the gentry, from *hoi polloi,* "the masses." With "the masses" now extensively engaged in banditry, "the unfortunate Jews, unable to endure the devastations that took place at the hands of the brigands, were forced to abandon home and country and flee, since anywhere at all among gentiles would be a better place to settle" (*Ant.* 20.255-56). Whatever Josephus's exaggerations, the bandit raids must have been hard on the gentry in the Galilean and Judean towns for them to have preferred residence in gentile territory, for sharp and even violent conflicts had already erupted between Jews and gentiles in Caesarea Maritima and other neighboring cities.

The evidence on bandit raids against foreigners is less susceptible of satisfactory analysis. The raids by Hezekiah and company along the Syrian border in the forties B.C.E. were very likely rooted in the recent displacement of Jewish peasants from the border areas by the Roman conquest and rearrangement of the social-political order, including reallocation of land to large landowners. The objectives or roots of the raids by Tholomaus and his band along the Arabian border are much less clear. Perhaps they represent places beyond the political jurisdiction of the Roman governors of Judea or objects of attack beyond the local Idumean peasantry on which the brigands depended for protection. The one case of attack on a foreigner that seems direct and clear from Josephus' account is the brigand robbery of (the imperial servant) Stephen of all the baggage he was transporting on the public road near Beth-horon. As an imperial servant, Stephen would have represented, to bandits and peasants alike, domination by the Roman government. It is not surprising that the local villagers protected rather than pursued the audacious robbers.

There is no direct evidence that the Jewish Robin Hoods always distributed their booty among the poor peasants, who supported them and even bore the violent consequences of having protected them. But we do have one important incident in which the peasants appealed to brigands as the champions of justice (*Ant.* 20.118-36; *J.W.* 2.228-31). Samaritans had murdered a Galilean on his way to a festival in Jerusalem. Masses of Judeans became enraged and impatient at the inaction of the governor, Cumanus, who did nothing to punish the Samaritans. The Judeans therefore appealed to the brigands led by Eleazar ben Dinai and Alexander (whom Josephus mentions only in this connection; see *J.W.* 2.235) for assistance in taking revenge. The brigands led an expedition into Samaria, where they sacked and burned some villages. Thus, in a situation where Cumanus would not (and thus the Jewish aristocracy could not) rectify the unjust state of affairs, the Jewish peasants looked to the brigands, themselves the victims of unjust circumstances and an alien law and order, as champions of justice. Moreover, as in the sequence of events following the robbery of the imperial servant Stephen, here again the peasants stood in solidarity and complicity with the bandits in their attempts to right wrongs. And the steps taken by the Roman procurators to punish the offenders and reestablish "order" only intensified the injustice and oppression experienced by the people and drove even more peasants into the ranks of the brigands.

Cumanus took from Caesarea one troop of cavalry called the "Sebastenians" and went to the rescue of those being plundered. He rounded up many of Eleazar's followers and killed even more. As for the rest of the crowd that had set out to fight the Samaritans, they were implored by the leaders in Jerusalem, dressed in sackcloth and ashes, to return home and not

provoke the Romans into attacking Jerusalem by their vengeful action against the Samaritans. . . . Yet many turned to
banditry out of recklessness, and throughout the whole country there were raids, and among the more daring, revolts.
(*J. W.* 2.236-38)

The story of the popular protest over the killing of
Hezekiah and his group illustrates how bandits could symbolize the Jewish peasants' basic sense of justice and their
religious loyalties. The protest took place not just in Galilee,
but primarily in Jerusalem. It was there in the temple itself
that the people appealed to the king-high priest to bring
Herod to trial in the Sanhedrin. The leading Pharisees and
other members of the Sanhedrin had somewhat different
concerns, which conveniently converged with those of the
Galilean peasants in this case. Judging from the speech
attributed by Josephus to the outspoken Pharisee Samaias,
the elders were in any case far more concerned about tyranny
from Herod and his father, Antipas, the prime minister, than
about disruption caused by brigands. They seized the opportunity of the widespread popular outcry to bring Herod to
account. The elders charged Herod before the king-high
priest, Hyrcanus, with killing Hezekiah and his brigands "in
violation of our law, which forbids us to kill a man, even a
malicious one, unless he has first been sentenced by the
Sanhedrin. But he has dared to do this without your authority" (*Ant.* 14.167). It would distort the evidence to claim that
Hezekiah and his followers were heroes for the whole Jewish
nation, i.e., for the Pharisees or Sadducees as well as the
common people. But it is clear that they were heroes to the
Galilean peasants, who viewed their murder as a gross injustice. In much the same way as Italian and other bandits and
their supporters looked to pope or king as the source of
justice, so here Galilean families journeyed to their holy city
looking to the central political-religious institutions as their
court of justice. Moreover, they were appealing to the king-
high priest and the Sanhedrin for redress of grievances with

apparent expectation of receiving satisfaction, i.e., of
obtaining the restoration of justice in a disrupted state of
affairs.

We have little or no direct evidence for the Jewish bandits'
religious beliefs. Judging from the popular prophetic movements and a great deal of other evidence, however, there is
no doubt that an apocalyptic orientation, at times intense,
had permeated Palestinian Jewish society during the first
century C.E. Thus, as banditry increased dramatically just
prior to the Jewish revolt against Rome, it may well have
fused with the escalating apocalyptic mood among the peasantry. This accords with another of Hobsbawm's principal
generalizations, that "social banditry and millenarianism—
the most primitive forms of reform and revolution—go
together historically."[13] A broader sketch of the apocalyptic
mentality of the Jewish peasantry must await a fuller treatment of its principal manifestations in popular prophets and
prophetic movements.[14] For the moment, a simple point and
an illustration must suffice. Peasant eschatological hopes
(and expectations) may appear more traditional than those
given more elaborate, literary form by Pharisees and Essenes.
In fact, peasant expectations may seem merely to focus on
the simple restoration of the legitimate, traditional state of
affairs. However, this can have rather revolutionary effects
when acted upon. Ever since the beginning of Herod's reign
(perhaps even since the "abomination of desolation" under
Antiochus Epiphanes), the high priests had been illegitimate in the sense that they were not of the proper Zadokite
lineage. When several brigand groups joined forces in Jerusalem as the "Zealots," they attempted to organize an
egalitarian social order in Jerusalem (see chapter 5). As
Hobsbawm explains, when "the great apocalyptic moments
come, the brigand bands, their numbers swollen by the time
of tribulation and expectation, may insensibly turn into
something else."[15] Just such a development among the Jewish peasantry can be traced.

JEWISH BANDITRY AND THE REVOLT AGAINST ROME

An upsurge of social banditry can lead directly into peasant revolt. This is not the usual outcome of banditry. Outlaw bands are ordinarily very limited in number, for obvious economic and organizational reasons. Most bandits last only a few years before they are apprehended or killed. Yet there are cases, some of them historically well-known, in which the spread of banditry led to or accompanied broad popular revolts. The disruption of a traditional society, politically, socially, or especially economically, can provoke a sudden escalation of banditry, as we have observed. The case of the Mexican revolution in 1910, led in the north by Pancho Villa and other former "bandits," is probably the best-known modern case. In late antiquity, the Bacaudae in Gaul and northern Spain (ca. 285 C.E.) provide an example of brigands leading a sizable and, for a while, effective rebellion against Roman rule. Although it has not been recognized as such, the Jewish revolt against Roman domination may be the most vivid and best-attested example from antiquity of a major peasant revolt preceded and partly led by brigands.

From the occurrence of ancient Jewish social banditry already examined, it is clear that at points it accompanied or almost led to a wider peasant rebellion. The cave-dwelling brigand forces in 38 B.C.E. were linked with other forms of continuing popular resistance to Herod's conquest of Galilee. In the mid-first century, Eleazar and Alexander's brigand bands provided leadership for Judean peasants in a punitive expedition; and the Roman governor's moves to suppress the uprising drove more of the insurgent peasants into the ranks of the brigands. Thus Jewish banditry had periodically threatened to trigger major disruptions.

The sudden increase of Jewish brigandage to epidemic proportions in the years just prior to 66 C.E., however, appears to have been a major factor leading to the outbreak and continuation of widespread peasant revolt. The upsurge brought growing numbers of peasants into active and unalterable opposition to the established order. In Josephus' reports of the first armed conflicts with Roman forces, we find sizable brigand groups playing a key role in the fighting. Brigand bands, moreover, often had effective control of certain areas soon after the outbreak of the revolt. Then more and more bands of brigands formed in the countryside in response to the general turmoil or Roman counterattacks.

As the revolt broke out, there were already several large groups of brigands active in Galilee. In addition, the Roman cavalry "ravaged the country, killing a great number of the people, looting their property and burning down their villages" (*J.W.* 2.509; see 2.503-5, 507-9). Such typical actions taken to suppress the rebellion only served to multiply the numbers of brigands.

Toward the beginning of the rebellion (September 66), a number of brigand groups and other rebel forces made a valiant stand against the Roman twelfth legion at a mountain stronghold in the middle of Galilee. Equipped with only light arms, they were no match for the professional Roman troops. Yet large brigand bands still prevailed in the countryside when Josephus arrived a few months later to take command in Galilee. These bands were particularly strong in northern Galilee, and they were probably joined by fugitives from the strife between Jews and gentiles in Syrian towns. The Roman ravages of the villages farther south had probably swelled their ranks even more. The strength and size of the Galilean bands were such that Josephus could not control, much less suppress, them.

Indeed, until the Romans regained control a year later, the bandit groups constituted the dominant force in Galilee. Josephus provides a variety of evidence for why this was so. First, of course, was their military strength. The presence of large, armed groups in the countryside was a force to be reckoned with. Recognizing the impossibility of subduing or disarming them, Josephus as commander attempted to

"employ" them as mercenaries (*Life*, 77). A large and independent group, however, could exert considerable political
leverage. The huge band of 800 brigands under the command of the brigand-chief Jesus initially sold its services to
the ostensibly pro-Roman town of Sepphoris, which was
resisting submission to Josephus' command. Josephus eventually won Jesus over, but he kept his sizable force intact.

The effectiveness of the brigands in dominating Galilee
did not lie simply in their own fighting strength, but in their
influence as well. In light of the generally evident sympathy
and respect that the peasantry had for social bandits, it is
quite credible when Josephus reports that brigands influenced numbers of peasants in small towns to join in the
rebellion:

> [In] the small Galilean town of Gischala . . . the inhabitants
> were peaceable, since they were mostly peasant farmers
> whose only concern was a good harvest. But they had been
> infiltrated by a sizable gang of brigands who had infected
> some of the townsmen. (*J.W.* 4.84)

The brigand groups, moreover, were quite capable of forming alliances with other rebellious elements. The Galilean
brigands made common cause both with the proletarian
party in Tiberias, led by Jesus, son of Sapphias, and with
groups of insurgent Galilean peasants (*Life*, 35, 66, 132-48).
In the latter case, of course, there may have been little difference, sociologically speaking, between brigands who were
fighting in the rebellion and peasant rebels who carried out
banditlike raids and guerrilla warfare (*Life*, 126-27; *J.W.*
2.595).

Thus, because of their own military strength, political
leverage on the Galilean peasantry, and their alliances with
other rebel forces, the brigand groups constituted the most
important insurrectionary force in Galilee. Josephus' real
strategy was to control the Galilean situation, with the assistance of its gentry, and to avoid direct military action against
the Romans until negotiations with them were possible.

From his own accounts, however, it appears that it was because of the strength of the bandit groups in Galilee that he continued his ostensible battle preparations until the expected Roman attempt to regain control. The result, of course, was a standoff between the brigands (who must have been aware of his double game) and Josephus himself with the Galilean notables, who were attempting to hold the lid on the rebellion. That standoff ended when the Romans reconquered Galilee the following summer (67), and Josephus was able to desert to the enemy and write his memoirs.

In Judea, as in Galilee, when the revolt broke out, several brigand groups immediately became involved. In terms of Josephus' accounts, Jerusalem was the scene of much of the decisive action at the outbreak. It was here in the religio-political center, the seat of the temple, that a committed coalition of priests led by the temple captain Eleazar, son of Ananias, had refused to continue the sacrifices for Rome and the emperor, a refusal tantamount to a declaration of war for independence (see *J.W.* 2.409-10). And it was here that the Roman garrison and Herodian troops, along with the Jewish aristocracy, had been besieged in the upper city; fortresses were stormed and archives burned as widespread and massive insurrection erupted.

Care must be taken in reading Josephus' accounts of the events in Jerusalem at this point, for he pejoratively labels as "brigands/bandits" a group of urban-based terrorists known as the "dagger-men" (Latin: *Sicarii*). These Sicarii were, sociologically speaking, a phenomenon different from ordinary banditry, bandits of a "different form," as Josephus had explained earlier (*J.W.* 2.254). As an important group in its own right, it should be pointed out only that when Josephus described "bandits" as aiding both in the siege of aristocratic Jews and Roman soldiers, and in the capture and execution of the high priest Ananias, he is apparently referring to the Sicarii.

The actual brigand groups at the outbreak of the revolt were still based in the countryside, which became the scene of their anti-Roman activities. Some brigands were among the insurrectionists who obtained weapons from the Herodian arsenal atop Masada when it was taken early in the revolt (*J. W.* 3.434.). Their most important military contribution early in the rebellion was their highly effective guerrilla-style attack on the army of Cestius Gallus (reminiscent of the victories of the Maccabees), as he retreated from his siege of Jerusalem in the late summer or fall of 66 c.e.:

> Because of this unexpected retreat, the brigands' hopes revived and they dashed out to attack his rearguard, killing many cavalry and infantry. . . . The next day, by retreating still further, he invited fresh attacks. Pursuing relentlessly, the enemy inflicted many casualties on his rearguard. They also pushed ahead on both sides of the road and threw spears at both flanks of the column. (*J. W.* 2.541-42)

The brigands thus touched off an absolute rout of the Roman army, which simply abandoned much of its war machinery and weapons in its flight. In one of the important results of their attacks, "the brigands and revolutionaries were now well stocked with arms" (*Life,* 28). This was a determining factor in the subsequent strategy of the Jewish aristocracy, according to one of their number (Josephus), for they now felt themselves forced to pretend to go along with the revolt while attempting to hold the rebellious forces in check until they could arrange a negotiated surrender. Again, as in Galilee, according to the participant-observer Josephus, the presence of strong brigand groups in a popular uprising could have an important, even determining, effect on the course of events.

More significant than the fact that the brigands played such a role at the beginning of the revolt in Judea, however, was the fact that they constituted the *form* that much of the peasant revolt as a whole assumed once the Romans began their reconquest. After they had sewn up the last pockets of resistance in Galilee, the Romans moved into Judea in the fall of 67 and were in full force there by the spring of 68. As they approached, systematically devastating the countryside, its villages, and inhabitants, the peasants had no alternative but to flee their homes. As the conditions of war made normal life impossible, numbers of peasants in village after village must have fled to join or form brigand bands. Josephus seems almost purposely to obscure this situation by his stylized portrayal of "civil strife" patterned after the great Greek historian Thucydides (*J.W.* 4.129-33), although he clearly indicates the Roman successes. Referring to northwestern Judea in the fall of 67, he notes,

> The various groups began by pillaging their neighbors; they then banded together in companies, and extended their raids throughout the countryside. (*J.W.* 4.134)

Then, in reference to the spring of 68, he offers a similar picture:

> Throughout the other districts of Judea there was a similar upsurge of guerrilla activity, which up to now had been dormant. Like the body, when the most important part is inflamed, all the others are infected too. Thus when there was insurrection and disorder in the capital city, the villains from around the countryside could plunder without restraint. Each gang would plunder their own village and then retreat into the wilderness. There they joined forces and formed companies—smaller than an army, but bigger than an armed gang—and fell upon sanctuaries and towns. Those attacked suffered as much as if they had lost a war and could not even retaliate, since the raiders, like bandits, fled as soon as they had their booty. (*J.W.* 4.406-9)

Judging from Josephus' overall account, it seems that these peasants-turned-brigands constituted the principal forces of rebellion in the Judean countryside.

Nor did these bands simply hide out in the hills or act only defensively to protect their own local interests.[16] As Josephus makes explicit, it was a coalition of precisely such brigand groups which moved into Jerusalem in the winter of 67-68 and formed the party called the Zealots. Similarly, some of the Judean bands apparently formed some of the early recruits of the movement led by the messianic pretender/popular king Simon bar Giora. Thus, both of the most important groups which successively took over Jerusalem and held out against the Romans were composed, largely or in part, of peasants-turned-brigands. Because of their importance, both groups will be discussed more fully later (Simon bar Giora in chapter 3, and Zealots in chapter 5). The points to be recognized here are (1) in the midst of the revolt against Rome, social banditry was the distinctive social form taken initially by the escalating peasant revolt in Judea, but (2) it was an intermediate form through which the Judean peasantry passed on into the more politically conscious, and more distinctively Jewish, social forms of peasant communal government (the Zealots), and messianic movement (the restoration of popular kingship under Simon bar Giora).

Brigand groups, finally, provided not only much of the fighting force in the revolt of 66-70, but some of the key leadership as well. In fact, the career of John of Gischala, who became one of the two principal leaders in Jerusalem before the end of the war, provides a link between the brigand bands so dominant in Galilee at the outset of hostilities and the resistance of the rebels who had gathered in the fortress city and temple to take their stand against the Roman military might. John began his career as a brigand leader in northern Galilee. Josephus' comment that he was a "man of mark" may mean that he came from a formerly distinguished family, but was now impoverished (or for some reason was an outcast). Toward the beginning of the rebellion, his band was expanded by fugitives from the Jew-Gentile conflicts along the border between Galilee and Tyre. During the first year of the revolt, before the Romans could attack Galilee in full force, John dominated Gischala and much of upper Galilee with his band of 400 brigands (for his early career, see

J.W. 2.587-94; *Life,* 71-76). Indeed, his influence was sufficiently strong that he rivaled Josephus for leadership of the
whole of Galilee (thus Josephus' extreme hostility in his
accounts of John's activities). It is unclear what to make of
Josephus' comment (*Life,* 43) that John was not originally in
favor of the revolt. It could mean that John was then merely
an apolitical brigand leader and took the opportunity of the
gentile cities' (Tyre, Soganaea, Gadara, and Gabara) attack
on Gischala to set himself at the head of the Jewish counter-
attack (*Life,* 44-45). Or it could mean simply that John originally resisted Josephus' leadership, the ostensible purpose
of which was to prepare for war, and actually agreed with
Josephus' hidden agenda, which was to disarm the rebels
and stall for negotiating time. Generally, Josephus portrays
John as "eager for revolution and ambitious of obtaining
command" (*Life,* 71). In many ways, the career of John of
Gischala is strikingly parallel to that of Pancho Villa in the
Mexican revolution of 1910. Both started as local brigands,
but both were entrepreneurs of sorts, taking the opportunity
of social turmoil to sell confiscated goods across the border
and to exploit the wealthy for the sake of the common
defense. They both rose to prominence as skillful leaders of
popular insurrections. In contrast with the Mexican outlaw
and hero, however, John was apparently seized by a strong
ambition to become a national, and not merely regional,
leader.

Accordingly, when John saw, amid the Roman siege of
Gischala, that resistance in Galilee was now futile, he
escaped to Jerusalem with a few thousand followers (*J.W.*
4.84-127). Once in Jerusalem, which was now being flooded
with brigands and other peasants seeking refuge from the
Roman advance, John allied himself with, and attempted to
take over, the leadership of the Zealots, the fighting group
composed of other, largely Judean, brigand groups. This created a conflict, and eventually a split, within the Zealot party,
with many members apparently preferring collective leader-

ship to John's autocratic leadership. At the head of the second most powerful fighting force, however, John rivaled Simon bar Giora for leadership of the resistance in Jerusalem until the final Roman conquest.

Ancient brigand chiefs such as Hezekiah and Eleazar ben Dinai were, in effect, the Robin Hoods of Palestinian Jewish society. In a number of significant respects the banditry described by Josephus resembles the social banditry of modern European agrarian societies as described by Hobsbawm. Besides providing a revealing window onto the disintegrating social-economic structure in Jewish society, this banditry also serves as an indicator of the conditions and attitudes of the peasantry from which they emerged and with whom they continued to interact. The mere occurrence of banditry indicates that numbers of people were being cut adrift from their traditional social roots, probably because of economic pressures (e.g., indebtedness, as Jesus' parables attest!), as well as troubles with the authorities. Stories about the authorities' attempts to suppress banditry indicate that the peasants were willing to take considerable risks in order to protect the brigands. The peasants, moreover, when their sense of justice was offended by the actions, or inactions, of the authorities, would not hesitate to call upon brigands (who, like the legends of Robin Hood, may well have been heroes of justice as well as symbols of injustice) to help them take vengeance and thus set things right. When conditions became increasingly severe following the great famine of the late forties, banditry escalated to epidemic proportions. Finally, "their numbers swollen by a time of tribulation and expectation," the Jewish brigand bands turned into something else: a widespread rebellion against Roman rule. At the outset of the great revolt, many of the fighting forces were the already existing bands of brigands. Without their fighting experience, it is unlikely that the Roman armies would have been driven out of Judea in the late summer of 66.

NOTES

1. See E. J. Hobsbawm, *Bandits,* rev. ed. (New York: Pantheon, 1981); *Primitive Rebels* (New York: Norton, 1965), esp. chap. 2, "The Social Bandit"; "Social Banditry," in *Rural Protest: Peasant Movements and Social Change,* ed. H. A. Landsberger (New York: Macmillan, 1974), chap. 4. His work has spawned a number of studies, attempting furtherance of his efforts through refinement, correction, and debate. A recent reflection of this development in scholarship can be found in B. D. Shaw, "Bandits in the Roman Empire," *Past and Present* 102 (1984): 3-52.

2. E. J. Hobsbawm, *Bandits,* 19-20.

3. For further details, see S. Applebaum, "Judaea as a Roman Province," *ANRW,* 2nd ser., 8 (1977): 355-96; F. C. Grant, *Economic Background of the Gospels* (Oxford: Oxford University, 1926).

4. E. R. Wolf, *Peasants* (Englewood Cliffs: Prentice Hall, 1966) 3-4.

5. See J. B. Pritchard, ed., *Ancient Near Eastern Texts Relating to the Old Testament,* 3rd ed. (Princeton: Princeton University, 1969), 68.

6. See discussions of relevant materials in R. de Vaux, *Ancient Israel* (New York: McGraw-Hill, 1965), 403-5; E. Schürer, *The History of the Jewish People in the Age of Jesus Christ (175 B.C. - A.D. 135),* vol. 2, rev. and ed. G. Vermes, F. Millar, and M. Black (Edinburgh: Clark, 1979), 257-74; S. Safrai and M. Stern, eds., *The Jewish People in the First Century,* Compendia Rerum Iudaicarum ad Novum Testamentum I (Assen: Van Gorcum, 1974 [vol. 1], 1976 [vol. 2]), 1.259-61, 330-36; 2.584-86, 632-38, 656-64, 691-99, 818-25; S. W. Baron, *A Social and Religious History of the Jews,* 2nd ed. (New York: Columbia, 1952), vol. 2, 276-84.

7. *J.W.* 7.253. See also chapter 5 in this book.

8. This reconstruction of the effects of Roman domination, beginning with Pompey's restructuring of Judea and vicinity, rests on the work of A. Schalit, *König Herodes,* (Berlin: de Gruyter, 1969), 323, 753-59, who rereads some difficult Josephus texts. See also S. Applebaum, "Judaea as a Roman Province," 360-61,

and S. Safrai and M. Stern, eds., "Economic Life in Palestine," *The Jewish People in the First Century,* vol. 2, 637-38.

9. The common translation of *lēstēs* here as "robber," as in the RSV, has some ambiguity. "Brigand/bandit" is more precise and avoids the possible implication of "(common) thief" (Greek: *kleptēs*), a different phenomenon.

10. C. G. Harper, *Half-Hours with the Highwaymen II* (London: Chapman & Hall, 1908), 235. See also such biblical texts as Lk. 1:46-55; 4:16-21; Mt. 25:31-46.

11. E. J. Hobsbawm, *Bandits,* 17.

12. *Il Ponte* 6 (1950): 1305, quoted in E. J. Hobsbawm, *Bandits,* 50.

13. E. J. Hobsbawm, *Bandits,* 29.

14. See chap. 4, p. 151-53.

15. E. J. Hobsbawm, *Bandits,* 29 and chap. 7.

16. In this respect they form an interesting contrast to the Sicarii, who sat out the revolt atop Masada, raiding the countryside for supplies, but contributing nothing to the resistance after the summer of 66. For further discussion, see chapter 5.

CHAPTER THREE

*Royal Pretenders
and Popular Messianic Movements*

The Romans executed Jesus on the charge of being "king of the Jews," according to Mk. 15:26. Pontius Pilate, however, was not the only Roman official in Palestine to deal with a popular Jewish leader who was viewed as king of the Jews. Both before and after Jesus of Nazareth (who is usually put in this category), there were several popular Jewish leaders, almost all of them from the peasantry, who, in the words of Josephus, "laid claim to the kingdom," "donned the diadem," or were "proclaimed king" by their followers. It thus appears that one of the concrete forms which social unrest took in the late second temple period was that of a group of followers gathered around a leader they had acclaimed as king. The principal concern of this chapter will be to examine these popular messianic movements in the context of the social-historical situation in which they arose. In order to understand why these movements took this particular social form we must also examine the cultural tradition out of which they responded to their situation. Thus, before focusing on the actual movements, we will attempt to delineate a tradition of popular kingship stemming from ancient Israel which most likely influenced the social form of these movements.

In dealing with popular Jewish movements it is important to avoid, indeed, to put out of our minds, three standard and interrelated concepts which have developed out of older, theologically determined studies. Not only do these concepts obstruct discernment of concrete social-historical forms, they also turn out to be unwarranted by historical evidence.

First, our understanding of the term *messiah* is heavily influenced by western christological doctrine. The term *christ* originated simply as the Greek translation of the Hebrew *messiah,* which means *anointed.* What later became the orthodox early Christian understanding of "Christ" was a creative synthesis of several different strands of Jewish expectation and Greek philosophical concepts. In their efforts to comprehend and articulate the meaning and message of Jesus, his crucifixion, resurrection, and imminently expected return, the early Christian communities juxtaposed and brought together a variety of Jewish hopes.[1] Even particular scriptural prophecies and psalms regarding eschatological figures were utilized, such as "a prophet like Moses," or "Elijah returned," the "suffering servant of the Lord," or "one like a son of man coming with the clouds of heaven," the "priest-king after the order of Melchizedek," and "the son of David." In pre-Christian Jewish literature and social-religious life, however, each of these eschatological figures was originally distinct and perhaps even the focus of divergent expectations. Some of these figures apparently also functioned as important images in the apocalyptic hopes of certain literate groups, such as the Essenes or Pharisees. Clearly, study of these different eschatological figures in Jewish literature is important for understanding how the early Christians interpreted the significance of Jesus, as well as for understanding the diversity of Jewish religion at the time. However, while literate groups produced images of various agents of redemption, the common people produced several concrete figures and movements actively pursuing their own liberation. These leaders and movements may be equally important for our understanding of Jesus and his movement.

Second, scholarly writing has compounded the potential for misunderstanding popular Jewish messianic and prophetic movements. Due largely to the prominence and connotations of "the Messiah" in traditional Jewish and Christian theological research, scholars often use the term "messianic" as a virtual equivalent for "eschatological."[2] Moreover, anthropologists, sociologists, and historians, partly because they have resorted to the superficially familiar Judeo-Christian tradition for analogies, have used the terms *messiah* and *messianic* as general concepts effectively synonymous with the equally vague *charismatic leader* and *millenarian.* To achieve a more precise analysis, however, we should attend to the specific tradition of expectation that influenced the form of particular movements. Therefore, besides avoiding the term as much as possible, we will confine application of *messianic* to those movements or expectations that focused on an "anointed" or popularly acclaimed king.[3]

Third, and most damaging to the old synthetic concept of "the messiah," recent studies have made clear that in pre-Christian times there was no general expectation of "*The* Messiah."[4] Far from being uniform, Jewish messianic expectations in the early Roman period were diverse and fluid.[5] It is not even certain that the term *messiah* was used as a title in any literature of the time. There was no uniform expectation of "the messiah" until well after the destruction of Jerusalem in 70 C.E., when it became standardized as a result of scholarly rabbinic reflection. In fact, the term is relatively rare in literature prior to, or contemporary with, Jesus. Moreover, the designation *messiah* is not an essential element in Jewish eschatological expectation. Indeed, a royal figure does not even occur in much of Jewish apocalyptic literature. Thus it is an oversimplification and a historical misconception to say that the Jews expected a "national" or "political" messiah, whereas early Christianity centered around a "spiritual" messiah—statements frequently found in New Testament interpretation. It would thus appear that the supposedly standard Jewish ideas or expectations of the messiah are a flimsy foundation indeed from which to explain early Christian understanding of Jesus.

The scarcity of the term *messiah* in the Jewish literature of the time does not mean, however, that there was no expectation whatever of an anointed royal leader. At certain levels of Jewish society, there was indeed some anticipation of a kingly agent inspired by God to bring deliverance to the people. Besides the infrequently attested *messiah,* there were other images which expressed this particular tradition of expectation, the most prominent of which was a Davidic king.

Here again a critical approach is necessary to avoid having our investigation determined by prominent elements of the old synthetic theological concept of the messiah. Two points are particularly important. First, the future Davidic king was not necessarily a *son* of David. Like the title "Messiah," the explicit term "Son of David" simply does not occur with any frequency in Jewish literature until after the fall of Jerusalem in 70 C.E.[6] Even if it had been a common expression for a future royal figure at the time of Jesus, it is difficult to imagine that this or any other imagery of a Davidic king meant a physical descendant or literal *son.* In contrast to the care and concern about legitimate descent and genealogy of the priestly and especially high priestly families in Jewish society at this time, it may be seriously doubted that there existed any families whose descent from the house of David could be confirmed.[7] The point is that the imagery of a Davidic king symbolized substantively what this agent of God would do: liberate and restore the fortunes of Israel, as had the original David.

Second, many discussions of messianic kingship in general,[8] and the Son of David in particular, have as their keystone the "Davidic covenant," God's unconditional promise

to David: "Your house and your kingdom shall be made sure
for ever before me; your throne shall be established for ever"
(2 Sam. 7:16). This prophecy by Nathan then became the
basis for the supposition that Jews at the time of Jesus
expected the coming of the messiah as the Son of David in
fulfillment of this ancient unconditional promise. This official royal ideology may have been important for the literate
strata of society (those who actually studied and interpreted
biblical texts, such as Pharisees and Essenes). However, we
suspect that for the common people, other strands of ancient
tradition were more important than the official ideology of
kingship.

THE TRADITION OF POPULAR KINGSHIP

These other strands of ancient tradition concerning kingship
are surely the most important for understanding the social
form taken by the popular messianic movements. Assuming
that the ordinary people, even if illiterate, had some substantial acquaintance with biblical stories and images, it is evident that they had memories of popularly recognized kings
and their followers which, precisely because they had
become embodied in the people's sacred traditions (the law
and the prophets), constituted the particular tradition of
popular kingship.[9] In examining the characteristics of this
tradition, we shall attempt to keep in mind our interest in
concrete social movements and not stray too far into a history
of ideas. The issue is how we can discern that one, rather
than another, particular social form is being embodied in
certain material. The issue and our approach to it can be
illustrated by examination of the source of the new social
form, namely, the traditions contained in biblical history.

As chapter 2 has shown, numerous bandit groups were
active in popular rebellions in the first century C.E., especially in the revolt of 66-70. There were also bandits among
the supporters of at least two of the popularly acclaimed
kings, Simon the royal slave in 4 B.C.E. and Simon bar Giora

in 68 C.E. It is important to determine why Josephus mentions "kingship" in these cases, and why we would discern here a special form, that of popular *messianic* movements, rather than unusually large bands of brigands. Many of the essential conditions for banditry and messianic movements are the same. In fact, there might well have been no difference between them had there not been among the Jews a *tradition* of popular kingship and historical prototypes of a popular "anointed one."

The difference in social form can be discerned right in ancient biblical history. During the period of the judges, before the rise of the monarchy under Samuel and Saul, there were at least two significant instances of brigands which were incorporated into Israelite historical traditions. Abimelech had hired a band of "worthless and reckless fellows" who followed his lead (Judg. 9:4), and Gilead's illegitimate son, Jephthah, collected a group of "worthless fellows" and led them in raiding expeditions (Judg. 11:3). During a period of intermittent war with the Philistines and the resulting social-economic turmoil, David, son of Jesse, got his start in exactly the same way. Because King Saul envied his martial prowess, David became a fugitive, an "outlaw." As a result, "everyone who was in distress, and everyone who was in debt, and everyone who was discontented, gathered to him; and he became captain over them—about 400 men" (1 Sam. 22:2). David, however, did not stop with mere banditry. He shrewdly maneuvered himself into recognition as the *anointed* king of Israel, the messiah. What may have started as banditry became a new kind of movement, a popular messianic movement, more politically conscious and deliberate than banditry. The elders of the tribes of Israel, eager for effective leadership in the flagging war against the Philistines, legitimated his kingship. The "shepherd king" David and his movement thus provided the historical prototype for subsequent popular messianic movements which, however many "worthless and reckless fellows" they included, deliberately opposed foreign domination or domestic oppression.

In order better to understand the form of these messianic movements, and the motivation of those who joined them, we must first examine this ancient Israelite tradition of popular kingship. We can then observe how the popular tradition survived alongside other images of kingship, and how some key texts of "expectations" manifest popular concerns, before we examine the reemergence of popular kingship in concrete form.

POPULAR KINGSHIP IN ANCIENT ISRAEL

Among the many strands and layers of biblical narrative one can still see evidence of the popular tradition of kingship. Kingship for the early Israelites was *conditional,* was by *popular election* or "anointing," and was *revolutionary.*

Tribal Israel adamantly resisted the institution of monarchy during the era of the judges. To the ancient Israelites, kingship, as established in the Canaanite city-states, meant a ruling military class in a stratified society, with little more than exploitation and oppression for the subject peasantry. According to their covenantal constitution, the true and only king of Israel was Yahweh, who had brought them out of slavery under the Egyptian Pharaoh and had established them as a free society in their own land. For one man, one family, or one tribe to have royal power and prerogatives over the rest would have been a basic violation of the egalitarian spirit and stipulations of the covenant. For nearly two centuries, temporary charismatic leadership and the inspired peasant militia proved sufficient to meet the periodic threats of subjection by the kings of Canaan. With the emergence of the Philistine domination of Palestine, however, Israel felt a need for more centralized authority and political power. So the Israelites groped toward their own adaptation of kingship. Since they were so profoundly suspicious of monarchy as they had experienced it in its Canaanite form, they made Israelite kingship conditional, in the sense that it was not dynastic and that it was subject to certain covenantal stipulations. As expressed in later historical narratives, the rights and duties of kingship were "written up in a book and laid up before the Lord [Yahweh]" (1 Sam. 10:25). Such conditions were also transmitted in covenantal (Deut. 17:14-20) as well as liturgical (Ps. 132:12) traditions.[10]

According to the idealized image of continuity with the old covenantal forms and principles, Saul, the first political-military "prince," was chosen *by lot* by the whole people under the guidance of Samuel, the last judge (that is, the last religious-political-military charismatic leader of tribal Israel). This election by lot was the actual way in which Saul emerged as "the one whom Yahweh has chosen." However, in the memory and symbolism of subsequent ages, it was David, not Saul, who was the prototypical *messiah*, the "anointed one." David's election as king, as well as the election of others, has less to do with casting lots than with his abilities and standing among his fellows—"skillful in playing, a man of valor, a man of war, prudent in speech, and a man of good presence, and Yahweh is with him" (1 Sam. 16:18). Another presupposition for election as popular king is an organized following, indeed, a fighting force. In David's case, in a time of social, political, and economic turmoil, he had become a leader of a sizable band of brigands. Such are the indispensable qualifications of a candidate for popular kingship. However, David (and subsequent popular messiahs) did not become king simply by force of arms. One was made messiah by *popular election,* either by all the people, or by the fighting men of the peasant militia, or by the representative assembly of elders.[11] In David's case it happened in stages, first by his own tribe of Judah, then by all Israel: "And the men of Judah came, and there [Hebron] they *anointed David king* over the house of Judah" (2 Sam. 2:4). Then, following further civil war, "all the elders of Israel . . . *anointed David king* over Israel" (2 Sam. 5:3). Moreover, just as the people made someone king by their anointing, so they could withdraw their recognition of kingship and elect someone else. Thus, when the ten tribes of northern Israel rejected the continuation of Solomon's oppressive rule by his son Rehoboam, they turned to Jeroboam and "all Israel . . . called him to *the assembly* and *made him king.* . ." (1 Kings 12:20).[12] It is a confirmation, not a contradiction, of the popular election or *anointing* of the king when the biblical narrative also includes stories of Yahweh's anointing of the king through the hand of an inspired prophet such as Samuel, Ahijah, or Elisha. Yahweh's anointing and that of the people are the same, or, Yahweh's anointing anticipates popular action, which action fulfills the will of Yahweh.

From Saul and David at the end of the eleventh century to Jehoahaz at the end of the seventh, it is clear that the anointing of a king by people or prophet was generally a *revolutionary act.* In its origins, Israelite anointed kingship was a means of securing and centralizing political-military power against foreign domination by the Philistines. Elisha's anointing of Jehu (2 Kings 9:1-13; see also 1 Kings 19:15-19), like Ahijah's designation of Jeroboam as king of the ten northern tribes (1 Kings 11:26-40; 12:16-20), was a revolutionary overthrow of an established regime that had become intolerably oppressive to the people and therefore illegitimate. Similarly, in 609 B.C.E., when "the people of the land" anointed Jehoahaz after his father, Josiah, was killed at the hands of the Egyptian army (see 2 Kings 23:30), it appears to have been a struggle of the people against a reactionary aristocratic or court party, as well as resistance to foreign domination.

THE OFFICIAL ROYAL IDEOLOGY AND ITS UNPOPULARITY

In sharp contrast to popular kingship, there emerged an official royal ideology, probably during the regimes of David and Solomon.[13] The understanding of the king as "the anointed of Yahweh" in all likelihood originated in popular traditions of kingship.[14] However, in the royal psalms, liturgical expressions of the official royal ideology, "the anointed of Yahweh" became identical with the Davidic king.[15] Moreover, in these psalms, which were heavily influenced by Canaanite and other ancient Near Eastern ideas of kingship, "the anointed of Yahweh," who was always the established Davidic monarch, was understood as secured in his position by divine adoption as "son of God." The Davidic Messiah-King was now *the* means by which the people had access to God and the one through whom God blessed the nation with military victories and domestic welfare. Central to the royal ideology, of course, was God's promise to David, understood not only as unconditional, but as lasting forever as well (2 Sam. 7:16). Thus, in contrast to the conditions and responsibilities of popular anointed kingship, the royal ideology viewed the Davidic monarchy, along with the temple established on the holy Mount Zion, as a divine guarantee of security for the nation, regardless of the justice or injustice of royal rule (2 Sam. 7:14-16).

The extreme difference and conflict between the popular and the official understandings of kingship emerged sharply in Jeremiah's interactions with the Davidic monarchs and their counselors during the last decades of the nation of Judah. The ruling class apparently trusted heavily in the promises to David. In the crises posed by impending Egyptian and then Babylonian invasion and conquest, the essential thing in their minds was the survival of the Davidic monarchy, upon which the nation as a whole was dependent, according to their ideology. When Jeremiah repeatedly delivered oracles of Yahweh that announced the punishment and end of the Davidic dynasty along with the destruction of Jerusalem and its temple, he appeared not only as a faithless heretic, but as an absolute traitor.

Jeremiah, a spokesperson for the common people in the villages of Judah—when he was not in prison, or wallowing at the bottom of a cistern, or otherwise persecuted by the king or royal officials—was consistently articulating the conditional popular understanding of kingship (see esp. Jer. 22:1-9, 13-19). Thus, while justice may also have been an ideal of royal ideology in theory, Jeremiah announced God's judgment precisely against the oppressive practices of the royal house. Indeed, for the common people of Judah, the established monarchy had become not only oppressive, but very dispensable. From their point of view, the welfare of the people, including the conditional monarchy, depended on the keeping of the covenant stipulations: just dealings, including attentiveness to the cause of the poor and needy. The fall of the Davidic monarchy could not have been as traumatic for the oppressed peasantry as it apparently was for the ruling elite, many of whom were taken into captivity along with the royal family.

"MESSIANIC" MEMORIES AND EXPECTATIONS

During the long period between the fall of Jerusalem in 587 and the first century C.E. we have very little clear evidence for what was happening among the Jewish aristocracy and literate groups, let alone what went on among the common people. We assume that very little by way of popular movements occurred during the time from the exile to the eruption of the Maccabean revolt. The lack of evidence, however, does not mean that the Judean peasantry had no problems or cherished no hopes for a better life. Any attempt to state what memories and hopes may have been entertained among the people, of course, involves extrapolation from limited textual evidence and comparative social analysis, as well as a good deal of speculation. In outlining what were the likely memories and expectations of the people, therefore, we must keep in mind not only that kingship may not have been the only or even primary focus, but also that we are extrapolating from literary evidence which was edited, if not actually produced, by the literate elite.

The fact that "the law and the prophets" were collected and edited into a sacred scripture means that the stories of popular anointed kings were remembered. Although it may not have been manifest in any actual movements, the tradition of popular kingship was not extinct, but dormant. It continued in the memory of the people. Considering how important memory is for informing people's hopes or expectations, the first and perhaps most important element to recognize is the continuing memory of stories of messianic movements from Israel's history. There is, for example, some evidence that although the Davidic dynasty had become oppressive to the common people, after its decline and fall the people looked back on the reign of David himself as a golden age of fulfillment and divine blessing. It is clear from texts such as Psalm 89 that courtly poets looked back to the victories of David as a glorious time of salvation, and embellished their expressions of nostalgia with extensive mythic elements borrowed from Canaanite culture. It is likely that memory of David's reign, a time when the ancient promises that Israel would be a great nation and possess its own land had been fulfilled, became the basis for popular as well as aristocratic hopes for the future.

Besides these all-important memories, there were numerous oracles, or simply images, which likely expressed the people's expectations. While taking into account the considerable diversity among the "messianic" prophecies, we will focus on some texts which contain expressions of what would have been the social-religious concerns of the common people. One of the central images of hope for renewed fulfillment of the promises was the "branch" God would raise for David. It is significant that the popular concerns of anointed kingship are incorporated in the principal prophecies of the Davidic branch or shoot. This can be seen in Jer. 23:5-6, and in the famous, idyllic prophecy in Is. 11:2-9, of the "shoot from the stump of Jesse," who shall "judge the poor with righteousness." In the prophecies of Micah there is no reference to the official royal theology, but there is a

more popular image of a future Davidic shoot. In the messianic prophecy, the coming king will be born, not in the royal
court of Jerusalem, but in a lowly clan of the town of Bethlehem, where David got his start (Mic. 5:2).

It is inappropriate to speak of a Jewish expectation of "The
Messiah" at this point because few of the extant late prophecies that shaped Jewish hopes even use the term *anointed*.
The focus on the new David or a descendant of David, moreover, was by no means the only image of Jewish hopes for a
revived or eschatological kingship. Some of the scriptural
texts most important to the hopes of later generations of
Judeans contained no explicit language of "anointed" or
"branch (shoot, horn, son) of David." There was rather, for
example, a focus on "the scepter" or "a star," as in Gen.
49:10 and Num. 24:17 respectively.

It is striking that many of the prophecies of a future king
either stem originally from tribal Israel or hark back to popular traditions from that period. Ezekiel, for example, in a
prophecy of fulfillment of the ancient promises to Abraham,
not only links renewed observance of the covenant ordinances with the new David, but prefers the term *prince*
(*nasi*), the term for the leader of the old tribal confederacy,
over the title *king* (*melekh*) as well (see Ezek. 37:24-26).
Another prophecy, but without explicit mention of the
Davidic line, is appended to the song of Hannah, one of the
great songs of victory stemming from early tribal Israel
(1 Sam. 2:10). Finally, there is the prophecy added to the
book of Zechariah. As it hails the future king, it evokes an
image of the leader of tribal Israel prior to the time it even
possessed the more advanced military technology of horses
and war chariots: "Lo, your king comes to you; triumphant
and victorious is he, humble and riding on an ass"
(Zech. 9:9-10).

The survival of, and later allusion to, such prophecies after
the destruction of Jerusalem constitute evidence that a hope
for a future king as God's agent to restore the fortunes of
Judah had endured—a hope for the fulfillment of the ancient

promises to Israel and for the realization of God's rule of justice in a revitalized society. However, although the hope for a future king was thus alive, it was apparently dormant for generations, even centuries. Prophets among those exiles who returned to Judea toward the end of the sixth century B.C.E. to rebuild Jerusalem and the temple had focused their hopes for restoration of the Jewish state and independence from Persian rule on Zerubbabel, the last scion of the Davidic line (Hag. 2:20-23; Zech. 6:12-13). Thereafter, there is little or no evidence for a lively expectation of a messiah during the period of Persian and Hellenistic domination. There may have been a general disillusionment with hopes focused on kingship as a result of the unfulfilled hopes placed in Zerubbabel after the return from exile.[16] After the reforms of Nehemiah and Ezra, the life of Judean society was centered on the temple and high priest. It is striking that throughout the whole Hellenizing reform, Antiochean persecution, and Maccabean revolt, there is no evidence of a revival of royal messianic hopes. The people and their leaders (e.g., the Hasmoneans Judas and Jonathan) must have been sorely disillusioned with the high priests. Moreover, since the Hasmoneans were not a Zadokite priestly family, Jonathan and Simon could not legitimately have assumed the high priesthood. Yet, instead of reviving royal imagery and titles, the Hasmonean leadership assumed the high priestly role; this act witnesses to the strength and centrality of the latter and perhaps the dormancy of the former at this time.

There is no question that the promises to David and the prophecies of a future king were known during the Persian and Hellenistic periods by the literate (see Sir. 47:11, 22; 1 Macc. 2:57), and probably also by the peasantry. Any expectation of a Davidic king, however, was relegated to the dim and distant future, not applied to the immediate political situation. This was true even during the intense distress of the persecution and resultant Maccabean revolt, at which time the apocalyptic "dream-visions" of 1 Enoch 83-90 must have been written. It is tempting to see the sprouting of "a great horn of one of those sheep" whom the "ravens" attack but cannot defeat (1 Enoch 90:9) as an almost certain reference to Judah the Maccabee described in Davidic (messianic) imagery. Like the simile of "the lion" in 1 Macc. 3:4, it may well be such an allusion. Yet the figure that plays the messianic role of the future ruler does not emerge until after the judgment and the advent of the New Jerusalem, at the very end of the vision (1 Enoch 90:37-38).

CONDITIONS OF THE REVIVAL OF THE TRADITION OF POPULAR KINGSHIP

Expectations of an anointed royal figure began to revive somewhat during the Hasmonean period. The fact that a resurgence had begun is evident in the Dead Sea Scrolls and Ps. Sol. 17. As noted at the beginning of this chapter, the occurrence of the terms *messiah* or *son of David* is still rare in Jewish literature prior to, and contemporary with, the rise of actual popular messianic movements. The very occurrence of the latter is evidence enough of the revival of the tradition of popular kingship. To appreciate how this tradition and related expectations of an anointed royal agent may have revived in popular circles, and thus influenced the social form taken by the popular movements, however, we must also examine the historical conditions in which those movements arose.

RESURGENCE OF MESSIANIC EXPECTATIONS AMONG LEARNED GROUPS

At Qumran, messianic expectations were as fluid as they were complex, far more complex than any previous tradition we have noted.[17] The Essenes, who had gone out to the wilderness at Qumran to form the community of the New Covenant in actual preparation of the way of Yahweh, expected the final fulfillment to involve three principal eschatological agents. According to their *Community Rule,* they were to be governed by their new covenantal ordinances until the coming of the prophet and the anointed (ones) of Aaron and Israel. The first figure, the eschatological prophet, promised by Deut. 18:15-18, will be discussed in the next chapter. For messianic expectations proper, the Qumranites apparently anticipated two anointed ones, a high priestly Messiah as well as the lay head of the eschatological community (the Anointed One of Israel).

The Anointed Priest is the more prominent figure and clearly takes precedence in all important matters. This is not surprising, considering that the Qumran community had formed in reaction to the "perversion" of national life and of God's will by the wicked (and illegitimate Hasmonean) Priest(s), and it was under heavy priestly influence in both conception and leadership.[18] In the age of fulfillment, the Anointed Priest will preside over the celebrations of the eschatological banquet (1QSa 2:11-22). In the final holy war against the Kittim (Romans), described in elaborate ritualized fashion in the *War Rule,* the eschatological high priest plays a prominent role, pronouncing blessings, marshalling the formations, and inspiring the troops.[19] The Prince of the Congregation is mentioned only incidentally (1QM 5:1). The Anointed Priest is also to be the final interpreter of the law. This teaching role appears even more important in the later texts, compared with the prominence of his ritual functions in the *Community Rule.* Along with the Qumran literature, the Testaments of the Twelve Patriarchs and the Book of Jubilees also exhibit an expectation of two anointed eschatological figures: an apparently superior, sacerdotal figure stemming from Levi, and a lesser royal figure from the tribe of Judah.[20]

Expectation of the Prince of the Congregation, the Anointed of Israel, also concerned the learned scribes at Qumran, who pored over biblical texts for insights into the eschatological mysteries of God. Many of the particular biblical prophecies of a future king noted earlier reemerge in the Qumran literature and are frequently juxtaposed. In some of the most interesting texts, we can see the Essene method of interpreting one prophetic text through another. Thus, the promise to David (2 Sam. 7) is clarified with the branch and tabernacle prophecies (Jer. 23 and Amos 9:11):

> . . . and I will raise up thy seed after thee, and I will establish his royal throne . . .[2 Sam. 7:12-14]. This is the Branch of David [see Jer. 23:5, etc.] who will arise with the Seeker of the Law and who will sit on the throne of Zion at the end of days; as it is written, "I will raise up the tabernacle of David which is fallen" [Amos 9:11]. This "tabernacle of David which is fallen" [is] he who will arise to save Israel. (4QFlor 1:10-13)

It is clear from this passage, as well as others,[21] that for Qumran the Branch of David was one of the principal agents of imminent eschatological fulfillment. He was expected to rescue Israel from domination by foreign rulers, even to achieve victory over the nations. He was to be honored with a glorious enthronement and was expected to rule over all peoples, as well as to establish justice within Israel. Here the priestly scribes at Qumran have picked up an important concern of the ancient popular tradition of kingship.

As strikingly as these passages indicate a revival of messianic expectations, such expectations by no means dominated the eschatological outlook of the community. Not only did the Anointed Priest and eschatological prophet or teacher have more prominent roles, but the Qumranites seem to have resisted placing messianic interpretations on what might appear to us as royal messianic texts. In one of the principal messianic passages of the *Damascus Rule* (7:14-21), for example, the fallen "tabernacle of David" (Amos 9:11) which is to be raised up is understood as "the books of the Law," "king" is found to mean the Assembly, and the "Star" from Jacob is understood as referring to the Prince of the Congregation. The Qumran texts generally resist using the word "king" in reference to the Anointed of Israel, following the usage of Ezekiel who prefers "prince." It would appear that in later Qumran literature, composed in Roman times, the royal figure is more prominent. Yet even in these texts the Branch of David will rule, not according to his own viewpoint, but as he is instructed by the priests, directly contradicting the Is. 11 text that is being interpreted (see 4QpIsa). In the priestly Qumran community, the anointed royal figure was always subordinated to their intense concern for careful interpretation of covenant law, as well as for calculating the historical application of God's eschatological mysteries.

Toward the beginning of the Roman period there was also a resurgence of expectation of an anointed royal figure in other literate circles. In the Ps. Sol. 17, the focus is on the actual earthly establishment of the Kingdom of God, following rule by illegitimate usurpers and conquest by foreign nations. The psalm is an appeal for, and an anticipatory description of, the rule of the future king, the son of David. Thus,

> Behold, O Lord, and raise up unto them their king, the son of David, at the time in which Thou seest, O God, that he may reign over Israel Thy servant. And gird him with strength, that he may shatter unrighteous rulers, and that he may purge Jerusalem from nations that trample [her] down to destruction. . . . He shall be a righteous king taught of God. . . . He will rebuke rulers and remove sinners by the might of his word. (Ps. Sol. 17:23-24, 35, 41)

The psalm is an original composition,[22] showing influence from, and allusion to, the traditional biblical prophecies, but it is not simply a repetition of biblical texts. The expectations in this psalm focus exclusively on a royal figure: a son of David, a righteous king. He is expected both to end the reign of unrighteous rulers within the society and to liberate Jerusalem from foreign domination. He is expected to destroy foreign enemies and bring the heathen nations under his own righteous rule. Within Israel he will bring an end to injustice and oppression so that the whole society will dwell in righteousness. The fact that the future king will be the "anointed of the Lord" is directly connected with the anticipation that justice will finally be established in the society.

Perhaps most noteworthy is the fact that the expectation is strongly spiritualized,[23] particularly the political-military imagery: he shall not place trust in military forces and technology, but in spiritual forces. The anointed king will rebuke or destroy unrighteous rulers *by the word of his mouth*. The Psalms of Solomon express an expectation of a *teacher-king*, a royal agent of eschatological Torah, an anointed one conceived, perhaps, in the author's own image, who would be able to bring the true kingdom of God into effect.

SOCIOHISTORICAL CONDITIONS AND POPULAR EXPECTATIONS

There remains the question of why there was this resurgence of expectations of an eschatological king in the literature of the Hasmonean period, after such expectations had apparently lain dormant for centuries. A commonplace response would view the Roman conquest and the resultant end of the Hasmoneans as the catalyst for such expectations. The initial cause, however, could just as well have been the Hasmoneans' own pretensions, with the situation then further aggravated by the Roman conquest and Herod the Great.[24] When the Hasmonean rulers Jonathan and Simon initially established themselves as high priests, they were considered illegitimate by both Qumranites and Pharisees. When subsequent Hasmoneans also assumed the title of king (and forcibly diminished the Pharisees' power), the usurpers simply compounded the illegitimacy of their rule. It may not be surprising, thereafter, to find yearnings for the fulfillment of the promise to David in Jewish literature such as Ps. Sol. 17. Conquest of Judea by the Romans must then have convinced many suffering under the Hasmoneans that they needed not only legitimate, but also effective, political leadership, namely the new David, anointed by God and empowered by God's spirit to liberate and rule the nations. The Qumranites and the authors of Ps. Sol. 17 expected their royal messiahs, however ceremonial or scribal their character, to implement their respective programs for the people, in sharp contrast to the utter failure of the Hasmoneans.

If the machinations of the Hasmoneans had stimulated the Essenes and other literate groups to focus their hopes partly on an anointed ruler, the even more arrogant pretensions and tyranny of Herod and direct Roman rule would have provided plenty of provocation for the revival of memories and expectations focused on popular kingship. The general conditions in Palestine that affected the peasantry have been detailed at the beginning of chapter 2, on banditry, and are directly relevant here. We may recall that under Herod and his successors the common people suffered a burdensome tax load, extreme social and political controls, famines, and severe tensions between the priestly aristocracy and peasantry, all of which ultimately spawned large-scale revolts in 4 B.C.E. and 66 C.E. Amid such trying conditions the juxtaposition of Herod's illegitimacy and posturing must have been highly provocative to the people's memory and expectations. For them Herod was an illegitimate king in every sense. Not only was he merely a "half-Jew" by birth—the offspring of a marriage between the Idumean Antipater and the Nabatean Cypros—he was also the furthest thing from a true leader. He was a mere puppet who had conquered his own people with the help of Roman troops. Herod thus ruled by the grace of Rome, not God.

It exacerbated matters when Herod, attempting to obscure his illegitimacy, created his own royal ideology. A speech put into his mouth by the historian Josephus probably reflects Herod's own propaganda. "I think I have, by the will of God, brought the Jewish nation to a state of prosperity it has never known before," says Herod, pointing to the peace and good fortune of the nation under his divinely blessed reign. As the king now rebuilding the temple, he perhaps even postured as another Solomon, the son of David who built the original house of God (*Ant.* 15.383-87). His propaganda, however, must have served only to sharpen the contrast between Jewish expectations and the actualities of his rule. If the popular legendary material behind the Matthean infancy narrative is any indication, far from being king by the will of God, Herod appeared to the people as the epitome of a tyrant, a wicked ruler who was, in effect, the anti-Messiah (Mt. 2:1-23).

Another story included by Josephus provides a vivid indication of how tensions had risen toward the end of Herod's reign. Although the story focuses on court intrigue and the misunderstanding of the discontented members of the royal family, it does provide a window on the mood at other levels of the society as well.

> [When the Pharisees], over six thousand of them, did not take this oath [of loyalty to Caesar and Herod's government], the king punished them with a fine. However, the wife of Pheroras [Herod's brother], paid the penalty for them. Returning her kindness, they foretold—for they were believed to have foreknowledge through manifestations of God—that the end of Herod's reign, both for himself and his lineage, was ordained by God, and that the royal power would fall to her and Pheroras, and any children they might have. All this was reported to the king—for it did not escape the notice of Salome—as well as the fact that they had corrupted some of those at the royal court. The king killed those most to blame, including the eunuch Bagoas and a certain Karos, who was outstanding among his contemporaries for his unusual good looks, and who was the king's lover. He also killed every one of his household who approved what the Pharisees said. Bagoas, it turned out, had been exalted by them in the belief that he would be called both father and benefactor[25] by the king who, in the foretelling, would be set over the people; for all things would be under his control, and he would give Bagoas the ability to marry and father his own children. (*Ant.* 17.42-45)

It is clear from this story that discontent with Herod had focused on hopes of a future king who would take charge of all things. Included were fantasies of the miraculous restoration of the people's life forces, such as those of fertility. Such

messianic expectations were lively and intense, whether in
the form of apocalyptic visions and prophecies articulated by
Pharisees, or in the way messianic prophecies may have reso-
nated in the minds of people such as the eunuch Bagoas. The
narrative also reveals that Herod's brutal repression was
more severe than ever. Living thus under an oppressive and
illegitimate king installed by an alien power, the people
were ready for an "anointed" charismatic leader from among
the peasantry, like David of old. It should not be surprising
that as soon as Herod died, the pent-up frustrations of the
people burst forth precisely in the form of messianic
movements.

Just how concentrated and intense the messianic expectations were under the Roman governers is difficult to determine. The Eighteen Benedictions, prayers spoken by the
people, may reflect (and may have helped to focus) popular
hopes during the first century C.E. The actual text that we
have of the *Shemone Esre* did not reach its final form until
after the fall of Jerusalem in 70, but it is thought to contain
prayers from earlier times.[26] Thus it is possible, and even
likely, that in pre-Christian times devout Jews prayed (three
times a day) for the shooting up of the branch of David and
the raising up of his horn, as in the fourteenth and fifteenth
benedictions:

> In thy great mercy, O Yahweh our God, have pity on Israel thy
> people. . . .and on thy Temple. . . .and on the kingdom of
> the house of David, the Messiah of thy righteousness. Let the
> shoot of David sprout quickly and raise up his horn with thy
> help. Blessed be thou, Yahweh, that thou dost cause a horn of
> help to grow.

Such prayers, centered on the hope of a new independence,
would have given expression to popular messianic hopes
during the early first century C.E.

As events began accelerating toward the outbreak of the
great revolt of 66-70, popular hopes for an anointed king
were apparently strong and widespread. There is no reason

to question Josephus' straightforward claim that "what
incited them to war more than anything else was an ambiguous oracle, also found in their sacred writings, to the effect
that at that time someone from their country would rule the
whole world" (*J. W.* 6.312). Indeed, this is confirmed, independent of Josephus, by Tacitus: "The majority firmly
believed that their ancient priestly writings contained the
prophecy that this was the very time when the East should
grow strong and that men starting from Judea should possess
the world" (*Hist.* 5.13). Josephus himself, of course, applied
this "ambiguous" oracle to his new patron, Vespasian, to
whom he had deserted following the siege at Jotapata. To the
Jewish masses in the mid-sixties, however, prophecy from
their sacred writings was not ambiguous. They were eagerly
longing for God to raise up the king who would defeat the
godless foreign nations, liberate the Jewish people, and
establish God's reign of justice and righteousness.

POPULAR KINGS AND THEIR MOVEMENTS

In contrast to the idealized branch of David hoped for by the
learned Essenes and others, the popular leaders actually recognized as kings by their followers led armed revolts against
the Romans and their upper-class Jewish collaborators.[27]
Unfortunately for our desire to know more about these
figures and the movements they led, we are dependent on a
few paragraphs from an extremely unsympathetic source.
Not only is Josephus hostile to all Jewish rebels against
Roman rule, but he studiously avoids the distinctively Palestinian Jewish conceptuality and patterns of thought in favor
of Hellenistic-Roman ideas. Thus we have to read between
the lines, or translate his Hellenistic conceptuality into the
apocalyptic idiom current among Palestinian Jews. Thus
when Josephus says that a figure "seized the opportunity to
seek the throne" or "was proclaimed king" by his followers,
we can reasonably surmise that these figures were messianic

pretenders. They are to be understood against the background of the long Israelite-Jewish tradition of popular anointed kingship and, in effect, as revivers of it.

POPULAR MESSIANIC UPRISINGS AT
THE DEATH OF HEROD

Immediately following the death of Herod, some Jews appealed to his son and heir apparent, Archelaus, to reduce the impossible tax burden and to release the many political prisoners still chained in various Herodian fortresses. A more organized group even demanded that he avenge the brutal murder of Judas, Matthias, and their followers who had pulled the Roman eagle down from the temple gate, and that he replace the illegitimate Herodian high priest with one who would serve more in accordance with the law. When the crowds from the countryside who were in Jerusalem for the Passover celebrations pressed these demands, Archelaus' anxious response was to send in the army, which massacred thousands of the worshiping pilgrims. Archelaus left shortly thereafter for Rome, to press for his appointment as Herod's successor, and the countryside virtually exploded in revolt.

At the festival of Pentecost in May, thousands streamed into Jerusalem from Galilee, Idumea, and Transjordan, as well as Judea itself, and besieged the Roman troops occupying the city. Although many of their number had gone to Jerusalem, in every major section of Herod's kingdom the peasantry rose in revolt—and these revolts took the form of messianic movements.

The key passages are as follows:

There was Judas, son of the
brigand-chief Ezekias (who
had been a man of great power and who had been cap-
tured by Herod only with
great difficulty). This Judas,
when he had organized at
Sepphoris in Galilee a large
number of desperate men,
raided the palace. Taking all
the weapons that were stored
there, he armed all of his followers and made off with all
the goods that had been
seized there. He caused fear
in everyone by plundering
those he encountered in his
craving for greater power and
in his zealous pursuit of royal
rank. He did not expect to acquire this prize by being virtuous, but by the advantage
of his superior strength.
(Ant. 17.271-72)

At Sepphoris in Galilee, Judas, son of Ezekias (the brigand-chief who once overran
the country and was sup-
pressed by king Herod), having organized a sizable force,
broke into the royal armories,
armed his followers, and attacked the others who vied
for power.
(J.W. 2.56)

There was also Simon, a servant of king Herod, but otherwise
an imposing man in both size and bodily strength, and he was
confident of distinguishing himself. Spurred on by chaotic
social conditions, he dared to don the diadem. When he had
organized some men, he was also proclaimed king by them in
their fanaticism, and he thought himself more worthy of this
than anyone else. After setting fire to the royal palace in
Jericho, he plundered and carried off the things that had
previously been taken (and stored) there. He also set fire to
numerous other royal residences in many parts of the country
and destroyed them, after allowing his followers to take the
confiscated goods in them as booty. He would have accomplished something greater had there not been swift intervention. For Gratus, leader of royal troops, took his forces, joined
the Romans and went to meet Simon. After a long and difficult

battle, a great number of the Pereans were killed, since they were in disarray and fought with more daring than skill. When Simon himself tried to seek safety by fleeing through a certain ravine, Gratus intercepted and beheaded him. (*Ant.* 17.273-76)

And then there was Athronges, a man whose eminence derived neither from the renown of his forefathers, nor from the superiority of his character, nor the extent of his means. He was an obscure shepherd, yet remarkable for his stature and strength. He dared to aspire to kingship on the grounds that having obtained it he would delight in greater wantonness. When it came to dying, he did not care if he risked his life in such circumstances. He also had four brothers; they too were large men, confident that they would also prevail by virtue of their feats of strength and expecting to provide solid support for his grip on the kingdom. Each of them led an armed band, for a great throng had assembled around them. Although they were generals, they served under him whenever they made forays into battle on their own. Putting on the diadem, Athronges held council on what was to be done, although everything ultimately depended on his own judgment. He held power for a long time, having been designated king and able to do whatever he wanted without interference. He and his brothers pressed hard in the slaughter of both the Romans and the Herodian troops, acting with a similar hatred toward both, toward the royal troops because of the outrages they committed during Herod's rule, and toward the Romans because of the wrongs they were thought to have perpetrated in the present circumstances. As time passed, they became ever more brutal, with no escape for anyone; sometimes they acted hoping to gain booty, and other times simply because they were accustomed to bloodshed. Once near Emmaus they even attacked a company of Romans carrying grain and arms to their army. After surrounding them, they struck down Arius the centurion, who led the brigade, and forty of his best infantry. Those who survived were alarmed by their predicament, but were able to escape when Gratus and his royal troops served as a shield for them; however, they left their dead behind. The brothers continued their guerrilla warfare

for a long time, harassing the Romans to no small degree and
ravaging their own nation. Some time later, however, they
were caught and taken prisoner, one in an encounter with
Gratus, and another in an encounter with Ptolemy. After
Archelaus caught the oldest one, the last brother, vexed by
the other's plight, and having no other way to save himself—
since he was now isolated, extremely fatigued and left
defenseless—surrendered to Archelaus after assurances and a
pledge of good faith. But this occurred later on.

Judea was infested with gangs of bandits. Whenever sedi-
tious bands came across someone suitable, that person could
be set up as king, eager for the ruin of the commonwealth,
doing little damage to the Romans, but causing extensive
bloodshed among their countrymen. (*Ant.* 17.278-85).

From these brief and vitriolic accounts, we can glean a few
important points about these popular messianic movements
and the royal pretenders at their head. First, they are centered around a charismatic *king,* however humble his origins. Although he is apparently quite familiar with the
distinctively Jewish "messianic" language, Josephus studiously avoids terms such as "branch" or "son of David" and
"messiah" (see *Ant.* 10.210; *J. W.* 6.312-13). Yet he does not
hesitate to use language of "kingship." Whether at the
beginning (see *J. W.* 2.55) or at the close (see *Ant.* 17.285) of
his accounts of these three movements, he provides summa-
rizing sentences: "The opportune circumstances induced a
number of persons to aspire to *kingship,*" or "Whenever sedi-
tious bands came across someone suitable, that person could
be set up as *king.*" Furthermore, Josephus uses the term
"diadem" in connection with both Simon and Athronges.
This term, by the Hellenistic period, had become an effective
synonym for kingship, and Josephus uses it accordingly with
Antiochus IV Epiphanes, Demetrius I Soter, Aristobulus I,
Hyrcanus II, and Herod, among others. When this term is
applied to Simon and Athronges, it is done without qualifica-
tion. Given Josephus' choice of the language of kingship,
anyone who is familiar with the tradition of popular kingship

is reminded of the popular election or "anointing" of the king and of the royal psalm

> I have set the crown upon one who is mighty,
> I have exalted one chosen from the
> people. . . . (Ps. 89:19)

Second, the people were not looking to the gentry or "distinguished" families for leadership, for most of the latter either owed their position to Herod or were otherwise involved in collaboration with the Herodian-Roman regime. The royal pretenders in all three of these movements were men of humble origins. One was a shepherd, as David had been according to the legend. Another had once been a servant of Herod. In Galilee, one generation's brigand leader had given birth to the next generation's royal pretender. Josephus' explicit mention of the physical stature or prowess of these figures may well be a reflection of the Davidic tradition that the leader elected by God or the people was to be a mighty man of war. This tradition probably evolved from the phenomenon of the charismatic "judge." David, like the "judge" Gideon before him, whom the Israelites wanted to recognize as king (Judg. 6:12; 8:22), was the prototypical "mighty man of valor" (1 Sam. 16:18).

The participants in the messianic movements were primarily peasants. These revolts occurred in the various country districts, in contrast with the metropolis, Jerusalem. A large number of the people involved may have been "desperate men." In the case of the Perean revolt led by Simon, it is not clear whether the phrase "the brigands he collected" is simply Josephus' pejorative terminology for those who responded to Simon's leadership, or it refers to peasants already driven to banditry before the eruption of the revolt. In any case, Josephus carefully distinguishes from these peasant movements the other groups that rebelled at that same time, such as the revolt of 2,000 of Herod's veterans (J.W. 2.55).

The movements appear to have been somewhat organized, at least into "armed bands" for military purposes. Athronges used his brothers to head the subdivisions of his apparently sizable force, and he held council to deliberate on their courses of action. In writing that the Pereans proclaimed Simon king "in their fanaticism," and that they fought with "more daring than skill," Josephus seems to suggest that such movements were fired by (divine) inspiration, or a special spirit.

The principal goal of these movements was to overthrow Herodian and Roman domination and to restore the traditional ideals of a free and egalitarian society. Thus, as Josephus seems to indicate, they stormed the royal palaces at Sepphoris and Jericho not simply as symbols of hated Herodian rule or to obtain weapons, but to recover property that had been seized by Herodian officials and stored in the palaces. Besides attacking both Roman and royalist forces, they also raided and destroyed the mansions of the gentry along with the royal residences. We can reasonably infer a certain resentment at prolonged social-economic inequity and exploitation, as well as a spirit of egalitarian anarchism, typical among peasant uprisings.

The size of these messianic movements and the seriousness of the insurrection can perhaps be gauged by the size of the military force that Varus, legate of Syria, deemed necessary to subdue the rebellion. In addition to the legions already in Judea, he gathered the two remaining legions in the province (about 6,000 each) and four regiments of cavalry (500 each), as well as the auxiliary troops provided by the city-states and client kings in the region. Varus had Sepphoris (where Judas' movement had been active) burned and its inhabitants reduced to slavery.

Abandoned by its inhabitants, Emmaus was also burned to the ground when Varus ordered it to avenge the slaying of Arius and his troops. He then marched on to Jerusalem where at the mere sight of him and his forces the Jewish armies dissolved and fled into the countryside. Those in the city, however, welcomed him and disclaimed all responsibility for the revolt. They explained that they had done nothing, but had been forced to put up with the swarm of visitors on account of the festival, so that far from joining the rebel attack they were themselves besieged, as were the Romans. . . . Varus dispatched parts of his army around the countryside to go after those responsible for the revolt, and among the many apprehended he imprisoned those who seemed to have taken a less active role, and crucified those most responsible—about two thousand in all. (*J.W.* 2.71-75)

The messianic movements, however, were not easily stamped out. At least that led by the shepherd Athronges continued for some time before the Roman or Herodian troops could eventually subdue one or another of the companies of followers, and before Archelaus could finally induce the last remaining brother (or Athronges himself?) to surrender. "But this occurred later on."

Because of the special interest that attaches to Jesus and his movement, it is worth noting, finally, that there were several mass movements composed of Jewish peasants from villages or towns such as Emmaus, Bethlehem, Sepphoris— people rallying around the leadership of charismatic figures viewed as *anointed kings* of the Jews. These movements occurred in all three principal areas of Jewish settlement in Palestine (Galilee, Perea, Judea), and just at the time when Jesus of Nazareth was presumably born. It is perhaps also worth noting that the city of Sepphoris, which was burned and its inhabitants sold into slavery in 4 B.C.E., was just a few miles north of the village of Nazareth, Jesus' home. Furthermore, the town of Emmaus, the location of one of the resurrection appearances according to the gospel tradition (Lk. 24:13-32), had been destroyed by the Romans in retaliation for another mass movement little more than a generation earlier. The memory of these popular messianic movements would no doubt have been fresh in the minds of most of the Jewish peasants who witnessed Jesus' activities.

ROYAL PRETENDERS AND MESSIANIC MOVEMENTS
DURING THE JEWISH REVOLT (66-70)

Because of the paucity of sources, it cannot be determined
whether there were any messianic movements—except, perhaps, for the followers of Jesus—during the seventy years
between the movements just discussed and the outbreak of
the great revolt of 66-70. The initial centers of the massive
rebellion were primarily Galilee and Jerusalem. Leadership
was at first provided by the many groups of brigands, their
ranks swelled by refugees fleeing the Romans' attempts to
suppress the uprising. Only two groups prominent during
the revolt can be identified as having taken the form of a
messianic movement. The first of these is perhaps better
described as a messianic incident within the long-standing
group of terrorists known as the Sicarii. Because of the considerable scholarly confusion surrounding the Sicarii and
Zealots, we must discuss both groups at length later (chapter
5). We should at this point, however, take into account the
climactic "messianic" episode in this group's long opposition to Roman rule and Jewish collaboration with it.

After years of terrorist activity, the Sicarii (dagger men)
were quick to join the insurgents in the city of Jerusalem
once the revolt erupted. In August of 66 some of them joined
the popular attack on the notables and chief priests in the
upper city and apparently participated in the burning of the
public archives, thus destroying the records of debts. In a
related or perhaps only parallel action,

> a certain Menahem, son of Judas the Galilean . . . took his
> followers and marched off to Masada. There he broke open
> king Herod's arsenal and armed other brigands, in addition to
> his own group. With these men as his bodyguards, he
> returned to Jerusalem as a king, and becoming a leader of the
> insurrection, he organized the siege of the palace. (*J.W.*
> 2.433-34; see 2.422-42)

It is somewhat surprising that the leadership of the Sicarii
here takes the form of kingship. As we shall see in chapter 5,

the Sicarii and their probable precursors, the Fourth Philosophy, featured "scholarly" leadership. Josephus calls the founder of the Fourth Philosophy a "teacher" (*sophistēs*), and Menahem is also known as a teacher (*J.W.* 2.433). We have no evidence, however, that Judas of Galilee or his successors, apart from Menahem, ever made any messianic claims. Thus the messianic pretensions of Menahem were apparently unprecedented and unique among the Sicarii. It seems reasonable to surmise, therefore, that this messianic episode at the climax of the struggles of the Sicarii for liberty was a function of the high level of excitement that must have prevailed in Jerusalem in the late summer of 66 C.E. The idea of a teacher-messiah, however, and expectations of such a figure had been articulated by the author(s) of Ps. Sol. 17, who were presumably scribes and teachers, like the leaders of the Fourth Philosophy and Sicarii. Thus in what appeared to be the time of general eschatological fulfillment, it is perhaps not so surprising to find this activist group of intelligentsia producing a "teacher" as their messiah. Contrary to Ps. Sol. 17, however, Menahem rebuked alien rulers and removed sinners more by the might of his sword than "by the might of his word."[28]

The second and far more extensive messianic movement emerged among the Judean peasantry nearly two years after the revolt had started. This movement focused on Simon bar Giora, who eventually became the principal Jewish commander in Jerusalem.[29] Although Josephus studiously avoids Jewish "messianic" language in his accounts, we can nevertheless discern a number of "Davidic" features in the rise of Simon. We can also determine through Josephus' account the important differences, as well as similarities, between a royal pretender (such as Simon bar Giora) leading a messianic movement, and a brigand chief (such as John of Gischala) who also provided leadership for the widespread popular rebellion. At the outbreak of the revolt, Simon bar Giora was the leader of a substantial fighting force, like John, his bandit counterpart in northern Galilee. In the battle against the Roman army advancing on Jerusalem in October, 66, he had led the attack from the rear, "cut up a large part of their rearguard, and carried off many of their baggage animals, which he then drove into the city" (*J.W.* 2.521). Also like John in Galilee, Simon was passed over for a command of provincial forces by the chief priests and leading Pharisees who controlled the government in Jerusalem. A popular leader of a rebellious peasantry was the last thing the Jerusalem authorities wanted if they were to moderate the revolt and negotiate with the Romans. However, again as in Galilee, the social revolution as well as the anti-Roman revolt was well underway.

> There was a young man from Gerasa, Simon bar Giora. He was not as unscrupulous as John, who had already gained possession of the city, but he was his superior in physical prowess and courage. . . . (*J.W.* 4.503-4)

> In the district of Acrabatene, Simon bar Giora organized a large number of revolutionaries and took up pillaging. Not only did he loot the houses of the wealthy, but he abused the people themselves. It was clear from the start that he was bent on tyranny. When an army was dispatched against him by Ananus and the leaders, he and his men took refuge with the brigands on Masada and stayed there until the death of Ananus and his other foes. (*J.W.* 2.652-53)

> Despite his efforts, he could not persuade the Sicarii to try anything more ambitious. They had grown accustomed to the mountain fortress and were afraid to go very far from their lair. He, however, sought supreme power and aimed at great things. When he heard that Ananus was dead, he withdrew to the hill country and proclaimed freedom for slaves and rewards for the free, collecting villains from everywhere. Since he now had a strong body of troops, he overran the villages in the hill country, and because more men were always joining up with him, he was confident in venturing down to the flatlands. He was soon an object of dread to the towns and many influential men were lured to his force and

the prosperous course of his achievements. It was no longer an army of slaves or brigands, but included many citizens who obeyed him like a king. He also overran both the district of Acrabatene and everything else up to and including greater Idumaea. At a village called Nain, he constructed a wall and used it as a fort for his protection. And at a ravine called Pheretae he enlarged a number of caves and, along with others already suitable, used them as storehouses for his treasures and booty. There too he stored the grain he had seized, and quartered most of his forces as well. It was thus clear that he was giving advance training to his corps and preparing for an attack on Jerusalem. (*J. W.* 4.507-13)

Although he now had a sizable army, before attempting to take Jerusalem he first sought to consolidate his position in southern Judea and take control of Idumea. Some of the Idumean leaders used their private influence to prepare the way for his assuming control there. His next move cannot have been made simply on strategic grounds.

Contrary to expectation, Simon invaded Idumea without bloodshed. In a surprise attack, he first overpowered the small town of Hebron where he seized a great deal of booty and carried away a vast quantity of grain. As the natives of Hebron say, the town is not only older than any of the other towns in the country, it is also older than Memphis in Egypt. . . . There Abraham, forefather of the Jews, had his home after his departure from Mesopotamia, and it was from there that his descendants went down into Egypt. . . . From Hebron, Simon advanced through all of Idumea, not only sacking villages and towns, but plundering the countryside as well, since his supplies were not adequate for such a huge multitude, his followers now numbering forty thousand, not counting his armed men. (*J. W.* 4.529-34)

In this account of Simon's rise from a leader of a local guerrilla band, to one followed as *king* by a train of thousands in addition to a sizable army, one can detect a number of remarkable parallels with the rise of David, proto- type of the ancient tradition of popular kingship. Both David and Simon began their careers as popular military leaders outlawed because they were a threat to the ostensibly legitimate national governments. Also, those who joined the respective bands of David and Simon at the outset were the "discontent" and villains. As in the case of the popular kings seventy years earlier, Simon's great physical strength and daring are emphasized. As in the original case of David, the people as a whole looked for effective leadership in a crisis situation. Large numbers of people, including some Jerusalemites, soon came to follow Simon "as a king." Finally, among the striking Davidic features of Simon's rise to kingship, he captured Hebron. Josephus goes out of his way to explain the local inhabitants' boast of the antiquity of the city. But to Jews in general the city was probably equally well or better known as the city in which David was anointed first as king of Judah, and then recognized as king over all of Israel, after which he proceeded to take Jerusalem and to liberate the whole country (2 Sam. 2:4; 5:1-7).

Like the messianic movements at the death of Herod, their actions indicate that Simon and his followers were strongly motivated by resentment of their previous exploitation by the wealthy. One of their principal goals seems to have been the restoration of social-economic justice. One must wonder to what extent there may have been, behind Josephus' Hellenistic conceptuality in *J.W.* 4.508, an apocalyptic tone to Simon's proclamation of "freedom for slaves and rewards for the free." However eschatological the tone may have been, equity for the meek and justice for the poor were essential things which the messianic king was expected to effect (see Jer. 23:5 and Is. 11:4). Moreover, there was precedent in the royal traditions for such a proclamation. In similar circumstances, with Judah under attack by the Babylonians, a Davidic king, Hezekiah, had made a proclamation of liberty: that no one should continue to enslave a Jew, his brother (Jer. 34:8-9). It would appear that Simon's plan included the establishment of a new social order or the restoration of the

"good old" socioeconomic order according to the original
Mosaic covenant.

It is also clear from Josephus' account that Simon and his
massive following were by no means merely a spontaneous
horde of peasants impulsively raiding the estates of the gentry and naively marching up to Jerusalem. Under Simon's
leadership they had become a trained and organized army,
with forethought and preparation given to the support system necessary for a prolonged war of liberation. No matter
how much Simon's Judean peasant followers may have
viewed the events as ultimately part of God's eschatological
holy war against oppression, they were quite clear about the
necessity of making preparations and fighting for their own
liberation.

With Simon in control of the whole Judean and Idumean
countryside, including the immediate environs of Jerusalem,
the high priests and the "citizen body" of Jerusalem took the
calculated risk of admitting Simon to the city to help overthrow the rule of John of Gischala and the Zealots.

> The resolution was carried out, and they sent the high priest,
> Matthias, to implore Simon to enter the city—the man they so
> greatly feared. The request was supported by those Jerusalem
> citizens who were trying to escape the Zealots and were anx-
> ious about their homes and property. Arrogantly consenting
> to rule, he entered the city as one who would expel the
> Zealots and was greeted as savior and guardian by the
> Jerusalemites [dēmos]. But once he and his forces were
> inside, his sole concern was to establish his own supremacy,
> and he looked upon those who had sought his help as his
> enemies as much as he did those he had been implored to
> suppress. Thus in the third year of the war, in the month of
> Xanthicus [April-May, 69], Simon became master of Jerusa-
> lem. But John and the bulk of the Zealots, because they were
> prevented from leaving the temple and had lost their posses-
> sions in the city—for Simon's followers had immediately
> seized them as plunder—saw no hope of safety. Simon now
> attacked the temple, with the aid of the Jerusalemites. . . .
> (J.W. 4.574-78)

Throughout the remainder of the war, nearly all of it spent with Jerusalem under siege by the Roman army, Simon was the principal leader in the city, while John and the Zealots occupied the temple. With the city under constant attack by the Romans, Simon had to maintain order in the city as well as the discipline of his army. Josephus sketches the contrast between Simon's devoted followers and the well-to-do citizens and high priestly elements who wanted to desert to the Romans. On the one hand,

> Simon was especially held in awe and respect, and each of his subordinates was so devoted to him that none would have hesitated to take his own life, had he ordered it. (*J.W.* 5.309)

On the other hand, members of high priestly families and other well-to-do citizens attempted to desert or even betray the Jews' cause to the Romans, especially as the prolonged siege brought famine and increased internecine strife.

> Some sold their most valuable treasures for very little, and others all their property. Then, to avoid detection by the brigands, they swallowed the gold coins, escaped to the Romans, and on emptying their bowels, had ample means for their needs. (*J.W.* 5.421)

The conflict eventually came to the point where the very man who had arranged Simon's entry into the city, Matthias son of Boethus, a member of a high priestly family, was accused as a traitor.

> Matthias was escorted in and accused of favoring the Romans. Simon allowed him no defense and sentenced him to death with his three sons. The fourth had already made his escape to Titus. . . .After their deaths, a prominent priest named Ananias son of Marbalus and Aristeus, the scribe of the council [Sanhedrin], a native of Emmaus, together with fifteen distinguished citizens, were put to death. They put Josephus' father under lock and key and issued an edict forbidding anyone in the city from conversing or assembling in the same place—for fear of treason. (*J.W.* 5.530, 532-33)

Josephus, who had long since deserted to the Romans and was rewarded with the return of his family's large estates, portrays this as ruthless tyranny. In the Jewish messianic movement, fighting for its life and liberation, however, this must have been understood rather in the vein of anticipations expressed even in the Psalms of Solomon. In the final war against, and victory over, the oppressive foreign nations, the king would "thrust out sinners from [the] inheritance" and "not suffer unrighteousness to lodge anymore in their midst," thus "purging Jerusalem, making it holy as of old" (Ps. Sol. 17:26, 29, 33, 36). One is also tempted to see here a holy war tradition rooted in ancient Israelite struggles, namely, the *ban* (Hebrew: *herem*), whereby the unholy had to be separated from the circle of the holy. To put it in more practical or mundane legal terms, Simon is here enforcing, in full public view, the criminal justice required to maintain national discipline in the desperate defense against Roman attack.

The movement led by Simon bar Giora was the longest-lived of all the messianic movements mentioned by Josephus. It lasted nearly two years from the time Simon proclaimed freedom for slaves and rewards for the free. Simon and his forces, however, were no match for the might of Rome. Titus brought Jerusalem under siege in April, 70 C.E. Simon and his followers, ultimately with the cooperation of John's forces and the Zealots against their common enemy, held out against fierce Roman assaults on the city walls and fortified temple for five months. By September, the temple as well as the rest of the city had fallen to the Romans, who butchered the helpless Jews and plundered and burned the whole city.

Even in Josephus' portrayal of Simon's surrender and his treatment by the Romans there is significant evidence for Simon as "king of the Jews." Simon and some of his most faithful friends, along with some stonecutters, attempted to escape through underground passages in the city, but found their way blocked.

So Simon . . . put on white tunics with a purple cape fastened over them, and popped up out of the ground at the very place where the temple had once stood. At first, those who saw him were dumbfounded and stood stock-still, but after a while they came nearer and asked who he was. Simon refused to tell them, and instead ordered them to summon the general. They ran to get him, and Terentius Rufus, left in command of the garrison, soon arrived. After learning the whole truth from Simon, he bound and kept him under guard and sent an account of his capture to Caesar. (*J.W.* 7.29-31)

When Caesar returned to Caesarea Maritima, Simon was brought to him in chains, and he commanded that Simon be kept under guard for the triumphal procession that he was preparing to celebrate in Rome. (*J.W.* 7.36)

As was the custom, the Emperor Vespasian and his son Titus celebrated their glorious victory over the rebellious Jewish people with a great procession in Rome, the imperial capital. After tremendous spectacles displaying the magnificence—and the raw power—of the Roman empire,

the triumphal procession concluded at the temple of Jupiter Capitolinus, where it came to a halt, for it was an ancient custom to wait there until someone announced the death sentence for the enemy's general. This was Simon bar Giora, who had just taken part in the procession among the prisoners, and, with a noose put over him, was dragged by force to the proper spot at the forum, all the while being tortured by those who led him. It was at that spot where Roman law required those sentenced to death for villainy to be slain. When his death was announced, it was greeted with universal acclamation, and the sacrifices were begun. When the customary prayers had been offered and the omens proved favorable, the princes departed for the palace. (*J.W.* 7.153-55)

These two events, Simon's ceremonial surrender and his ritual execution at the climax of the imperial triumphal procession, reveal both that Simon understood himself as the messiah and that the conquering Romans recognized him as the leader of the nation. When Simon suddenly appeared, in the place where the temple had stood, clothed in royal robes, he may well have been sacrificing himself as an offering to God. His purpose in this may have been either to bring about divine apocalyptic intervention or else to lighten the punishment that would befall his people through the self-sacrifice of the leader. In any case, he appears in royal robes as the king of the Jews (see Mk. 15:17-18; Lk. 23:11;[7] Rev. 19:13-16). Similarly, from the Roman side, whereas John of Gischala was simply imprisoned, Simon was ceremonially captured, scourged, and executed as the king of the Jews— now once again a people under Roman domination.

THE BAR KOCHBA REVOLT (132-135 CE): THE FINAL MESSIANIC MOVEMENT IN JEWISH ANTIQUITY

The actual king ruling over Jewish society was once again Caesar. Much of the country was devastated by the war, and a sizable portion of the Jewish population of Palestine had been either killed or sold into slavery. Rome had suppressed the revolt and the messianic movement led by Simon bar Giora, but Rome could not suppress messianic hopes and expectations. In fact, Jewish eschatological hopes seem now more exclusively focused on expectations of a messianic king as the central eschatological agent. It would seem that Yohanan ben Zakkai and most of the other rabbis, sobered by the defeat by the Romans, had little or no interest in apocalyptic revelations. Yet a few scholars must have continued the apocalyptic traditions of the Essenes and Pharisees. In the apocalypse 4 Ezra, some Jewish sages toward the end of the first century produced more vivid and highly developed expectations of "The Messiah" than those expressed in earlier literature, although still not in the standardized doctrinal form that appeared in later rabbinic literature.

There is no way of knowing whether the Jewish peasantry shared or appreciated the more fantastic features of the literary apocalyptic expectations, but there can be no question about the form of the popular rebellion that again erupted little more than sixty years after the end of the first great revolt.[30] The aged and revered Rabbi Akiba, who had not lost touch with his peasant origins, proclaimed that the leader of the renewed rebellion was the eschatological king.

> R. Simeon ben Yohai said: R. Akiba my teacher used to explain the passage, "a star shall go forth from Jacob" [Num. 24:17] thus: Kosiba goes forth from Jacob. Again when R. Akiba saw Bar Kochba [Koziba], he cried out, "This is the king, the Messiah."

Other rabbis, perhaps the majority of them, wanted nothing to do with the movement.

> Rabbi Yohanan b. Torta answered him: "Akiba, grass will grow out of your cheek-bones and the Son of David will still not have come." (J. Ta'anit 4.8 [68d 48-51])[31]

Subsequent rabbinic traditions further denigrate the royal pretender by referring to him, with a pun on his name, as bar Kozibe, i.e., "Son of the lie," or "Liar." But Akiba's proclamation is eloquent testimony to the *form* that the popular rebellion again assumed, a messianic movement. Akiba's application of the Star prophecy to Simeon bar Kosiba is unequivocally royal-messianic in contrast to Qumran, where the Star had not been understood as a prophecy of the messiah. Moreover, coins provide corroborating evidence that Simeon bar Kosiba was understood as the chosen royal agent of God. He has the title "Prince (*nasi*) of Israel." Although there also seems to be a priestly leader, "Eleazar, the Priest," Simeon clearly takes precedence.

A large proportion of the Judean peasantry must have responded readily to Simeon's movement, undeterred by the rabbinic rejection of its messianic pretensions. For, in effect, Simeon and his followers enjoyed independent self-government for over three years while defending themselves against the Roman reconquest of Judea. They minted coins inscribed "Year I of the Liberation of Israel." Such inscriptions also indicate that Simeon bar Kosiba and his followers believed that a new era had been inaugurated with independence from Roman rule. The time had come for the fulfillment of ancient prophecies, for Israel to be liberated from Roman domination.

Recent archaeological discoveries in the Judean desert[32] also provide evidence that the leadership of the second revolt emphasized strict observance of traditional religious stipulations. These documents also indicate that Simeon exercised firm military and administrative discipline.

From its outbreak, Simeon's revolt spread quickly throughout Judea (Galilee continued under Roman occupation). Where they did not completely control an area, Simeon's followers would operate out of caves or other strongholds, fighting for their traditional way of life and harassing those who did not join the resistance. "Bar Kochba's" people must have occupied the ruins of Jerusalem, and exercised control over much of the Judean countryside for a time as well. Even when the Romans sent in a massive force to resubjugate the Jews, Simeon and his forces, by skillful guerrilla operations based in their caves and other mountain strongholds, forced the Romans into a prolonged war of attrition. Only after extended campaigns and costly individual battles could the Romans finally "annihilate, exterminate, and eradicate" them from the land (see Dio Cassius 59.13.3).

It thus becomes clear that around the time of Jesus there was a great deal more than a mere expectation of an eschatological king cultivated by literate groups such as the Essenes and others. Indeed, popular royal pretenders and messianic movements were very different from figures expected by the Qumranites and others, even though they were informed by the same general tradition of expectation of an anointed king as God's agent of liberation.

The Psalms of Solomon and the Dead Sea Scrolls are products of literate, reflective communities. Like the people generally, both groups opposed Roman domination and Hasmonean and Herodian tyranny. For their part, the Qumranites had long since rejected the wicked establishment and withdrawn from the futile political process "to prepare the way of the Lord" in the wilderness of Qumran. Many of the Pharisees and other sages, after opposing Alexander Jannaeus, also spoke out against Herod. Under the procurators as well, they were prominent dissenters against increased Roman encroachments, especially in attempting to preserve Jewish religious privileges. Yet they were increasingly excluded from effective participation in the political process from the beginning of Herod's rule and began to concentrate more and more on the cultivation of personal piety and interpretation of the Torah. Their character as scholarly groups and their withdrawal or exclusion from political affairs may be reflected in their conception of anointed kings. Although the Qumranites celebrated ritual warfare against the Kittim (Romans), whom they expected God to defeat in apocalyptic battle, there is little or no evidence that their participation was anything other than anticipatory ritual. Correspondingly, the messianic expectations expressed in their literature have an almost unreal, transcendent tone, similar to that found in Ps. Sol. 17. The imagery of warfare is present, but it is mostly rationalized or idealized to an ethereal plane. The future king would destroy the godless nations with the *word of his mouth.* There is no evidence that the anointed figures of the literate groups were expected to have any real military function. The messiahs of the Qumranites and the scribes who produced Ps. Sol. 17 have either primarily ceremonial functions or scribal features.

More important than literary expression for the actual course of events, however, were the concrete popular messianic movements. The messianic pretenders, however, do not appear to have been the genteel, spiritual figures looked for by the Essenes or author(s) of the Psalms of Solomon. In fact, these popularly acclaimed kings were armed leaders against the Romans. With the exception of the royal pretender Menahem and his Sicarii, moreover, these were movements among the Jewish peasantry. While the Essenes had withdrawn to the wilderness and the Pharisees cultivated piety in their brotherhoods, the Jewish peasantry steadily bore the direct burden of economic pressure and the frustrations of alien rule. It appears that the ancient Israelite tradition of popular anointed kingship, though dormant during the Persian and Hellenistic periods, remained alive. It certainly reemerged in vigorous form just before and after the life of Jesus of Nazareth. In response to foreign domination, severe repression, and illegitimate Herodian kingship, peasant attempts to set things right took the form of messianic movements. They destroyed or took back the excesses of wealth that the ruling class had gained by exploiting their labor. They fought against the hated foreign domination by the Romans so that, led by the king whom they themselves had recognized or acclaimed, they could once again be free to live under the rule of God, according to the traditional covenantal ways. In some cases (Athronges, Simon bar Giora, Bar Kochba), before the Roman troops could suppress these large-scale movements, they were able to control and, apparently, govern their territories for several months, even years.

NOTES

1. This is recognized in New Testament christological studies which proceed by way of titles (see the work of O. Cullmann and F. Hahn, referred to in the Introduction, n. 10).
2. For example, R. Meyer, "*Prophētēs*," *TDNT* 6 (1968): 826, can speak of a "messianic prophet"; see also D. Hill, "Jesus and Josephus' 'Messianic Prophets,'" in *Text and Interpretation: Studies in the New Testament Presented to Matthew Black,* ed.

E. Best and R. McL. Wilson (Cambridge: Cambridge University, 1979), 143-54.

3. A restriction found recently, for example, in J. A. Fitzmyer, *The Gospel According to Luke I-IX,* AB 28 (Garden City: Doubleday, 1981), 197-98. "Anointed" can also, in some literature, refer to a priest, although it predominantly refers to a royal figure.

4. See M. de Jonge, "The Use of the Word 'Anointed' in the Time of Jesus," *NovT* 8 (1966): 132-48; D. C. Duling; "The Promises to David and Their Entrance into Christianity—Nailing Down a Likely Hypothesis," *NTS* 20 (1973-74): 68.

5. See J. Neusner, *Messiah in Context: Israel's History and Destiny in Formative Judaism* (Philadelphia: Fortress, 1984).

6. See D. C. Duling, "The Therapeutic Son of David: An Element in Matthew's Christological Apologetic," *NTS* 24 (1977-78): 407-8.

7. The data that may be adduced as evidence for real genealogical knowledge at this time all fall under the suspicion, and sometimes proper judgment, of having political or theological motives. See the various assessments, G. Vermes, *Jesus the Jew* (New York: Macmillan, 1973), 156-57; R. E. Brown, *The Birth of the Messiah* (Garden City: Doubleday, 1977), 505-12; J. Jeremias, *Jerusalem in the Time of Jesus* (Philadelphia: Fortress, 1969), 276-77.

8. See S. Mowinckel, *He That Cometh* (New York: Abingdon, 1956).

9. See the references in chapter 1, n. 4, for this standard anthropological concept of the difference and interrelationship between the "great" and "little" tradition.

10. On these matters, see further, F. M. Cross, *Canaanite Myth and Hebrew Epic* (Cambridge: Harvard University, 1973), 222-37.

11. See C. U. Wolf, "Traces of Primitive Democracy in Ancient Israel," *JNES* 6 (1947): 105-7; Z. Weisman, "Anointing as a Motif in the Making of the Charismatic King," *Bib* 57 (1976): 382; H. Tadmor, "The People and the Kingship in Ancient Israel: The Role of Political Institutions in the Biblical Period," *Cahiers d'histoire mondiale (Journal of World History)* 11 (1968): 46-68.

12. This incident also illustrates the conditional character of popular anointed kingship.

13. See F. M. Cross, *Canaanite Myth*, 241-64.
14. E.g., 1 Sam. 26:9, 11, 16, 23; 2 Sam. 1:14, 16; 19:22.
15. See Ps. 2; 18; 20; 45; 132.
16. See F. M. Cross, "A Reconstruction of the Judean Restoration," *Int* 29 (1975): 199.
17. See R. E. Brown, "The Messianism of Qumran," *CBQ* 19 (1957): 53-80, and "The Teacher of Righteousness and the Messiah(s)," in *The Scrolls and Christianity*, TC 11 (London: SPCK, 1969), 37-44.
18. After all, for nearly 400 years the high priest had been the symbolic and actual head of the Judean people. This renders intelligible some of the postexilic prophecies of the Davidic Branch, which include a priestly figure alongside the royal figure, e.g., Zech. 6:11; Jer. 33:14-18.
19. See 1QM 2:1; 15:4; 16:13; 18:5; 19:1.
20. E.g., *T. Reuben* 6:7-12; *T. Simeon* 7:1-2; *T. Levi* 8:11-16; *T. Issa.* 5:7; *Jub.* 31:9-21; see further, J. Liver, "The Doctrine of the Two Messiahs in Sectarian Literature in the Time of the Second Commonwealth," *HTR* 52 (1959): 149-85.
21. See also 1QpIsa fragment D; 1QSb 5:20-29.
22. Authorship is uncertain, but possibly Pharisaic; see R. H. Charles, *Apocrypha and Pseudepigrapha of the Old Testament*, vol. 2 (Oxford: Clarendon, 1913), 630; R. Wright, "Psalms of Solomon," in *The Old Testament Pseudepigrapha*, vol. 2, ed. J. H. Charlesworth (Garden City: Doubleday, 1985).
23. As also in the Isaianic prophecy of the shoot from the stump of Jesse (Is. 11).
24. For the Pharisees' attitude toward the Hasmoneans see J. Neusner, *From Politics to Piety*, (Englewood Cliffs: Prentice-Hall, 1973), 48-50.
25. For a brief discussion of this obscure line concerning Bagoas, see E. Schürer, *The History of the Jewish People in the Age of Jesus Christ (175 B.C. - A.D. 135)*, vol. 2, rev. and ed. G. Vermes, F. Millar, and M. Black (Edinburgh: Clark, 1979), 505.
26. See E. Lohse, "Der König aus Davids Geschlecht: Bemerkungen zur messianischen Erwartung der Synogoge," in *Abraham Unser Vater: Festschrift für Otto Michel*, ed. O. Betz, et al. (Leiden: Brill, 1963), 337-45; D. C. Duling, "The Promises to David," 63-64.

27. See R. A. Horsley, "Popular Messianic Movements Around the Time of Jesus," *CBQ* 46 (1984): 471-95, esp. 473-80.

28. See R. A. Horsley, "Menahem in Jerusalem: A Brief Messianic Episode among the Sicarii—Not 'Zealot Messianism,'" *NovT* 27 (1985).

29. There are two complementary treatments of Simon bar Giora: C. Roth, "Simon bar Giora, Ancient Jewish Hero," *Commentary* 29 (1960): 52-58, and O. Michel, "Studien zu Josephus," *NTS* 14 (1967-68): 402-8. Roth focuses on Simon's heroism, while Michel concentrates on the social form and motivation of Simon's leadership.

30. See J. A. Fitzmyer, "The Bar Cochba Period," in *Essays on the Semitic Background of the New Testament* (Missoula: Scholars, 1974; orig. 1962), 305-54.

31. With this application of the Balaam oracle to Simeon bar Kosiba, Akiba also coined the term by which this messianic movement became known to subsequent (Christian) history [bar Kochba = Son of the Star].

32. Namely, Murabba'at, 1951; Nahal Hever and Nahal Ze'elim, 1960-61; see P. Benoit, J. T. Milik, and R. de Vaux, *Discoveries in the Judean Desert II: Les grottes de Murabba'at* (1961), esp. nos. 22-46; N. Avigad et al., "The Expedition to the Judean Desert, 1960," *IEJ* 12 (1962): 167-262; E. Schürer, *History of the Jewish People,* vol. 1, rev. ed., 512, 515, 534-57.

CHAPTER FOUR

Prophets and Prophetic Movements

Judging from several reports by Josephus, there were a number of prophetic figures that appeared among the people around the time of Jesus. Indeed, Jesus was understood as a prophet (see Mk. 6:15-16). Although our sources are fragmentary and, in the case of Josephus, hostile, careful analysis indicates that these popular prophets were of two fairly distinct types. The principal function of the one, the oracular prophet, was to pronounce the impending judgment or redemption by God. The characteristic feature of the other, the action prophet, was to inspire and lead a popular movement to vigorous participation in an anticipated redemptive action by God.

The peasantry, from whose ranks the popular prophets and their followers came, were probably acquainted with the expectations of an eschatological prophet, especially those of the fiery Elijah. However, none of the popular prophets appear in any distinctive way to be a fulfillment of this expectation of Elijah as the eschatological prophet. The Jewish popular prophets of the first century appear rather to be a revival of certain types of prophets portrayed in biblical traditions. Both the oracular prophets and the popular movements led by prophets of action are social forms distinctive to Jewish society. We cannot satisfactorily explain them

through a comparative study or through recourse to a concept such as "charisma." In order to account for the distinctive forms these concrete prophets and prophetic
movements assumed, we must examine the distinctively Jewish historical traditions out of which they responded to their
situation. In particular, the oracular prophets who
announced judgment or redemption appear to be a continuation of the ancient Israelite tradition of oracular prophets
known from Hebrew Scriptures. The activist prophetic movements, which anticipated God's new redemptive action,
appear to be at least informed by the memory of the great
liberation movements led by Moses, Joshua, and the judges,
and perhaps even a revival of an older tradition of prophetic
movements such as those led by Elijah and Elisha.

Examination of the prophetic prototypes from biblical history as well as the continuation of prophetic traditions in the
postexilic period will enable us to discern how the popular
prophets and prophetic movements at the time of Jesus may
have been influenced by the distinctive types of prophets in
Jewish biblical tradition.

TRADITIONS OF TWO TYPES OF POPULAR
PROPHETS AND PROPHETIC EXPECTATIONS

THE PROTOTYPICAL CHARISMATIC LEADERS
OF EARLY ISRAEL:
THE JUDGES, MOSES, AND JOSHUA

Early Israel had no established state institutions. The Israelites' only government was their covenant with Yahweh,
which held the Israelite tribes and clans in minimal coherence, and their common actions necessary for survival.
Indeed, one of the distinctive, even constitutive, factors of
Israel as a society was its liberation from the oppressive political institutions of the Egyptian empire and the Canaanite
city-states. For the independent Israelites, Yahweh was their

true and only king. All of them, individually and collectively, were directly responsible to God as servants of the divine King.

During times of political crisis, however, when the Canaanite kings threatened to force Israelites back into subservience, or when foreign nations threatened to conquer them, "the Spirit of Yahweh" would rush upon charismatic leaders who would rally the people to a revival of Yahwism and call out the peasant militia. In their response to such crises, the people had the feeling that Yahweh himself was leading them in liberation or in defense of their freedom. The inspired leader, called a *shophet* (judge), was usually both God's messenger, to announce what action Yahweh was taking, and the leader of the people obediently following God's course of action. His/her authority was inherent in the way s/he responded to the crisis and was not hereditary. Thus, combining both message and action, the *shophet* was not simply an individual messenger, but also the leader of a religiopolitical movement, what modern social scientists might call a revitalization movement.[1] The book of Judges contains several condensed and stereotyped descriptions of these charismatic leaders (see Judg. 3:9-10; 3:15; 3:27-28). Indeed, one of the oldest segments of Hebrew Scriptures, the "Song of Deborah" (see Judg. 5:2-3, 6-7, 10-11, 13), is a song celebrating the victory of one of these movements, led by the "prophetess" Deborah (Judg. 4:4). During the over 200-year existence of Israel prior to the rise of the monarchy, there were many such "prophetic movements."

The most prominent such movement in biblical tradition, indeed, the prototype of the rest, was the great liberating exodus from Egypt through the sea, led by the larger-than-life figure of Moses. A close second was Joshua's conquest of the promised land across the Jordan. Moses, through visions and direct communication of God's will, was commissioned to lead the liberation of the enslaved Israelites from Egypt. Preaching a trust in Yahweh to a despairing people, he organized the movement of liberation. It was successful, with great signs and wonders, climaxing as the sea engulfed the Pharaoh's armies. Then Yahweh, through Moses, led his liberated people through trials and preparations in the wilderness to the very entrance to the promised land. On the way, Moses mediated the basic organization and constitution of Israel, the covenant with Yahweh. Through Joshua, disciple and successor of Moses, Yahweh guided the entry into the promised land. Like Moses, Joshua led the people with great signs and wonders (stopping the waters of the Jordan; commanding the sun to stand still; the victory over Jericho). Throughout, Yahweh fought for the people, causing panic among their enemies. Finally, Joshua mediated the covenant renewal at Shechem, which renewed the people's mutual commitment to a just social order in the land of promise under the rule of Yahweh. In Joshua, and then in the periodic appearance of a charismatic *shophet,* or prophet (Judg. 4:4), we can see the significance of Moses' declaration in Deut. 18:15: "Yahweh your God will raise up for you a prophet like me from among you, from your brethren—him you shall heed."

PROPHETS AS BOTH MESSENGERS AND LEADERS OF MOVEMENTS

With the rise of the monarchy in Israel, a split developed between the prophetic functions of message and action. Whereas the last *shophet,* Samuel, was still both messenger and political-military leader, the prophet Nathan was simply the messenger of Yahweh, while the anointed king David assumed the military and political leadership. When the institution of the monarchy became firmly established, it appeared that the prophet would surely be confined to the role of a spokesperson. Indeed, by the time of the great eighth- and seventh-century prophets Amos, Isaiah, Hosea, and Jeremiah, the prophet was simply a messenger pronouncing the word of Yahweh. However, the covenantal traditions and social forms of early Israel were not immediately and completely suppressed by the monarchy. The biblical narratives about Elijah and his successor, Elisha, indicate that prophets as both messengers and leaders of movements continued long into the monarchical period in the northern kingdom of Israel, if not in the kingdom of Judah.

These prophets continued to serve as *messengers*, communicating the will of Yahweh to king and people in oracular form (see 1 Kings 17:1). The source of their oracular pronouncements was their experience of standing in the heavenly council of Yahweh (see 1 Kings 22:19-22). As with their successors, the classical oracular prophets, the burden of the prophecies of Elijah, Elisha, and others appears to have been the pronouncement of judgment on king and court and sentence for faithless violation of the covenant with Yahweh, often as a result of strong foreign cultural influence. For example, Yahweh's withholding of rain (and therefore fertility) is punishment for King Ahab's program of transforming Israel into a Canaanite kingship legitimated by fertility religion (see 1 Kings 16:29-17:2). At the time of Elijah and Elisha, however, the prophets also performed one of the traditional functions of the judge (*shophet*) in communicating Yahweh's redemptive action, his protection of his people against foreign invasion and domination. Elisha gave oracles of deliverance from the invading Syrian army and assisted the defensive war effort generally with insights into the tactical moves of the enemy forces and with a prayer of intercession asking Yahweh to "strike the enemy with blindness" (2 Kings 6:8-10, 18). An important component of such prophecy was the vision of Yahweh's heavenly armies fighting for his people, in one case allaying fears about the massive siege of the city of Dothan (see 2 Kings 6:16-17; see also 7:6 and 2:11-12).

Political circumstances and social structure had changed considerably since the time of Moses or Deborah. The monarchy now provided institutionalized government as well as the primary political-military leadership. Nevertheless, some of the prophets still became, periodically, "leaders" of prophetic movements with a popular social base and a distinctive social form. From the Elijah-Elisha narratives we learn that there were groups or guilds of "sons of the prophets" residing in or around major towns such as Gilgal and Jericho, probably under the leadership of a prominent figure such as Elijah or Elisha.[2] Besides providing prophetic "services" to the people, these groups provoked or led political action, as called for by the social-political situation. Indeed, the Elijah-Elisha stories portray these prophetic groups as popular movements against the monarchy. The king and court, under strong influence from the surrounding monarchies, had become oppressive, in violation of the Mosaic covenant. Ahab and his Sidonian queen, Jezebel, brought in hundreds of "prophets of Baal" and killed or otherwise persecuted prophets of Yahweh. Seen as enemies or "troublers of Israel," Elijah and other loyal Yahwists even had to go into hiding for a time. No wonder they may have believed that there was only a remnant of a few thousand in Israel who had remained faithful to the covenant (1 Kings 19:18).

This oppression and persecution of the popular prophets of Yahweh under Ahab and his sons may provide a context in which we can understand some of the prophetic actions reminiscent of earlier themes of liberation under Moses and Joshua. Elijah withdrew into the wilderness to Sinai-Horeb, the very mountain of revelation. There he received both personal strength and a prophetic commission to return to his people as the agent of revolution against an oppressive regime (1 Kings 19). Elijah and Elisha, accompanied by fifty of the "sons of the prophets," went out on Yahweh's instructions to the Jordan River:

> Then Elijah took his mantle, and rolled it up, and struck the water, and the water was parted to the one side and to the other, till the two of them could go over on dry ground. (2 Kings 2:8)

Then after Elijah was taken up by a whirlwind into heaven, and Elisha had assumed his mantle, he in turn "struck the water, the water was parted to the one side and to the other, and Elisha went over." These are clearly prophetic signs of imminent deliverance reminiscent of Moses and the crossing of the sea and of Joshua and the crossing of the Jordan.

Against the oppression and its strong foreign cultural basis, the prophets Elijah and Elisha and their followers, the "sons of the prophets," fomented a popular rebellion. The apparently widespread opposition to the house of Ahab finally climaxed in outright revolution led by the military commander Jehu (2 Kings 10:15-27), who was anointed as the new king by the prophets (1 Kings 19:15-16; 2 Kings 9:1-13). What began as a movement led by prophets gave rise to a popular messianic movement led by the prophetically anointed Jehu. However, it is significant that it was not the new messiah Jehu but Elijah (2 Kings 2:11-12) and Elisha (2 Kings 13:14) who were associated closely with the heavenly armies and the great saving acts by which Yahweh liberated his people anew.

THE CLASSICAL ORACULAR PROPHETS

The great prophets of the eighth and seventh centuries, whose oracles are preserved in the Bible, were primarily messengers or spokespersons for Yahweh. They discerned what actions Yahweh was taking and interpreted their significance, but they did not gather movements about them or lead group actions. They were all deeply rooted in the Mosaic covenant, which had constituted social policy in Israel during the period of the judges and which continued to inform and determine social relations among the peasantry long after the rise of kingship and its imposition of monarchical political and religious institutions. Indeed, these oracular prophets could be called "messengers of the covenant." Many, if not most, of their pronouncements can be discerned as fragments of "covenant lawsuits," in which

Yahweh, as both prosecutor and judge, accuses and pronounces sentence on his people or their royal leaders for breaking the covenant (see Hos. 4:1-3; Mic. 6:1-5). In the prophetic assessment of both kingdoms, Judah and Israel, the people, especially the powerful, had failed to observe the basic principles of social policy stated in the decalogue (for example, Amos 2:4; Jer. 7, esp. vv. 5-10). Not only were the egalitarian economic and social relations not maintained, but the powerful persistently exploited the poor and weak (see Amos 2:6-7).

Because the covenant had been broken, the prophets were constrained to announce Yahweh's punishment for faithlessness. The prophets discerned that a particular defeat or destruction of the kingdom of Israel or Judah was really the form of Yahweh's punishment for failure to maintain covenantal justice and trust within the society. Occasionally, the prophets accompanied their pronouncements of judgment with desperate pleas to the people, and especially to their rulers, to reestablish just social-economic relations. Besides these pronouncements and pleas, the classical oracular prophets often dramatized their message with symbolic actions that struck their contemporaries as peculiar or even as evidence of madness. Even the supposedly respectable Jerusalemite Isaiah, with his connections at court, walked about the city naked and barefoot for three years "as a sign and portent" against the court placing false hopes in Egypt for defense against the Assyrians (Is. 20). Jeremiah wore yoke bars around his neck symbolizing the necessary submission to the Babylonian emperor Nebuchadnezzar (Jer. 27).

Yahweh's judgment announced by the prophets frequently focused on Jerusalem and the temple (or "Zion") and on the kings, the princes, and the powerful. Prophetic woes uttered against Jerusalem became sharper and more vehement toward the end of the classical prophetic period, as in the oracles of Zephaniah (see Zeph. 3:1-2), and especially those of Jeremiah, not only in his famous "Temple

Sermon" (Jer. 7), but in several other oracles as well (see Jer. 6:1-8, esp. v. 6; chap. 19, esp. vv. 14-15). Though reluctant and torn, Jeremiah felt compelled to speak such woes over Jerusalem and the temple; for as he tells the princes following his arrest because of the Temple Sermon, "Yahweh sent me to prophesy against this house and this city all the words you have heard" (26:12; see further chaps. 7 and 26; 9:11; 38:23).

Even more prominent a feature of the prophetic message were oracles against the king, princes, and priestly or governmental officials. In fact, the injustices and oppression committed by the rulers and wealthy is often given as the reason for God's judgment on Jerusalem. This is the basis of Amos' proclamation of Yahweh's judgment on king and kingdom—just forty years before the Northern Kingdom was destroyed by Assyria (Amos 7:11; see also vv. 16-17).[3] Even Isaiah, who so closely identified with the temple cult and associated with the king, delivered rather sharp oracles (see Is. 1:21-23; 3:14-15; 7:10-17). Sharpest of all is Micah: "Hear this, . . . you rulers of the house of Israel, who build Zion with blood . . . and eat the flesh of my people . . . because of you . . . Jerusalem shall become a heap of ruins . . ." (Mic. 3:1-3, 9-12).

Indeed, from the consistently sharp prophetic indictments of the kings and ruling class and the vehement defense of the exploited common people, we can infer the prophets' orientation toward the peasantry. Many of the prophets were, at the least, spokespersons for the peasantry. Despite the paucity of information regarding their personal social status, it is clear that they were not professional court or cultic prophets, as Amos insisted in his own case (Amos 7:14). Micah was probably himself a peasant. And Jeremiah, descended from the priestly line of Abiathar, who had been deposed from high priestly office by Solomon, was from a village northeast of Jerusalem. Moreover, as with the prophets' oracles of judgment, accusation and punishment were most sharply directed at kings, the gentry, and the sacerdotal and courtly

aristocracy (see Zeph. 3:3-4; Mic. 7:3). The wealthy, too, so
full of violence against the needy, were the object of prophetic criticism (see Mic. 6:11-12; Amos 6:1, 4-7; Is. 5:8;
10:1). Accordingly, the expensive military forces and
defenses, supported by or built by peasant labor, also fell
under prophetic indictment (see Hos. 10:13-14; Mic. 5:10-
11). Even the priests and their elaborate cultic apparatus
were condemned, for the priests forgot or suppressed the
law, and their exploitation of the people was nothing but
robbery and murder (see Hos. 4:4-6; 6:9; 10:1; Amos 5:21-24).

It is not surprising, therefore, that kings and ruling groups
were hostile, even repressive, to these prophets. The wealthy
and powerful had no desire to hear oracles against themselves (see Mic. 2:6). In fact, by the time of Amos and Hosea,
there had already been a long history of prophetic warnings
and a long history of official suppression or persecution of
the unofficial popular prophets. From the prophets' own
viewpoint, their oracles were Yahweh's continuing attempts
to redeem and care for his people, parallel to the liberation
from Egypt and guidance through the wilderness: Yet the
prophets were hated, ordered not to prophesy (see Amos
2:10-12; 5:10; Hos. 9:7-8). In a few cases, we have records of
the (official) royal or priestly persecution of prophets.
Micaiah had been thrown in prison by Ahab (1 Kings 22:27).
Amaziah, apparently the chief priest and high royal officer at
Bethel under Jeroboam II, attempted to drive Amos out of
Israel (see Amos 7:12-13). Jeremiah was arrested more than
once and threatened with death or imprisonment for his
outspoken and persistent prophecies against the city, monarchy, and temple. At one point, the chief temple officer,
Pashur, had Jeremiah beaten and put in stocks (Jer. 20). He
escaped execution after his Temple Sermon only because he
had an influential defender at court named Ahikam (Jer.
26:24). Because of his prophecy of the defeat of Jerusalem by
the Babylonians, Jeremiah was accused of treason (see Jer.
38:4-6). In at least one case, a prophet was actually killed and
remembered as a martyr (see Jer. 26:20-23).

The classical oracular prophets and others like them, whose memory is preserved in prophetic traditions, can thus be discerned as spokespersons for the peasantry and the covenantal social-economic policy that served to protect their interests. Because of the blatant exploitation of the peasantry, these prophets felt compelled to oppose the ruling class, which was failing to observe the covenantal order. Rather than heed the prophetic warnings, the ruling groups appear to have responded with repression and persecution.

Although oracles of punishment and judgment dominate in the classical prophetic books of the Bible, there were also oracles of salvation and victory. Many of the prophets who gave them were professionals, attached to the court or temple cult, without any apparent base among the people. These oracles were usually favorable to the monarch, capital city, and temple.[4] This should not lead, however, to the conclusion that "true" prophecy is uniformly doom-oriented, or that salvation oracles are necessarily false, especially when they concern particular events and therefore seem predictive. The criterion implicit in classical (preexilic) prophecy that is remembered as true (and included in the canon) is that of a covenantal interpretation of social-economic relations and political events. Thus, the prophets whose oracles have been remembered as true were not the official cult or court prophets, but rather the popular prophets who articulated Yahweh's concern for covenantal justice and indicted those who exploited and oppressed the people.

Once this is clear it is possible better to understand the few oracles of salvation which are extant from the classical prophets. It is important to realize that although the prophets interpret the decline and defeats of kingdoms as their deserved punishment for not maintaining just (covenantal) socioeconomic relations, there was not always a simple relationship between covenant-breaking and military defeat. That the rulers' actions deserved punishment did not mean that there was no hope for the people's future. For example, Isaiah had condemned Judah's ruling class for its oppression of the people, and pronounced God's purifying judgment against rulers and holy city. Yet when Assyria attacked Jerusalem, Isaiah proclaimed that Yahweh would protect Jerusalem from the siege by Sennacherib and announced that God was about to punish the arrogant Assyrian empire[5]—a prophecy that later played an important role in subsequent crises for the city and people centuries later.

POSTEXILIC PROPHETS AND PROPHETIC EXPECTATIONS

The defeat of the nation and the destruction of Jerusalem and its temple did not mean the end of prophecy, but the confirmation of the prophets' oracles of judgment. It also meant the need for further prophetic interpretation of the new situation of the Jewish people now under foreign domination. Especially important was an answer to the question of whether Yahweh had abandoned his people or was still caring for them. Prophetic activity and lore from the fall of Jerusalem to late second temple times has several important features that facilitate our understanding of the two types of popular prophets active at the time of Jesus.

In terms of social history, there has been a good deal of misunderstanding regarding prophecy and prophets in the "intertestamental" period. This is partly because of the serious lack of sources. But it is also due to the traditional dominance of theological (christological) interests and a "history of ideas" approach within biblical and intertestamental studies. We must therefore carefully differentiate historical analysis of prophetic activity in the second temple period from certain traditional generalizations found frequently in biblical studies, which may have some theological validity but are historically misleading. From at least the first century C.E. onward, the ancient rabbis and scribes held that true prophecy had ended with Haggai, Zechariah, and Malachi. Josephus, a Pharisee as well as a historian, shared this view (see *Ag. Ap.* 1.37-41). Moreover, such a view prevailed in the emerging "canonical" thinking regarding which writings were to be recognized as authoritative scripture, as reflected in the prophetic books finally included in the Hebrew Bible. Because true prophecy had ceased, according to some theologically oriented views in the intertestamental period, there were no prophets during the second temple period. The resulting vacuum, according to such views, was filled by lively expectations of an eschatological prophet to come at the end-time, and by apocalyptic visions of judgment and salvation. The following reconstruction of postexilic prophecy attempts to avoid misconceptions by its focus on four points.

The Continued Appearance of Oracular Prophets

Contrary to the official doctrine of later scribal or courtly circles,[6] the line of oracular prophets did not cease with the destruction of Jerusalem or within a few generations thereafter. The crisis brought on by the destruction stimulated the collection and adaptation of oracles of the classical prophets. Some of this activity was carried on by prophetic schools or disciples loyal to their masters. But by no means was prophetic activity confined to such schools. As had been the case under the monarchies, some of the postexilic prophets were closely related to the temple (rebuilt in the sixth century) and the official leadership of the Judean community. Others must have been more popularly based and independent of, if not in active opposition to, the new established order.

Oracles of judgment continued, but no longer dominated, at least in the postexilic prophetic books included in the biblical canon. Prophets now emphasized oracles of liberation. After the Babylonian destruction of Jerusalem, the end of the Davidic monarchy, and the exile of the ruling class to Babylon, the situation of a society in disarray and a people languishing under foreign rule called for oracles of comfort and new redemption. In these circumstances, prophets such

as the "Second" Isaiah (Is. 40-55) interpreted the imminent
Persian conquest of Babylon and release of the Jewish cap-
tives as presaging the imminent restoration of Zion/Jerusa-
lem. Second Isaiah even assured the Jewish people of their
own world-historical role—precisely in their own long-suf-
fering situation of oppression—as Yahweh's chosen means
of bringing justice and light to the nations.[7] Similarly, the
prophets Haggai and Zechariah, who appear to be closely
associated with the new ruling group of Jewish society, saw
in the international upheavals of their times indications that
Yahweh's action to rescue the people and restore
Zion/Jerusalem was imminent.

Not all postexilic prophetic activity, however, was confined to those of "respectable" demeanor or those associated
officially with the restored temple cult and government, or
the prophetic schools. Prophetic visions and oracles by more
popular figures continued, as can be seen in Zech. 13:2-6,
which derides spiritually inspired prophets clad in hairy
mantles. Since we owe the preservation of prophetic materials from this period to the respectable scribal circles or prophetic schools, it is not surprising that there is little or no
material surviving from such rustics, who were despised and
not recognized. But these "tillers of the soil" (Zech. 13:5)
appear to stand more directly in the tradition of Elijah and
Micah than do their more respectable contemporaries, such
as those in the school of Zechariah, whose vision of the "day
of Yahweh" now entailed the end of crude prophets with the
"unclean spirit" and "hairy mantles." Indeed, the harangue
against them by the disciples of Zechariah provides evidence
that, far from having died out, the line of popular prophets
based in the peasantry had continued right into the postexilic period.

Expectation of a Future Prophet

The fall of Jerusalem must have provided a vindication of the
"prophets like Moses," messengers of the covenant who

defended the covenantal constitution of Israelite society against internal oppression and foreign domination. With Judean society now in disarray and under the rule of successive Babylonian, Persian, and Hellenistic empires, there was all the more need for a messenger who would articulate the will of God or even reestablish the rule of God in the community. With the monarchy destroyed, and perhaps discredited, it is not surprising that hopes did not spontaneously focus on a royal figure. Rather, some focused on a prophet as Yahweh's agent of judgment and restoration. The memory of Yahweh's promise to Moses provided the basis of this expectation:

> I will raise up from them a prophet like you from among their brethren; and I will put my words in his mouth, and he shall speak to them all that I command him. (Deut. 18:18)

A remarkable claim by the "Third" Isaiah (Is. 56-66) reflected this hope and provided another vivid expression of it (Is. 61:1-2, 8).

Despite these striking texts, there is little evidence that expectations of an eschatological prophet were very prominent in Jewish society.[8] There is evidence only of some focus on the returning Elijah, perhaps because he had been translated into heaven, and therefore could be expected to return in order to set things right (see Mal. 3:1-3; 4:4-6). The memory of Elijah's wondrous deeds and the idea of his eschatological return were still current two centuries later, as indicated by its inclusion in a recitation of the great heroes of the past by the scribal Jesus ben Sira, who included little else of eschatological content or tone in his "wisdom" book (see Sir. 48:1, 7-10). However, the expectation of Elijah's return must not have gained prominence in scribal circles. In apocalyptic literature dating from the Maccabean rebellion, as in the Hasmonean court history, Elijah is simply remembered for his great zeal for the law (along with other heroes) and for his translation into heaven—no mention being made of his future role in redemption and restoration.[9]

Memory of Yahweh's Great Acts of Deliverance
through the Leadership of a Prophet

There appear to have been no actual prophetic movements during the exilic period, although this may simply be a function of the extreme lack of evidence for this period in general. We do know, however, that the memory of Yahweh's great acts of salvation—in the exodus, the way through the wilderness, the conquest of the promised land, and the several defensive holy wars led by the judges—was prominent in Judean society from the Persian period on. For it was during this time that the biblical narratives, including the Priestly edition of the books of Moses and the Deuteronomic history (i.e., the books of Deuteronomy through 2 Kings), were given their final form. The "reforms" led by Ezra and subsequent generations of official scribes, moreover, attempted to make the covenantal traditions generally, along with the law of Moses in particular, known among the people.

One of the principal reasons this memory was important for the Judean people is that it would have directly informed their expectations regarding future liberation. The most important events of deliverance in memory and anticipation were the exodus, the way through the wilderness, and the gift of the land. The memory of these events had already been emphasized by the classical oracular prophets. They referred prominently to these events as a reminder of Yahweh's liberation and care for the people and the basis of the people's obligation to keep the covenant.[10] The exodus and way through the wilderness thus became especially prominent as a model or prototype of purification, renewal, and God's new acts of redemption.[11] By the time of Second Isaiah in the mid-sixth century B.C.E., the memory and anticipation of Yahweh's acts of liberation had become a fundamental pattern of Judean historical-eschatological thinking. According to this pattern, God's future acts of deliverance were anticipated on the model of the wondrous events that originally constituted Israel as a free nation in its own land. One significant illustration of this pattern is the familiar opening oracle of Second Isaiah, "in the wilderness prepare the way of Yahweh" (Is. 40:3-5), which became a focal text for the Essene exodus to the wilderness at Qumran, as well as for the early Christian understanding of the role of John the Baptist.

The Relation of Prophets and Apocalypticism

Contrary to the common generalization that prophets and prophecy died out and were replaced by apocalypticism, it is clear that prophecy and prophets, at least of the oracular type, did not die out at all, but continued to function right into the late second temple period. It has also been claimed that, whereas classical Israelite prophecy addressed concrete historical situations, apocalypticism was alienated from history. It may be useful, therefore, to clarify the relationships between prophets and apocalypticism, especially since the latter term can encompass literature (texts), theological outlook, and social groups possessing a particular orientation toward imminent redemption.[12]

In a number of respects, apocalyptic visions and visionary literature appear to be an outgrowth of traditional Israelite prophecy. The ecstatic experience of elevation to the heavenly court of Yahweh was a development of the classical prophetic experience, as illustrated in the cases of Micaiah ben Imlah (1 Kings 22) or Second Isaiah (Is. 40-55). Further, apocalyptic dream-visions, while far more elaborate, apparently also stood in a long line of similar visions of earlier prophets such as Amos (Amos 7-8) and Jeremiah (Jer. 1). Much of the standard imagery used by the earlier prophets was also used and elaborated in apocalyptic literature, for example, the image of the divine warrior and his heavenly armies coming to the rescue of the beleaguered people. Furthermore, apocalyptic literature emerged in response to historical circumstances similar to, if more extreme than, those that evoked earlier prophetic oracles and movements, that is, situations of social oppression and foreign threat.

Insofar as the later situations were more extreme, it is understandable that the imagery of salvation would correspondingly become more fantastic. The similarity and continuity lie in the fact that both prophets and apocalyptic visionaries were addressing concrete social-historical situations and announcing that God was still concerned about, and active in, those situations. It is this rootage in, and relevance to, particular concrete circumstances that is the most important aspect of apocalypticism with regard to the later revival of oracular and action prophets in the time of Jesus. As discussed at somewhat greater length in chapter 1, apocalypticism as a general orientation in society, or at least influential groups within it, could arise out of and address situations in which Jewish faith was pushed to the brink of despair. In what were, to some, seemingly hopeless situations, such an orientation enabled people not only to endure in their traditional faith, but even to take action against overwhelming odds, such as the persecution by the Hellenistic armies of Antiochus Epiphanes.[13] Particular pieces of apocalyptic literature provide expressions of, and insights into, this general mood among the people, at least among literate circles. At other times apocalypticism probably subsided. But it was there to be rekindled in times of new crises. Thus, far from being mutually exclusive in a social-historical sense, apocalypticism and prophecy went hand in hand. Prophets were the human vehicles through which apocalypticism could be revived in response to a particular situation. Among the literate, revelations could take the form of apocalyptic literature. The same or similar theological outlook and confidence in God's imminent deliverance or judgment, however, could be articulated among the common people by popular prophetic figures such as the rustic ecstatics castigated in Zechariah and the two types of prophets to be examined below. The standard, older theological approaches understood prophecy to have been replaced by apocalypticism. A social-historical approach looks instead to the particular historical situation and the apocalyptic orientation as an important dimension of how the people involved responded to their situation.

THE ABSENCE OF THE TWO TYPES OF POPULAR PROPHETS AMONG THE LITERATE GROUPS

It is commonly observed that there was considerable prophetic activity in Jewish society in the late second temple period.[14] Not surprisingly, given the general scarcity of evidence for the period, much of our sense of prophecy is based on materials from the literate groups. There was indeed prophetic activity among these groups. There is little evidence among Essenes or Pharisees, however, either of any significant expectation of a prophetic deliverer or of actual prophetic figures who fit the oracular or the action type of prophets known from biblical traditions. When we inquire after the particular social forms, it is clear that among the Pharisees and especially among the Essenes, prophetic activity was channeled primarily into (inspired) interpretation of traditional biblical prophecies. Moreover, the only prophetic figures, a few Essenes mentioned by Josephus, appear to have been seers who made narrowly focused predictions about future events or personal destinies.

Seers and Scriptural Interpretation among the Essenes

On the surface, the Dead Sea Scrolls might appear to offer evidence of lively expectations of an eschatological prophet in Jewish society. In the *Community Rule* found at Qumran is the following enigmatic passage:

> [The men of holiness who walk in perfection] . . . shall be ruled by the primitive precepts in which the men of the Community were first instructed until there shall come the prophet and the messiahs of Aaron and Israel. (1QS 9:11-12)

The scribes of the community seem to have in mind here the same trio of figures as in the *Testimonia* (a collection of scriptural texts referring to future agents of salvation). The key text of Deut. 18:18, about the prophet like Moses, is cited along with references to an apparent royal messiah and an anointed priest (4QTest). Just what and how much we should make of these passages, however, is problematic. Eschatological expectations at Qumran were fluid, sometimes focusing on two figures, sometimes on three. Moreover, there are only these few brief references to a prophet among the many scrolls left by the community. Hence we cannot really conclude that the Qumran community itself focused much hope on such a future prophet, much less use this as evidence for Jewish society generally.

Indeed, from what we know of the Essenes from Josephus and the Dead Sea Scrolls themselves, it seems unlikely that they would have entertained any vivid expectations of future prophets or produced any prophets of their own, whether of the oracular or action type. The Qumranites saw themselves as being a new exodus into the wilderness (in fulfillment of Is. 40) and as the new covenant community patterned after the original Mosaic covenant. As leader and founder of the community, the shadowy Righteous Teacher seems to have performed the functions of a new Moses. In particular, the key to all revelations from the past had been disclosed through him (1QpHab 7:1-2). Thus, the community members, convinced that biblical prophecies had been addressed to their own situation, busily pondered the application of those prophecies to contemporary events and figures. Judging from the literary remains, the scribal community devoted much of its energy to interpreting the biblical prophecies and recording its interpretations in its scrolls. Emphasis among the Essenes, therefore, fell on the interpretation of revelation already received from the past. Thus, one would not expect prophets of the action type because the Righteous Teacher had already led the decisive move to the wilderness "to prepare the way of the Lord." One would not expect new oracular prophets from the Qumranites because the function formerly served by prophecy (discerning the meaning of the present situation) was now being served by interpretation of historical prophecies. Moreover, one would not expect a community which had cut itself off from the "degenerate" society at large (as hopelessly under the sway of evil powers) to engage in a prophetic ministry to that same society.

The kind of prophecy the Essenes did produce, judging from Josephus' reports, fits the group's emphasis on application of scriptural prophecies to contemporary events and figures. The Essene prophets mentioned by Josephus are all seers who make *predictions*—and not leaders of movements, or deliverers of oracles.[15] In assessing his accounts of Essene seers, however, we must take into account Josephus' own view of prophecy. He had clearly been influenced by the Hellenistic concepts he uses. Compared with classical biblical prophecy, the concept of prophecy in Josephus has been reduced to one of prediction and foreknowledge. Yet such prediction was no simple matter, as Josephus explicitly notes:

> Some of them [Essenes] profess to foretell the future [*ta mellonta proginōskein*], after life-long study of the sacred books, different kinds of purifications and the sayings of the prophets. (*J.W.* 2.159)

Josephus' comment thus accords with the more precise information we now have from the Dead Sea Scrolls about the predictive value of the Qumranites' application of historical revelations to their own situation. Two Essene seers mentioned by Josephus easily fit into this context.

> A certain Judas, of the Essene group, who had never been proven wrong in his predictions [*en hois proeipen*] . . . cried out to his friends and disciples who were with him to get instruction in foretelling the future. . . . He had foretold that Antigonus [son of John Hyrcanus and brother of the King-High Priest Aristobulus]

would die at the place called Strato's Tower. . . . (*Ant.* 13.311-12; see also *J.W.* 1.78-80)

Judas' prediction can easily be understood as a rather precise application of some biblical prophecy to a figure in his own situation. Josephus' account of the second seer, Menahem (*Ant.* 15.373-76), seems more legendary in character, but its kernel is the prediction of Herod's eventual kingship. Like Judas' prediction of the death of Antigonus I, such foreknowledge was a concern of the Essenes, as they pondered the application of biblical revelation to contemporary figures and events.

What seems surprising about the reports of these two seers is that they portray Essenes engaging in ordinary social intercourse around the temple in Jerusalem. While the Dead Sea Scrolls indicate that the Essenes had rejected and withdrawn from the social order after the Hasmoneans had established themselves in power, Josephus' accounts may be plausibly explained by suggesting that the Essenes had relaxed their guard once the original Hasmonean "Wicked Priest" (Jonathan or Simon) had left the scene, and had established minimal contact with society at large. By the time of Herod, the Essenes may have accommodated themselves to the "sons of darkness"—perhaps to Herod in particular, since he systematically destroyed the Hasmoneans, the bitter enemies of the Qumranites.

The Essene seers may seem to have some superficial similarities with the oracular type of prophets. To judge from Josephus, however, they simply predicted narrow future happenings, whereas the classical oracular prophets brought God's judgment to bear on the present situation of an entire society. The Essene seers' predictions focused narrowly on the fortunes of individual rulers, whereas the classical oracular prophets addressed broad social relationships and placed judgment on royal behavior in an all-inclusive covenantal context.[16] Such seers, moreover, appear to have been confined to, and distinctive of, the Essene group. Indeed, from the Dead Sea Scrolls we know that the Qumran community provided a very intelligible social-cultural background for the focus, form, and content of such prediction regarding contemporary figures.

Although Qumran manifested little prophetic expectation, and apparently produced no prophets of either the oracular or the action type, the origin of the group itself—a type of exodus to the wilderness—may be significant for our survey of prophetic movements. It might be argued that Qumran provides the first instance of a prophetic movement since Elijah-Elisha and the "sons of the prophets." One might even claim that the Essenes constitute a prophetic movement among the literate strata nearly 200 years prior to the emergence of such movements among the Jewish peasantry. The long interval between them, and the fact that they had become, by the first century C.E., so well established that Josephus can refer to them as one of the three principal "philosophies" or "sects" of the Jews, makes it unlikely that the origin of the Qumran community served as the model for the later popular prophetic movements. Qumran does show, however, that the typological pattern of interpretation and action—as was God's great act of deliverance in the past, so will be the great new act of deliverance—was very much alive in Jewish society at the time. It also indicates that the *memory* of the older tradition of liberating movements led by a Moses or a Joshua was still vital among the people, even if there apparently had been no prophetic movements since Elijah-Elisha.

The Relative Lack of Prophecy among the Pharisees

From what we know of the distinctive concerns and social characteristics of the Pharisees we would not expect them to produce anything like a prophetic movement. They believed that the decisive revelation had occurred on Sinai through Moses; it was now up to them and other sages to interpret this

revelation of God's will for their own situation. The Pharisees pursued personal purity in their own associations and at
the outset at least attempted to have the rule of God realized
by working through established political processes. There is
also little or no literary evidence for any expectations of an
eschatological prophet among the Pharisees, although it is
likely that Pharisaic circles entertained at least the belief in
the eschatological return of Elijah. Even Elijah, however, was
not a central concern for them. In the two great apocalypses
written near the end of the first century C.E. by visionaries
who must have had connections with Pharisaic circles, he is
little more than part of the general apocalyptic lore, one of
those who, taken up at death, shall return at the end (2 Bar.
77:24; 4 Ezra 6:26; see also 7:109). This means, in effect, that
the Pharisees were deferring any prophetic or other political
action to correct current injustices. Neither here nor later,
however, in the eventual standardization of eschatological
doctrine by the rabbis in the second and third centuries C.E.
is there much "burning fire" of judgment and restoration in
the Pharisaic or rabbinic view of Elijah as eschatological
prophet.

Finally, there is little evidence for oracular prophets from
among the Pharisees. Possibly stemming from the intense
apocalyptic mood of sages during the Hellenistic persecution and Maccabean revolt, the Pharisees had a strong reputation for having foreknowledge of events through visions
imparted by God (see *Ant.* 17.43). Such visionary activity
found literary form toward the end of the first century C.E.
among at least some sages (i.e., 2 Baruch and 4 Ezra). The
basic reason why the Pharisees were unlikely to produce or
be receptive to oracular prophets of the more traditional
kind was their firm conviction that the decisive revelation of
the will of God had already been given in the Torah. Their
principal task, their own *raison d' être,* was to interpret and
realize the provisions of the law in the life of the community.
Inspiration that had previously taken the form of prophetic
oracles now was channeled into interpretations of the law

and explications of Torah narratives. Somewhat like the Essenes (but far less compulsively or extensively), the Pharisees may have attempted to interpret and apply biblical prophecies, such as those of an anointed king. An example of such activity is the court intrigue involving Herod's brother Pheroras, his wife, and the eunuch Bagoas (*Ant.* 17.43).[17] Aside from the general gift of prophecy that Josephus describes, however, the main textual evidence for oracular prophetic activity by a Pharisee is Josephus' account of the statement made by Samaias at the trial of the young Herod for the murder of Hezekiah, the brigand-chief. Samaias blamed Hyrcanus and the rest of the Sanhedrin for kowtowing to the arrogant young tyrant-to-be.

> Be assured, however, that God is great; and this man, whom you now want to set free because of Hyrcanus, he will one day punish you and the king himself. (*Ant.* 14.174)

Beyond this, however, there is simply no evidence of the traditional forms of prophetic activity among the Pharisees. Content to work through the ordinary political processes as long as they could, they would have had little interest in any apocalyptically inspired prophetic movements. Although they undoubtedly shared points of eschatological doctrine with other Jewish groups of the time, they "realistically" deferred action themselves until such time as God would clearly intervene in human affairs. Focused as they were on the interpretations and the social realization of the law in community life, they found little reason for interest in oracular prophets.

Thus, although there was indeed prophetic activity among the literate groups, there is little evidence for a significant expectation of a prophetic agent of salvation among Pharisees or Essenes. More importantly, there is no evidence of actual prophetic figures of the two types found in biblical traditions, the oracular or the action prophets. This may mean, judging from the available evidence, that the appearance of several prophetic figures who fit one or the other of the two traditional biblical types was a distinctively popular phenomenon.

TWO TYPES OF POPULAR PROPHETS AT THE TIME OF JESUS

For the bulk of the Jewish peasantry, the Spirit took more spontaneous forms than it did among the scholars. Although for the literate groups the inspired communicaton of God's will was the interpretation of the covenant law given by Moses and the application of ancient oracles, the common people were far less constrained by the scriptural tradition. Spontaneous popular prophecy, however, was by no means formless. Although few among the peasantry would have been able to read the Scripture, they were quite familiar with the revered traditions, covenantal principles, and prophecies of the people of Yahweh. These traditions and traditional forms were still very much alive among the peasants at the time of Jesus. Indeed, during the first century C.E. the memory of ancient prophetic movements of liberation informed new prophetic movements, and traditional oracular prophecy was revived among the people.

As indicated in the first part of this chapter, however, there is simply very little evidence for Jewish expectations of an eschatological prophet prior to the time of Jesus. There is no documentation whatever for expectations of *the* eschatological prophet, and very little for expectations of the prophet like Moses based on Deut. 18:18. There is reason to believe that at least some people, such as Pharisees and the earlier scribe Jesus ben Sira, held expectations of a returning Elijah. The Christian Gospel tradition also indicates that this expectation was present, ready to be applied to figures such as John the Baptist and Jesus of Nazareth. Outside the Christian Gospel tradition, however, there is no evidence to indicate that any of the actual prophets who appeared among the people during the first century were understood as the returning of Elijah. The point to be recognized is that with the popular prophets who appeared at the time, we are dealing with more than simply a fulfillment of some particular expectation. Prophecy was very much alive among the Jewish people. Judging from the particular social forms it assumed, the two types or popular prophets at the time of Jesus were a continuation or a revival of the principal traditional forms known from biblical history.

POPULAR PROPHETIC MOVEMENTS

The action prophets led movements of peasants in active anticipation of divine acts of deliverance.[18] The hostile Josephus suggests that there may have been several such movements around the mid-first century C.E. In his general comments we can discern some of the principal characteristics of these movements.

> Impostors and demagogues, under the guise of divine inspiration, provoked revolutionary actions and impelled the masses to act like madmen. They led them out into the wilderness so that there God would show them signs of imminent liberation. (*J.W.* 2.259; see also the parallel in *Ant.* 20.168: For they said that they would display unmistakable signs and wonders done according to God's plan.)

Josephus' Hellenistic terms and concepts cannot quite hide the apocalyptic features of the prophets and movements that shine through here. What were imposters and demagogues with mere pretense of inspiration to the aristocratic Pharisee and deserter to the Romans were, in the ordinary Palestinian Jewish context, prophets filled with the Spirit. Thus fired by the Spirit, these prophets and their followers thought they were about to participate in the divine transformation of a world gone awry into a society of justice, willed and ruled by God: exactly the revolutionary changes Josephus feared and despised. Like Josephus, the Roman governor Felix had well-founded anxieties about the potential disruption of the

Roman imperial order, for such prophets apparently proclaimed to the people that God was finally bringing an end to their oppression and restoring their freedom.

Large numbers of people, inspired and convinced of the imminence of God's action, abandoned their work, homes, and villages to follow their charismatic leaders out into the wilderness. They knew from the sacred traditions that it was in the wilderness that God had shown signs and wonders of redemption in earlier times, and that the wilderness was the place of purification, preparation, and renewal. Thus their procession into the wilderness and the marvels and signs anticipated there as tokens of their own deliverance were surely conceived in analogy with the great liberating acts of God in the formative history of Israel: "Yahweh . . . saw our oppression . . . and Yahweh brought us out of Egypt with a mighty hand and an outstretched arm, . . . with signs and wonders" (Deut. 26:7-8). Underlying such prophetic movements, moreover, was a basic trust in "God's design." Like the Qumranites, who articulated their faith in more sophisticated and elaborate form, the common people also believed that despite external appearances of oppression and suffering, God had not abandoned his people. Indeed, a *mystery,* an eschatological *plan* of redemption, was about to be revealed. God had now revealed that plan to the popular prophets, and through them to their followers, and they proceeded into the wilderness in anticipation of God's action. It is in this sense of apocalyptic prophetic movements that we should understand Josephus' further reports of three particular prophets and their followers.

The first of these movements occurred under Pontius Pilate, not among the Jews proper, but among the Samaritans. Despite the mutual distrust and conflict that existed between the two peoples, the Samaritans, like the Jews, were an outgrowth of, and were loyal to, the same Israelite people and heritage. The Samaritans were the descendants of the Israelite tribes which had composed the northern kingdom of Israel. Thus they too looked back to the exodus from

Egypt and to Moses as *the prophet,* the mediator of the cove-
nant revealed on Sinai. Samaria had been conquered by (the
Jews under) the Hasmoneans, who had also attempted to
Judaize the population, whence some of the intense feelings
between Jews and Samaritans. Samaria had been part of
Herod's domain and, at the death of Archelaus, came under
the direct rule of the Roman governors. No less than the
Jews, the Samaritans resented foreign rule and oppression.
They too cultivated hopes for a future prophet, the "restorer"
(*tahev*) who was thought of as a new Moses. The *Tahev* was
expected to restore the ancient temple on Mount Gerizim
and the people as a whole to independence and prosperity.
Thus both the Samaritan situation and the Samaritan traditions and expectations were very similar to those of the Jews,
and the prophetic movement described by Josephus appears
to fit the same pattern as the parallel movements a few years
later among the Jews.

> Nor was the Samaritan nation free from disturbance. For a
> man who had no qualms about deceit, and freely used it to
> sway the crowd, commanded them to go up with him as a
> group to Mount Gerizim, which is for them the most sacred
> mountain. He promised to show them, when they got there,
> the holy vessels buried at the spot where Moses had put them.
> Those who thought his speech convincing came with arms
> and stationed themselves at a village called Tirathana. There
> they welcomed late-comers so that they might make the
> climb up the mountain in a great throng. But Pilate was quick
> to prevent their ascent with a contingent of cavalry and armed
> infantry. They attacked those who had assembled beforehand
> in the village, killed some, routed others, and took many into
> captivity. From this group Pilate executed the ringleaders as
> well as the most able among the fugitives. (*Ant.* 18.85-87)

Although for once Josephus does not cite an exaggerated
number, his account gives the impression that this movement was indeed large. Word had apparently spread quickly
among the villages in the area, and the populace, responding
readily to word of impending deliverance, flocked to the

base of the sacred mountain. Josephus writes, moreover, as though the movement were large enough and sufficiently organized to have had several "ringleaders." Behind Josephus's description of the nameless man who could "sway the crowd," we can discern a prophet, received as divinely inspired and whose message of deliverance struck a resonant chord among the vast number of the Samaritan peasantry. The anticipated action, ascending the holy Mount Gerizim to recover the sacred vessels deposited there by Moses, indicates that this prophet was understood as a restorer, Moses' eschatological counterpart. Josephus' mention that they assembled in arms, if trustworthy, may mean that they were gathering in anticipation of some sort of eschatological holy war. The report that they proceeded up the mountain despite being blocked by Roman troops suggests that the yearning for liberation had reached a fevered pitch and emphasizes their absolute trust in the prophet's message of divine deliverance.

As in all non-Christian reports of his character and actions as governor, Pontius Pilate was hardly the indecisive weakling portrayed in the Christian Gospels. He responded to the emergence of this movement with sizable military force and aggressively suppressed what he feared was a popular uprising. Not content simply to disperse the movement, he attacked and slew many followers of the Samaritan prophet.

About a decade later, perhaps in 45 C.E., appeared the second major prophetic movement described by Josephus:

> When Fadus was governor of Judea, a charlatan named Theudas persuaded most of the common people to take their possessions and follow him to the Jordan river. He said he was a prophet, and that at his command the river would be divided and allow them an easy crossing. Through such words he deceived many. But Fadus hardly let them consummate such foolishness. He sent out a cavalry unit against them, which killed many in a surprise attack, though they also took many alive. Having captured Theudas himself, they cut off his head and carried it off to Jerusalem. (*Ant.* 20.97-98)

In Acts, the distinguished Pharisee Gamaliel, in a speech to allay the anxieties of the Sanhedrin about the followers of Jesus of Nazareth, cites Theudas' movement as an earlier analogy, concluding that Theudas "was slain, and all who followed him were dispersed and came to nothing" (5:36). The implied dating of Theudas before Judas of Galilee (6 C.E.) in Acts is surely confused. But the fact that (by the end of the first century when Acts was written) Theudas' movement is remembered alongside that led by Judas of Galilee (the "Fourth Philosophy"; see chapter 5) as one of the two most significant movements analogous to the growing "Jesus movement" must mean that it had been an important event.

We are not confined to mere speculation as to why such a movement occurred under Fadus (44-46). During the previous five years, Palestinian Jews had gone through an experience of alternating extreme tension with Roman rule, a relaxation of that tension, and a restoration of direct and repressive Roman rule. In 40 C.E. Caligula's attempt to have his statue placed in the Jewish temple in Jerusalem had provoked national resistance, including a peasant strike. Then, in a relaxed but all too brief interlude, Agrippa I had ruled as king over the whole of Jewish Palestine, Judea as well as Galilee. Symbolically at least, Agrippa must have formed a buffer between the Jews and the direct Roman rule they so resented. According to Josephus, the "Jewish" king scrupulously observed the Jewish traditions and formed a welcome contrast to the hated Herod. Economically, however, he must have exploited his realm to an extreme degree, imitating his grandfather Herod's flair for costly building projects and lavish gifts to gentile cities (*Ant.* 19.299-311, 327, 331-52). And whatever his observance of Jewish laws had been earlier, Jews must have deeply resented Agrippa's manipulation of a pagan spectacle in honor of Caesar so that he himself was acclaimed as divine. His death almost immediately thereafter was interpreted as punishment by God. After three years without direct Roman rule, the symbolic significance of its reimposition was compounded by the repressive administration of the new governor, Fadus. He moved swiftly and harshly against the Perean Jews in their quarrel with Philadelphia, one of the Hellenistic cities, killing or exiling only the Jewish leaders (*Ant.* 20.2-4). He suppressed brigand groups throughout Judea, including the famous brigand-leader Tholomaus. He reclaimed control of the sacred high priestly vestments which had been in Jewish custody under Agrippa. The fact that the emperor Claudius reversed Fadus in the latter case indicates that even in Rome his policies were viewed as overly severe. The Jews surely experienced Fadus' administration as a renewal of sharply repressive Roman rule.

Theudas' movement was both large and serious in its long-range eschatological purpose. Josephus' phrase "most of the common people" is somewhat vague. One wonders if the account in Acts does not minimize the extent of the movement in fixing their number at 400. That the movement was not a mere demonstration or temporary sally into the wilderness is indicated by the report that the company had taken their possessions with them. Theudas' claim indicates just how serious their purpose must have been. The precise historical analogy does not come through from Josephus' account, but possibilities are suggested. Theudas, parting the waters of the Jordan as the new Joshua, can be seen as leading a reverse conquest, a retreat into the wilderness in order to be purified and prepare the way of the Lord. Or Theudas can be seen as leading a new exodus: parting the waters of the Jordan, as Moses had the Red Sea, thus liberating the people from the bondage imposed on them (in their own land!) by the Romans. Or Theudas' movement can be seen as a combination of exodus and conquest. It is worth recalling that during the period of the judges, the Israelites apparently celebrated a ritual conquest of the promised land, damming up the Jordan so that, symbolically, the liberating exodus from Egyptian slavery was juxtaposed with the entry into the land of promise. These two most significant events

in the constitutive history of the people had been symbolically juxtaposed in earlier prophecies of new redemption,
such as Is. 51:9-11. It may also be of significance to recall that
Elijah and Elisha, leaders of great liberation movements of
the past, had parted the waters of the Jordan (2 Kings 2:6-8).
The precise intention of Theudas and his followers cannot
be reconstructed, but it is clear that in some way Theudas
anticipated a new, perhaps eschatological, action of deliverance by God, analogous to the ancient acts of redemption,
the exodus and conquest.

Fadus, no less efficient in handling prophetic movements
than in suppressing banditry and quarrelsome Perean Jews,
dispatched a squadron of cavalry (500 to 1,000 mounted
men), perhaps the hated Sebastenians that Claudius had supposedly ordered transferred out of Palestine (*Ant.* 19.365-66;
see also *J.W.* 2.52 and *Ant.* 20.122). That Theudas and company were attacked and slain unexpectedly suggests that, in
contrast to the popular messianic movements, this prophetic
movement was not an armed rebellion. The ceremonial
parading of Theudas' severed head into Jerusalem, of course,
was meant as a stern warning to any other Jew who might act
out his passion for liberation.

The third movement was headed by a Jewish prophet who
had come originally, or returned recently, from Egypt, and
for whom the apostle Paul was purportedly mistaken in the
temple precincts on his last journey to Jerusalem (see Acts
21:38). It must have taken place, therefore, around 56 C.E.,
during the administration of Felix, sometime prior to Paul's
visit to the city. As in the case of Theudas, we can supplement
Josephus' account in the *Antiquities* with his earlier narrative
from the *Jewish War,* a more sharply worded and exaggerated
account.

At this time, a certain man from Egypt arrived at Jerusalem, saying he was a prophet and advising the mass of the common people to go with him to the Mount of Olives, which is just opposite the city. . . . He said that from there he wanted to show them that at his command the walls of Jerusalem would fall down and they could then make an entry into the city. But when Felix learned of these things, he commanded his soldiers to take up their weapons. Marching from Jerusalem with many horsemen and foot-soldiers, he attacked the Egyptian and his followers, killed four hundred of them and took two hundred alive. The Egyptian himself fled the battle and vanished without a trace.

(*Ant.* 20.169-71)

The Egyptian false-prophet . . . when he arrived in the countryside, though an imposter, made himself credible as a prophet and rallied about thirty thousand dupes and took them around through the wilderness to the Mount of Olives. From there he intended to force an entry into Jerusalem, overpower the Roman garrison, and become ruler of the citizen body, using his fellow-raiders as bodyguards. Felix anticipated his assault and met him with heavily armed Roman troops, with the whole citizen body joining in the defense. In the aftermath, the Egyptian escaped with a few of his followers, but most of them were killed or captured; the rest scattered and hid out in their homes.

(*J. W.* 2.261-63)

As was the case with the movement of Theudas a decade earlier, again the social and economic circumstances were those that might well have led to a movement seeking liberation from oppression and distress. The people had recently undergone a disastrous famine in the late forties. Then the repressive measures taken by Cumanus (49-52) against minor incidents had the effect of escalating tensions and increasing needless bloodshed. His less than judicious handling of violent conflicts between Jews and Samaritans provoked widespread outcry, and his general actions tended only to multiply the ranks of the brigands and increase the spirit of rebellion. His successor, Felix, continued the repressive measures against brigands and others, but such measures probably further exacerbated rather than ended the distress and turmoil.

From Josephus' more explicit reports in this case, it is possible to reach a clear sense of the size and composition of this movement. Even if his figure of 30,000 is an exaggeration, the group probably numbered in the thousands, not simply hundreds. Moreover, it was composed of peasants from the villages of Judea. In his other accounts of these movements, Josephus typically used vague terms such as "the masses" or "crowd" with reference to the participants. His explicit comment (*J.W.* 2.261) that the Egyptian appeared "in the countryside" clearly indicates that this movement—and almost certainly the others like it—involved primarily the Judean peasantry.

The symbolism that shines through Josephus' reports suggests that the movement of the "Egyptian" understood itself as participating in a new "conquest" of the promised land. The historical prototype must have been the battle of Jericho led by Joshua. In the great "battle of Jericho," after the people had marched around the city walls and the priests had blown the trumpets, "the people raised a great shout, and the wall fell down flat, so that the people went into the city, . . . and they took the city" (Josh. 6:15-20). Thus, the new Joshua, the prophet from Egypt, declared that "at his command the walls of Jerusalem would fall down, and they [his followers] could then make an entry into the city." The roundabout route by which the prophet led his followers to the Mount of Olives probably also had a symbolic purpose similarly patterned after God's great acts of salvation under Joshua or Moses. It was probably either a ritual march around the city, or a reenactment of "the way through the wilderness."

Although we know of no special significance that the Mount of Olives would have had in the great formative events under Moses and Joshua, it had acquired a highly important role in contemporary Jewish apocalyptic lore. The movement, its symbolic location (Mount of Olives), and its apparent purpose of the liberation of Jerusalem should be compared to the prophecies in Zech. 14. A "day of the Lord" is anticipated, indeed the day when the kingdom of the Lord will be established over all the earth, on which the Lord will finally engage in battle against the alien nations occupying Jerusalem; and "on that day his feet shall stand on the Mount of Olives which lies before Jerusalem on the east" (14:1-4, 9). An earlier prophet had imagined it; now several thousand peasants, eager to be freed from alien domination, followed another prophet in order to participate in the realization of such a fantasy.

The report that the "Egyptian" and his followers expected the walls of Jerusalem to fall down on command indicates that this movement, like that of Theudas', was not one of armed rebellion. Luke's statement in Acts that the "Egyptian" had stirred up a revolt and led 4,000 men of the Sicarii out into the wilderness (Acts 21:38) can be explained simply as his confusion of the prophetic movement led by the "Egyptian" with the terrorism being conducted by the Sicarii during this very same time under the procurator Felix. Nothing in Josephus' language suggests that these "common people" from the countryside were bearing weapons, let alone that they were identical with the Sicarii he has just finished describing (*Ant.* 20.163-66, 169-71; *J. W.* 2.254, 261-63). The Roman heavy infantry, however, was well armed and well trained in the use of its arms. Even allowing for some exaggeration by Josephus, the slaughter was extensive.

These three prophetic movements, along with the others about which Josephus generalizes, all follow the same general pattern. A popular prophet with some magnetism and a message collects a large following among the common people in the countryside. The frequency and facility with which such movements arose suggest that the peasantry must have been predisposed to heed such a message of imminent deliverance by God. Not just the ruthless Pilate, but Fadus and

Felix as well, suppressed the movements quickly and brutally, apparently because they believed them to pose a serious threat to public order and to be fostering "revolutionary actions," as Josephus suggests. Certainly the peasants participating in these movements were not out on a temporary holiday, however festive their mood may have been. Both prophets and followers were apparently acting on the firm conviction that they were about to participate in an act of divine liberation. It is indeed likely that they were marching out to experience a decisive eschatological act of deliverance, for there is plenty of evidence that a strong apocalyptic mood pervaded the society during this period of acute distress and tension.

Most significant is the clear pattern of symbolic correspondence between the great historical acts of redemption and the new, eschatological acts anticipated by these prophetic movements. As was the mighty act of God in the formative history of early Israel, so would be God's imminent eschatological act of deliverance. Just as Moses led the people through the divided waters and into the wilderness, so would the prophet Theudas lead a new exodus through the waters of the Jordan and into the wilderness. As God's agent Joshua led the battle of Jericho, so the prophet from Egypt would lead the people to the Mount of Olives, expecting the walls of Jerusalem to fall so they could "liberate" the city. This very pattern of interpreting and anticipating history had been important in Jewish tradition at least since Second Isaiah, who interpreted the anticipated liberation from Babylonian captivity as a new exodus and procession through the wilderness (e.g., Is. 40:1-11; 51:9-11).

This historical-eschatological typology is certainly in evidence as a pattern of interpretation and anticipation in later apocalyptic literature.[19] It also became a standard and central pattern of interpretation in the early Christian movement.[20] It may be of some significance that the literarily productive groups displayed a considerable interest in Moses' prophetic message to their own situation, as well as in his ancient actions. The implication seems to be that a recounting of the ancient historical acts of redemption is directly relevant to *interpretation* of the present situation. The Dead Sea Scrolls, of course, have now dramatized the existence of this pattern and elucidated its significance. In the popular prophetic movements, however, the historical-eschatological typology was a pattern of *action*. These movements enacted this understanding of God's new acts of deliverance. Moreover, the frequent appearance among the peasantry of actual movements shaped according to this pattern is significant in the attempt to understand Jesus of Nazareth and his movement. Whether or not the early church was (or was conscious of itself as) such a movement, it was certainly aware of its "competition":

> False messiahs and false prophets will arise and show signs and wonders, to lead astray, if possible, the elect. (Mk. 13:22)

And the Gospel of Matthew adds what may be an even more specific reference:

> So, if they say to you, "Lo, he is in the wilderness," do not go out. (Mt. 24:26)

ORACULAR PROPHETS

Besides the movements led by Theudas, the prophet "from Egypt," and others, a number of popular oracular prophets appeared during the first century, especially just before and during the great revolt. Because they share a number of distinctive characteristics with the biblical prophets, it makes sense to consider them as a continuation of the long-standing Israelite-Jewish tradition of oracular prophets (i.e., of prophets who delivered messages from God to the people, especially during times of crisis). The question of "true" versus "false" prophecy is not under consideration here. Rather, this is simply an attempt to appreciate the reality and significance of oracular prophets who appeared among the Jewish people during the first century C.E. There were prophets who, like most of their classical predecessors, preached repentance and pronounced judgment; and there were those who announced God's impending deliverance, like Second Isaiah and Zechariah.

As was the case with the leaders of prophetic movements, there were more such figures during this period than our sources describe in any reliable detail. The only two figures about whom we have much information prior to the last few months before the outbreak of the massive revolt are John the Baptist and Jesus son of Hananiah. Josephus provides a fairly lengthy description of the "simple peasant" Jesus:

> Four years before the war, when the city was enjoying great peace and prosperity, a certain Jesus, son of Hananiah, a simple peasant from the lower classes, came to the festival at which all Jews traditionally make booths to God. Standing in the temple, he suddenly began to cry out, "a voice from the east, a voice from the west, a voice from the four winds; a voice against Jerusalem and the temple, a voice against bridegrooms and brides, a voice against the whole people." He went roving through all the byways with his dirge day and night. Some of the gentry, irritated by his ominous words, seized the man and beat him severely. But without a word in his own defense, even to those who struck him, he incessantly repeated his cry as before. Thus the authorities, thinking his agitation had a supernatural cause, which indeed it did, took him to the Roman governor. There, despite being lashed to the bone he did not plea for mercy or shed a single tear, but, as best he could, mourned with each blow, "woe to Jerusalem." And when Albinus, the governor, questioned him as to who he was and where he came from, and why he cried out like this, he said nothing at all, but only continued to repeat his cry of woe until Albinus, thinking him a madman, released him. During the period before the war, he approached no citizen, nor was he seen conversing; he simply continued his daily lament, "woe to Jerusalem," just as if he were practicing a traditional prayer. He did not curse any of those who daily struck him, nor did he thank those who gave him food; but to everyone he gave the single reply, the same

gloomy omen. He was especially vociferous during the festivals. Thus for seven years and five months he persevered, never falling silent or growing weary. It was only when he saw his forebodings fulfilled with the beginning of the siege that he was made to cease. For as he was going around the walls, crying out with a piercing voice, "again, woe to the city and to the people and to the temple," he added a final word, "and woe also to me." At that point, a stone from one of the missile-engines was let loose; it struck and killed him instantly. Thus indeed he was uttering those laments to the very end. (*J.W.* 6.300-9)

To the superficial observer from the Jewish ruling class in the early sixties C.E., the sociopolitical situation may have had the appearance of "peace and prosperity," just as it had several centuries earlier when the sharp-tongued Amos prophesied judgment in the ancient (northern) kingdom of Israel. However, like Amos and later Jeremiah, in a situation which bears an even greater similarity to that of Jesus son of Hananiah, the prophet knew better. Also like his precursors Amos and Jeremiah, Jesus goes straight to the temple precincts with his message of judgment. His subsequent behavior, as he continues his dirge on the doomed city, recalls that of the naked and barefoot Isaiah uttering his warnings or that of Jeremiah with the yoke around his neck before the impending Babylonian siege of the holy city. Again, like Jeremiah, Jesus was mistreated and imprisoned for his oracles and behavior. Although the Roman governor, Albinus, did not know what to make of the bizarre figure and dismissed Jesus as a raving maniac, the Jewish ruling group knew what a threat to the established order was posed by such a prophet and his message. It is interesting that Josephus mentions attempts to silence Jesus only by Jerusalem's aristocratic ruling group—collaborators with the Romans. But he makes no mention of opposition by the Judean peasant groups and their leaders (e.g., the Zealots, Simon bar Giora) who took control of the city and led the resistance to the Roman siege.

Like his relations with the established ruling group, Jesus' message is reminiscent of the judgment and lament pronounced on the city by the classical prophets, especially Jeremiah (e.g., 7:34; 19; 22:1-9; 26). One also thinks of the lament over Jerusalem attributed to another Jesus thirty years earlier:

> O Jerusalem, Jerusalem, killing the prophets and stoning those who are sent to you! How often would I have gathered your children together as a hen gathers her brood under her wings, and you would not! Behold, your house is forsaken and desolate. (Mt. 23:37-38)

Yet another popular prophet of judgment was one John, called the Baptist.[21] John was certainly not originally understood as Elijah come back as the prophetic forerunner of the Messiah. The very idea that Elijah would return at the end of time as the forerunner of the Messiah was apparently not yet current at the time of John's career. The Christian Gospel tradition is by no means unanimous that John is "Elijah who is to come" (Mt. 11:14). There is certainly no evidence that John saw himself—or that his immediate followers (including Jesus of Nazareth) viewed him—as Elijah returned. However, John most definitely was a prophet who, like Jesus son of Hananiah after him, displayed many characteristics similar to the classical biblical prophets, especially Elijah.

In comparison with the other prophets mentioned by Josephus, we have a good deal of material on John the Baptist, although we should like to have considerably more. Besides Josephus' account, we possess independent materials on John from the Gospel of Mark, from the sayings source (Q) common to both Matthew and Luke, and from Luke's own special sources.

> John the Baptizer appeared in the wilderness, preaching a baptism of repentance for the forgiveness of sins. And there went out to him all the country of Judea, and all the people of Jerusalem; and they were baptized by him in the river Jordan, confessing their sins. Now John was clothed with camel's

hair, and had a leather girdle around his waist, and ate locusts and wild honey. (Mk. 1:4-6)

But when he saw many of the Pharisees and Sadducees coming for baptism, he said to them, "You brood of vipers! Who warned you to flee from the wrath to come? Bear fruit that befits repentance, and do not presume to say to yourselves, 'We have Abraham as our father'; for I tell you, God is able from these stones to raise up children to Abraham. Even now the axe is laid to the root of the trees; every tree therefore that does not bear good fruit is cut down and thrown into the fire." (Mt. 3:7-10)

John answered them all, "I baptize you with water; but he who is mightier than I is coming, the thong of whose sandals I am not worthy to untie; he will baptize you with [the Holy Spirit and with] fire. His winnowing fork is in his hand, to clear his threshing floor, and to gather the wheat into his granary, but the chaff he will burn with unquenchable fire." (Lk. 3:16-17)

King Herod heard of it; for Jesus' name had become known. Some said, "John the baptizer has been raised from the dead; that is why these powers are at work in him. . . ." But when Herod heard of it he said, "John, whom I beheaded, has been raised." For Herod had sent and seized John, and bound him in prison for the sake of Herodias, his brother Philip's wife; because he had married her. For John said to Herod, "It is not lawful for you to have your brother's wife." (Mk. 6:14, 16-18)

And though he [Herod Antipas] wanted to put him to death, he feared the people, because they held him to be a prophet. But when Herod's birthday came, the daughter of Herodias danced before the company, and pleased Herod, so that he promised to give her whatever she might ask. . . . He sent and had John beheaded in prison, and his head was brought on a platter and given to the girl, and she brought it to her mother. (Mt. 14:5-7, 10-11)

It seemed to some of the Jews that God had annihilated Herod's [Antipas] army . . . for his punishment of John, called the baptist, since Herod had him executed. John was a good man, who demanded that the Jews be intent on virtue, and conduct themselves with justice towards one another and piety towards God, and to come together in baptism. . . . But when others rallied behind him—for they were greatly stirred up by his speeches—Herod feared that such convincing eloquence among the people might lead to some sort of uprising, for they seemed to heed his every word. Anticipating trouble, he decided to eliminate him before he provoked a rebellion. . . . Thus John, because of Herod's suspicion, was sent in chains to Machaerus, the fortress . . . and executed. (*Ant.* 18.116-19)

John appeared in the wilderness, the symbolic place of purification and renewal (apparently along the lower Jordan in Perea). His hairy garment and girdle are reminiscent not just of Elijah, but of the biblical prophets in general. The popular prophets castigated in Zech. 13 wore such attire, as had Isaiah and all the faithful prophets, according to the Martyrdom of Isaiah.

The central thrust of John's message is that eschatological judgment is at hand. Since Elijah and Amos, the popular prophets had pronounced God's impending punishment for failure to keep covenantal justice. At least since the prophet Malachi (fifth century B.C.E.), oracles of judgment had borne an eschatological tone. Like that of the biblical prophets, John's imagery of judgment is drawn from peasant agricultural life. The imagery of harvest and threshing floor has also now taken on an ominous tone of eschatological judgment— "the chaff will be burned with *unquenchable fire.*" In John's prophetic warning, "the wrath to come" is now imminent. The mightier one who is coming after him will baptize with the fire of final judgment.

The impending judgment requires the baptism preached and administered by John. Judgment is now not only inevitable, but imminent, because Israel has not been faithful and borne fruit. Only by completely changing their direction, by a complete return to just, covenantal social practices ("repentance"), can they escape the impending wrath of

God. Baptism in the Jordan was the rite by which that change
of direction was symbolized, by which persons passed into
the eschatologically reconstituted community of Israel
which would survive God's judgment. Nothing in our texts
indicates that John intended to found a sect or lead a mass
movement in a decisive eschatological event of deliverance.
In preaching the baptism of repentance he was attempting to
prepare the people, apparently even across class and sectarian lines, for the impending judgment.

The criteria of judgment are implicit in the requirements
John demands for membership in the repentant remnant. In
order to endure God's wrath, people must bear fruit that
befits repentance. That is, the requirement for membership
in the eschatological people is, very concretely, social and
economic, and not vaguely "spiritual." Like Amos or Jeremiah before him, John demands that the people observe
God's will for the satisfaction of people's basic needs and the
realization of simple social-economic justice.

John's message of impending eschatological judgment is
clearly addressed to all the people, the whole nation. But,
who is it that John castigates as "You brood of vipers" and
warns that being descendants of Abraham is no guarantee of
salvation? It was surely not "the multitudes" now in the text
of Luke. For the multitudes readily responded to John, whom
they believed was a prophet (Mk. 11:32 and par.); it was the
common people who repented and underwent baptism by
John. In Matthew's text, it is "the Pharisees and Sadducees"
whom John castigates as "vipers." But this phrase may be
suspect, especially "the Pharisees," because the Pharisees
are the standard, typical enemy of Jesus (and John) throughout Matthew's Gospel (Matthew's church probably viewed
the Pharisees as their principal rival). Moreover, the Pharisees themselves, far from relying on any descent from Abraham, devoted their whole energy to stressing the keeping of
covenant law as the condition for any eschatological fulfillment of God's promises to Israel. Thus those who presume to
say to themselves, "We have Abraham as our father," must be

the priestly aristocracy. One detects here a similarity with the situation of Jeremiah centuries earlier. In the time of Jeremiah it was the royal court and priestly aristocracy who placed absolute trust in God's supposedly unconditional promise to the Davidic dynasty and the temple on Zion—as God's judgment broke over their heads. So now in the situation John the Baptist addresses, it is the same social strata, the priestly aristocracy and gentry (perhaps indicated by "the Sadducees"), who trust in their supposedly sacred lineage and sacral position. John, by contrast (like Jeremiah), is the spokesperson for the common people, from whom comes the demand for simple justice—and whose demand has now turned to God's eschatological wrath for its vindication. To suggest that there is a note of class conflict in John's message is perhaps a bit of an understatement. A sharp exchange between "the chief priests and the elders" and Jesus of Nazareth provides another good illustration of the intense class conflict expressed explicitly in John's preaching.

> As he was walking in the temple, the chief priests and the scribes and the elders came to him, and they said to him, "By what authority are you doing these things, or who gave you this authority to do them?" Jesus said to them, "I will ask you a question; answer me, and I will tell you by what authority I do these things. Was the baptism of John from heaven or from men? Answer me." And they argued with one another, "If we say 'From heaven,' he will say 'Why then did you not believe him?' But shall we say, 'From men'?"—they were afraid of the people, for all held that John was a real prophet. So they answered Jesus, "We do not know." And Jesus said to them, "Neither will I tell you by what authority I do these things." (Mk. 11:27-33)

The priestly aristocracy knew very well that prophetic preaching such as John's was a direct challenge to their authority and power, considered both illegitimate and oppressive by "the multitude."

The circumstances of John's execution described in the Gospel accounts are patently legendary. Josephus' account provides more reliable access to the general historical circumstances and events. The Gospels' report that Herod Antipas' arrest and execution of John had been occasioned by the prophet's sharp denunciation of the king's divorce of his own wife (the daughter of Aretas, the king of Nabatea) and remarriage to his brother Philip's wife, Herodias, is highly credible. John's indictment that "it is not lawful" fits exactly with the rest of his sharpened insistence of observance of the covenant law in the face of the impending judgment. John's denunciation of Antipas' second marriage, however, is only the occason for his arrest and execution. The broader and more basic reason for the Tetrarch doing away with John is indicated by Josephus. Antipas was concerned that John's continued preaching would lead to a revolutionary uprising by the people. Here we must return to the Gospel accounts of John's preaching to see what is behind Josephus' cosmetic portrayal of John as simply a virtuous preacher of morality and piety. Hiding behind Josephus' "justice towards others" is John's preaching of God's judgment based on the criteria of covenantal justice. John was, in effect, announcing God's imminent overthrow of the established order as headed by the sacerdotal aristocracy and Herod Antipas. And we must not imagine that John's preaching of eschatological judgment (unquenchable fire) or old-fashioned marital morality was remote from the politics of his day. Antipas' first marriage to the Arabian princess was in effect a diplomatic alliance with her father, Aretas IV, king of Nabatea, one of the strongest Near Eastern kingdoms of the time, which was quite capable of mounting an attack on Antipas' realm, a region then forming part of the eastern flank of the Roman Empire. In the potentially explosive international circumstances created by Antipas' second marriage and the flight of the Nabatean princess, condemnation by the popular prophet posed a special threat to Antipas. There was a definite possibility that John's preaching could provoke the Jewish inhabitants of Perea (Transjordan) into common action with his Arabic subjects, i.e., a popular insurrection parallel to, or perhaps in response to, invasion by Nabatean forces which might be sent by Aretas to avenge Antipas' abuse of his daughter. Indeed, Antipas' fears were well-taken. To the Jews, Antipas' subsequent defeat by Aretas was only the just divine vengeance for his treatment of John the Baptist, as Josephus explains. As we can see from this brief sketch of current political affairs, far from being simply an old-fashioned marital morality, John the Baptist's prophecy had such immediate implications for political affairs that he was arrested and executed as a threat to the regime.

That is, no less than the earlier biblical prophets such as Amos, Micah, or Jeremiah, John the Baptist was a prophet called by God from among the people to address the social and political conditions and the events of the day. Moreover, although John's message was one of less total gloom than that of Jesus son of Hananiah thirty or so years later, it was clearly an announcement of impending eschatological judgment.

Not surprisingly, the popular prophets who announced imminent divine deliverance were concentrated just before and during the great revolt. Josephus claims that there were many prophets at this time bidding the people to "await help from God." Originating in apocalyptic visions, the messages delivered by these prophets held out hope for the people suffering under increasing oppression prior to the rebellion, or for those struggling against overwhelming odds once the Romans brought their massive forces to suppress the revolt (see *J.W.* 6.286-87).

The portents that appeared in the months prior to the beginning of and in the years during the revolt, and the seriousness with which their meaning was pondered, provide dramatic indications of the intense apocalyptic mood that pervaded the populace as the political-social order began to break down completely.

Before the uprising and surge toward war, while the people were assembling for the feast of unleavened bread—it was the eighth of the month of Xanthicus, during the ninth hour of the night—there was such a bright light around the altar and the sanctuary that it seemed as bright as day. This lasted for half an hour. To the inexperienced it seemed a good portent. . . . At the same feast, a cow brought for sacrifice gave birth to a lamb in the middle of the temple precincts; and the eastern door of the inner temple court—it was made of brass and so massive that at evening twenty men could barely close it—this door was seen opening all by itself at the sixth hour of the night. . . . Again, this seemed to the uninitiated a most glorious omen, because, as they understood it, God had opened for them the door of prosperity. . . . (*J.W.* 6.290-95)

Josephus, who so successfully deserted, and "the expounders of holy books" and other "learned men," of course, interpreted such occurrences "on the basis of later developments . . . as portent[s] of devastation" (*J.W.* 6.291, 295-96). To the common people, however, such happenings appeared to portend God's imminent intervention against the Romans on their behalf. Similarly, during the war, "when a star stood over the city, resembling a sword, and a comet lasted for a year," it was interpreted by the prophets and taken by the people not as a warning, but as a hopeful sign of God's protective presence (*J.W.* 6.288-89).

Indeed, just prior to the outbreak of the revolt, the apocalyptic mood was so pervasive and intense that some of the "revelations" were, in effect, collective visions.

Not many days after the festival, on the twenty-first of the month of Artemisium, an unbelievable heavenly portent appeared. What is about to be told would seem to be an invention, I suppose, were it not for the fact that it was reported by those who saw it and that the events which took place afterwards matched the omens. Before the sun went down, chariots were seen high in the air all around the country and armed battalions rushing through the clouds and

encircling the cities. (*J. W.* 6.297-99; see also Tacitus, *History*
6.13)

Here are collective fantasies of God and the heavenly armies
rushing through the clouds in anticipated relief of the
oppressed—and about to be embattled—chosen people.
This belief in the heavenly armies fighting in defense of the
people of Israel was rooted in a long-standing tradition. The
earlier prophets (judges, etc.) had been the messengers of
Yahweh to announce that "the Lord had given the enemy
into their hands." But the expectations and prophetic
announcements of eschatological deliverance by the divine
warrior and the heavenly armies had become increasingly
important among proto-apocalyptic prophets such as Second
Zechariah (chaps. 9-14). The War Scroll from Qumran is a
vivid expression of the confidence that the heavenly armies
would finally defeat the oppressive enemies of the elect. The
vivid expectations of the heavenly armies, moreover, were
not confined to the literate groups, such as the prophetic
schools and Essenes. The common people, too, trusted
firmly in the heavenly hosts—as illustrated in the reported
saying of a peasant prophet to his followers overly eager to
resist his arrest:

> Put your sword back into its place. . . . Do you think that I
> cannot appeal to my Father, and he will at once send me more
> than twelve legions of angels? (Mt. 26:52-53)

Apparently the common people were also highly receptive to
visions of the heavenly hosts or to the announcement of
visions and prophecies that the time was imminent when
God would finally lead the heavenly armies in victory over
the forces of evil and oppression.

There is one final prophecy, again a collective fantasy,
reported by Josephus from just before the rebellion that
could have been understood in its immediate historical context as a warning of judgment.

> At the festival of Pentecost, when the priests were going into
> the inner temple court at night to perform their traditional
> duties, they said they first noticed a commotion and a rum-
> bling, and then they heard a sound of many voices at once,
> saying, "we are going away from this place." (*J.W.* 6.299-300)

This collective experience of the priests breathes more of the
same sense of foreboding expressed by the weird fellow
Jesus son of Hananiah. The divine presence, the heavenly
host, was departing from the temple (supposedly, to an interpreter such as Josephus), since it was about to be destroyed.
However, even this could have been understood in the historical circumstances by some as meaning that, since the
temple remained the scene of corruption and control by an
illegitimate and oppressive high priesthood, God was
removing his presence until, leading the forces of liberation
and renewal, God again made the temple a sacred place
worthy of the presence. This may not be idle speculation,
considering what the various rebel forces did once they took
control of the temple and upper city: one group immediately
burned the archives which contained the official records that
supported the oppressive political-economic order, and the
bandits-turned-Zealots held a popular election of a new and
legitimate high priestly officer, choosing the illiterate village
priest, Phanni, son of Samuel, as officiating high priest (*J.W.*
2.426-27 and 4.151-57, and chapter 5 below).

During the war, especially the prolonged siege of Jerusalem, numerous prophets delivered oracles of encourage-
ment, promising the defenders of the city that the
anticipated help would surely come from God (*J.W.* 6.286).
As Josephus suggests (in a decidedly backhanded way), such
oracles must have been an important factor in the ability of
the defenders to maintain their hopes and morale as their
situation worsened month by month. Unfortunately,
Josephus describes only one of these prophets of deliverance in specific terms, and then very briefly. Toward the end

of the siege, as the Romans were successfully pressing their attack,

> a mixed crowd of people, including women and children, totaling about 6000, had taken refuge [on the only remaining colonnade of the outer court of the temple]. The soldiers, carried away by their fury, torched the colonnade from below. . . . As a result, of that vast number not a one escaped. The cause of their destruction was a certain false prophet, who that very day had proclaimed to those in the city that God had decreed that they should go up to the temple to receive there the signs of their deliverance. (*J.W.* 6.283-85)

In conclusion, it is clear that among the peasantry in the first century C.E. there were two distinct types of prophets, both of which were continuations or revivals of older biblical types. The action prophets, such as Theudas and the "Egyptian," led sizable movements of peasants from the villages of Judea in anticipation of God's new, eschatological act of liberation. These prophets and their followers conceived of the new act of liberation on the model of, and as corresponding to, those which originally constituted the people of Israel as a free people with their own land. Thus, it is not surprising that these movements appear as a revival of the ancient prophetic movements led by Moses, Joshua, the judges, and Elijah or Elisha. The Roman governors, apparently viewing these movements as popular insurrections, simply sent out the military to suppress them.

The prophets of the other type delivered oracles, either of judgment or deliverance, much as had the classical oracular prophets such as Amos or Jeremiah centuries earlier. The oracular prophets who announced imminent deliverance are concentrated in the period just before and during the great revolt, when social and economic conditions for the peasantry were deteriorating even as official behavior became increasingly erratic and repressive. These prophets of deliverance were simply dismissed as raving lunatics or castigated

as fanatical deceivers of the masses by the upper-class collaborators with Rome such as Josephus. The popular oracular
prophets who pronounced judgments, such as John the Baptist and Jesus son of Hananiah, were seen as a political threat
by the Jewish ruling groups, who attempted to silence them
(Jesus) or even had them killed (John)—again much as the
ruling groups of an earlier age had killed or attempted to
silence prophets such as Uriah son of Shemaiah, Amos, or
Jeremiah.

> O Jerusalem, Jerusalem, killing the prophets
> and stoning those who are sent to you!
>   (Mt. 23:37; Lk. 13:34)

According to traditional canonical views of biblical revelation, the succession of inspired prophets ceased after Malachi, i.e., long before late second temple times. The social life
and creativity of the common people continued, however,
regardless of whether the guardians of the official biblical
tradition took notice. Our survey of prophetic activity in late
second temple times indicates that actual leaders and movements among the people were at least as important as scribal
interpretations and expectations, both for the social history
of the period and for interpretation of Jesus of Nazareth.
Indeed, there turns out to be little clear literary evidence that
expectations of a new Moses or a returning Elijah or another
eschatological prophet were especially prominent in Jewish
society at the time. Moreover, prophetic activity among the
principal literary groups was focused primarily on interpretation and application of scriptural prophecy, with the only
actual prophetic figures being more like seers or diviners
than the traditional biblical prophets. By contrast, there
emerged during the first century C.E. among the Jewish common people several prophets of two distinctive types. The
individual prophets of the oracular type appear to be a continuation of the classical biblical oracular prophets, while
the action prophets and their movements appear to be heavily influenced by biblical traditions of the great historical

acts of liberation led by Moses and Joshua. Their significance for Jewish society at the time and their enduring historical significance are indicated by the large numbers of people involved, by the serious efforts of the Roman and/or Jewish authorities to suppress them, and by their figuring prominently in Josephus' histories of the period as well as in the New Testament. One of them, of course, was understood as the predecessor and perhaps even the mentor of Jesus of Nazareth.

NOTES

1. "Revitalization movements are . . . deliberate . . . organized efforts by members of a society to create a more satisfying culture." Such movements are usually conceived "in a prophet's revelatory visions, which provide him [and his movement] a satisfying relationship to the supernatural and outline a new way of life under divine sanction." In the case of Israel, this meant a return to genuine convenantal practice and independence. See A. F. C. Wallace, "Revitalization Movements," in *Reader in Comparative Religion*, 3rd ed., ed. W. A. Lessa and E. Z. Vogt (New York: Harper & Row, 1972), 503-12, reprinted and abridged from *American Anthropologist* 58 (1956): 264-81.
2. See 2 Kings 2:3, 5, 7, 15-18; 4:1-7, 38-44; 6:1-7.
3. See R. B. Coote, *Amos Among the Prophets: Composition and Theology* (Philadelphia: Fortress, 1981).
4. E.g., the 400 prophets who prophesied victory for Ahab (1 Kings 22:6), and Hananiah, son of Azzur, who prophesied restoration of monarchy and temple (Jer. 28:1-4).
5. Is. 31:4-5; 29:1-8; chap. 37. And earlier, Elisha still prophesied victory for Israel and Judah against the Moabites, even though he despised and condemned the anti-Yahwist policies of Jehoram, son of Ahab (2 Kings 3).
6. See 1 Macc. 9:27; T. Sotah 13.2; Josephus, *Ag. Ap.* 1.37-41.
7. See Is. 42:1, 4, 6, 7; 49:1, 6.
8. Contrary to the claims of some of the secondary literature, such as R. Meyer, "*Prophētēs,*" TDNT 6(1968): 826. For support for the contentions here, see R. A. Horsley, "'Like One of the

Prophets of Old': Two Types of Popular Prophets at the Time of Jesus," *CBQ* 47 (1985): 435-63, esp. 437-43.

9. 1 Enoch 89:52; 90:31; 93:8; 1 Macc. 2:58.

10. E.g., Amos 2:10-11; Hos. 2:14-15; 11:4-5; 12:9, 13; Mic. 6:3-4; see also B. W. Anderson, "Exodus Typology in Second Isaiah," in *Israel and Its Prophetic Heritage: Essays in Honor of James Muilenburg,* ed. B. W. Anderson and W. Harrelson (New York: Harper, 1962), 177-95.

11. See R. A. Horsley, "'Like One of the Prophets of Old.'"

12. See in general J. J. Collins, *The Apocalyptic Imagination* (New York: Crossroad, 1984); G. W. E. Nickelsburg, *Jewish Literature Between the Bible and the Mishnah* (Philadelphia: Fortress, 1981); D. E. Aune, *Prophecy in Early Christianity and the Ancient Mediterranean World* (Grand Rapids: Eerdmans, 1982), 103-6, 112-14; D. Hellholm, ed., *Apocalypticism in the Mediterranean World and the Near East* (Tübingen: Mohr, 1983), which contains many fine essays. All of these works reflect the great strides that have been made in the study of apocalypticism in the last decade.

13. See J. J. Collins, *The Apocalyptic Vision of the Book of Daniel,* HSM 16 (Missoula: Scholars, 1977), 201-18.

14. Many studies have approached the issue abstractly, in terms of Jewish "prophecy" at the time of Jesus, e.g., P. Vielhauer, "Introduction" [to Apocalypses and Related Subjects], in *New Testament Apocrypha,* vol. 2, ed. E. Hennecke and W. Schneemelcher (Philadelphia: Westminster, 1965), 581-607, esp. 601-7; R. Meyer, *"Prophētēs"*; and, to a degree, D. E. Aune, *Prophecy in Early Christianity.* We are focusing more concretely on the occurrence or nonoccurrence of actual prophets in attempting to discern their distinctive characteristics.

15. See further, Horsley, "'Like One of the Prophets,'" 446-49.

16. For the narrowed covenant theology among the Essenes, see G. Vermes, *The Dead Sea Scrolls: Qumran in Perspective* (Philadelphia: Fortress, 1981), 163-69, esp. 165.

17. The relevant passage is quoted on p. 108. Note also how Josephus can apply such biblical prophecy to himself (*J. W.* 3.352); see J. Blenkinsopp, "Prophecy and Priesthood in Josephus," *JJS* 25 (1974): 240-47, 257.

18. P. W. Barnett, "The Jewish Sign Prophets—A.D. 40-70—Their Intentions and Origins," *NTS* 27 (1980-81): 679-97, labels

these figures "sign prophets," but this elevates to undue prominence what was incidental to their main concern or activity. Barnett also reads the sources (e.g., Gospels, Josephus) uncritically.

19. E.g., 4 Ezra 13:44-47, in comparison with the Theudas movement.
20. E.g., 1 Cor. 10:1-4; 5:7; 1 Pet. 3:20.
21. See W. Wink, *John the Baptist in the Gospel Tradition,* SNTSMS 7 (Cambridge: Cambridge University, 1968).

CHAPTER FIVE

Fourth Philosophy, Sicarii, Zealots

Because the synthetic concept of the "Zealots" has generated such a misunderstanding of first-century C.E. Jewish society (see Introduction), it will be useful to clarify the two "zealous" anti-Roman and antiestablishment groups which were *not* peasant movements, i.e., the Fourth Philosophy and the Sicarii. For a fresh approach to these groups, it is helpful to avoid many of the component ideas that have been synthesized into the Zealot concept. For example, "zeal" for God and the law did not characterize any one group more than another. There is no evidence for prophets or prophetic activity among either the Fourth Philosophy or the Sicarii. And there is no evidence for a royal or messianic posture among either group until the brief episode in 66 involving Menahem.[1] The obvious place to begin is with an examination of Josephus' accounts of the Fourth Philosophy.

THE FOURTH PHILOSOPHY

After deposing Herod's son Archelaus as client ruler of Judea, the Romans imposed their own direct rule in Judea and Samaria and charged Quirinius, the legate of Syria, along with Coponius, the new governor, to conduct an assessment of how much revenue could be extracted from the territory. Then, according to Josephus' first history, the *Jewish War,*

190

A Galilean named Judas was urging his countrymen to resistance, reproaching them if they submitted to paying taxes to
the Romans and tolerated human masters after serving God
alone. Judas was a teacher [*sophistēs*] with his own party, in no
way similar to the others. (*J. W.* 2.118)

In his later work, the *Jewish Antiquities,* Josephus vastly
expanded his account and corrected, or simply contradicted,
the claim that Judas' party had nothing in common with the
others:

Although the Jews were at first intensely angry at the news of
their registration on the tax lists, they gradually calmed down,
having been persuaded to oppose it no further by the high
priest Joazar son of Boethus. Those who succumbed to his
arguments unhesitatingly appraised their property. But a certain Judas, a Gaulanite from the city of Gamala, in league with
the Pharisee Saddok, pressed hard for resistance. They said
that such a tax assessment amounted to slavery, pure and
simple, and urged the nation to claim its freedom. If successful, they argued, the Jews would have paved the way for good
fortune; if they were defeated in their quest, they would at
least have honor and glory for their high ideals. Furthermore,
God would eagerly join in promoting the success of their
plans, especially if they did not shrink from the slaughter that
might come upon them. The people listened with relish and
their daring scheme made real headway. . . . Indeed, Judas
and Saddok established an alien fourth school of philosophy
among us. When their numbers grew, they filled the nation
with unrest, and were at the root of the afflictions which
ultimately enveloped it. (*Ant.* 18.3-9)

Judas the Galilean established himself as the leader of the
fourth philosophy. They agree with the views of the Pharisees
in everything except their unconquerable passion for freedom, since they take God as their only leader and master.
They shrug off submitting to unusual forms of death and stand
firm in the face of torture of relatives and friends, all for
refusing to call any man master. Since most people have seen
their unwavering conviction under such circumstances, I can
omit further comment. For I have no doubt that anything said

against them will be believed. The real problem would be that the report about them would understate their contempt for suffering pain. The mania that began to wreck the nation from then on was the result of Gessius Florus, the governor, who had driven it to a desperate revolt against the Romans by his outrageous abuse of power. (*Ant.* 18.23-25)

Josephus takes the occasion of the Roman tax assessment and the resistance party organized by Judas and Saddok to digress into a discussion of the Jewish religiopolitical parties: the Pharisees, Sadducees, and Essenes. In writing to a Hellenistic readership, he portrays these Jewish groups, which are more than simply religious sects, in terms of traditional Greek philosophies. Because he is eager to blame the Jewish revolt on a minority of agitators among the people, and because he himself had been a Pharisee, he initially claimed that Judas' party had nothing in common with any of the other Jewish parties. In the later *Antiquities,* he claims that the Fourth Philosophy was unprecedented and intrusive. But he also reveals there that the party led by Judas and Saddok agreed with the Pharisees in all respects except their unusually strong passion for liberty. It is thus tempting to see here simply an offshoot of the Pharisees, i.e., a group led by Pharisees (e.g., Saddok) and other teachers (e.g., Judas) who were more prepared than others to take an active stance of resistance to Roman rule. In any case, the group, or at least its leadership, was composed of intellectuals who articulated a coherent religiopolitical rationale for their position.

Judging from Josephus' accounts, their advocacy of resistance to Roman rule was rooted in four interrelated basic ideas:

(1) To cooperate with the tax assessment, i.e., to acquiesce in paying tribute to Rome, amounted to slavery for the Jews. The Jewish people should be striving for their own liberation, for they were the chosen people of God. Symbolized in the call and migration of Abraham, and especially in the exodus from slavery in Egypt, the Jews were called by

God into freedom from foreign overlords. The scribal leadership, moreover, was surely aware of the explicit biblical sanction against a tax assessment for the people of Israel (2 Sam. 24).

(2) The understanding of the tribute as slavery was rooted in the fundamental Jewish faith that the people (of Israel) had been called to live directly under the rule of God, as expressed in the Mosaic law. The "First Commandment" in the covenantal stipulations expressed in the Decalogue was unambiguously clear: "You shall have no other gods besides me." Submission to any foreign ruler was an infringement of that principle. Possible Jewish awareness that the Roman emperor (Augustus), like the Hellenistic emperors before him, was understood in the Hellenistic East as divine would only have compounded the resolve of sensitive Jews not to submit to human masters, since God was their only true ruler (see *J.W.* 2.118, 433). Jewish society was supposed to live directly under the rule of God.

(3) One of the Pharisaic principles shared by the Fourth Philosophy was belief in "synergism" with God. That is, although all things are ultimately in the control of, or due to, the providential guidance of God, humans are responsible for acting according to the will of God, and God accomplishes his purposes by working through people.[2] When it came time for living out this belief under the stipulation expressed in the first commandment, however, Judas, Saddok, and their followers exhibited an "unconquerable passion for freedom," whereas most Pharisees apparently were ready to make adjustments to certain circumstances and contingencies. Judas and his party apparently "practiced and observed what [the Pharisees] said, and not what they did," to borrow from Jesus' words (Mt. 23:3). They were prepared to "shrug off submitting to unusual forms of death and stand firm in the face of torture of relatives and friends, all for refusing to calling any man master" (*Ant.* 18.23), because they trusted that God "would eagerly join in promoting the

success of their plans" if they stood firm in their resistance (*Ant.* 18.5).

(4) The Fourth Philosophy's "unconquerable passion for freedom" would appear to be informed by a certain eschatological orientation. A few allusions to this seem to shine through Josephus' Hellenistic language. If we "translate" Josephus' phrasing back into the apocalyptic idiom current among Pharisees, Essenes, and other Palestinian Jewish contemporaries, Judas, Saddok, and company appear to have understood their actions as an attempt to realize the kingdom of God. Thus, Josephus' statement that they argued that "if successful, the Jews would have paved the way for good fortune" would mean more or less that the Fourth Philosophy believed that by carrying out God's eschatological will they would be helping to bring about the Kingdom of God. Similarly, "if they were defeated in their quest, they would at least have honor and glory for their high ideals" would mean that if defeated, tortured, and killed before the final fulfillment of the Kingdom, they would be seen as glorious martyrs to God's cause.[3]

Furthermore, besides sharing the teachings of the Pharisees and other Jewish sages, Judas and his party stand in a long tradition of organized resistance to foreign rule by Jewish scribes and teachers. That is, besides traditions of popular resistance to oppression, whether domestic or foreign, there was a long line of intellectuals (scribes, etc.) who had offered deliberate and even organized rebellion or other acts of defiance. As the Maccabean revolt got under way, scribes among the Hasidim[4] had apparently been among the first, not simply to resist the Hellenistic reform imposed by the Jerusalem aristocracy, but to organize active rebellion against forced Hellenization by Antiochus Epiphanes. Other teacher-sages, the Maskilim, left a theology of martyrdom developed in that struggle (Dan. 11:32-35; 12:1-3) which may have provided inspiration to subsequent generations of teachers, such as Judas and Saddok. Under the Hasmonean monarchy two generations later, the Pharisees, among

others, were driven to civil war in their attempt to resist the
arbitrary use of power by Alexander Jannaeus in particular.
The Pharisee Samaias spoke out sharply against the nascent
tyranny he perceived as manifested in the arrogant young
Herod's slaughter of the Galilean brigands led by Hezekiah.

The most dramatic recent example of resistance by intellectuals occurred just ten years before the emergence of the
Fourth Philosophy, as Herod lay dying.

> In the midst of his troubles, there was now a popular demon-
> stration.[5] In the city were two teachers [*sophistai*], Judas son of
> Sepphoraeus and Matthias son of Margalus who had an enor-
> mous reputation for their meticulous care for their ancestral
> customs, and were thus accorded great respect by the whole
> people. . . .When they learned that the king was physically
> and mentally wasting away, they dropped the word to their
> disciples that now would be an opportune time to strike a
> blow for God and pull down the structures built contrary to
> their traditional laws. . . . The king had put up a golden
> eagle over the great gate. The teacher now urged them to tear
> it down, even if it might be dangerous to do so, for it was
> noble to die for one's ancestral laws. . . . While they were
> making this exhortation, it was rumored that the king was
> actually dying. This caused the young men to tackle their
> plans even more confidently. At midday, then, when the tem-
> ple was bustling with people, they let themselves down from
> the roof with heavy ropes and began to hack the golden eagle
> down with hatchets. This was immediately reported to the
> king's officer who hurried to the spot with a large force,
> seized about forty young men and brought them before the
> king. He first asked if they had dared to cut down the golden
> eagle. They confessed they had. So he pressed them for
> whose orders they had followed. The laws of their fathers,
> they said. He then asked why they were so joyous since he was
> about to have them executed. Because, they said, they knew
> they would enjoy greater blessings after their death.
>
> (*J. W.* 1.648-53; compare *Ant.* 17.149-54)

The Jerusalemites, fearing wholesale prosecutions, implored
Herod to first punish those who suggested the deed, then

those who were caught in the act, and to take no action
against the rest. The king reluctantly agreed. He burned alive
those who came down from the roof, together with the two
teachers; the rest of those who were arrested he turned over to
his assistants to be executed. (*J. W.* 1.655)

Like his portrayal of the founders of the Fourth Philosophy,
Josephus' account of Judas' and Matthias' exhortations to
their followers is reminiscent of the martyrological tradition
exemplified by the Maskilim over a century and a half before.
The point here is that with such predecessors, the founders
of the Fourth Philosophy were by no means the first Jewish
teachers to advocate and practice resistance to foreign
tyranny.

Resistance to alien rule and refusal to cooperate in the tax
assessment, however, does not mean armed rebellion. In
much of the standard secondary literature in New Testament
studies and Jewish history of the second temple period, it is
claimed that Judas (and the Fourth Philosophy, often understood as "the Zealots") not only advocated a revolt against
Rome but actually led an armed rebellion—it is even
claimed that he advocated violence and murder.[6] Neither
Josephus nor the book of Acts provides any basis for this
claim. In Acts 5:36-37, Luke has Gamaliel, in a speech to the
Sanhedrin, compare the early Jesus movement (hardly a revolutionary group) with the movement led by Theudas (far
from a leader of violent rebellion) and the movement led by
Judas of Galilee.

In *Jewish War,* as cited above, Josephus has indicated that
Judas' advocacy of resistance consisted of two interrelated
elements: reproaching his countrymen for consenting to pay
tribute to the Romans, and for tolerating mortal masters after
having God as (sole) Lord. Josephus repeats exactly the same
elements when he later mentions Judas in passing:

The formidable teacher, Judas the Galilean, who once
reproached the Jews for recognizing the Romans as masters
when they already had God. (*J. W.* 2.433)

Judas . . . persuaded many Jews not to register in the census tax assessment. (*J. W.* 7.253)

And the later *Antiquities,* as also cited above, reiterates precisely the same points (*Ant.* 18.4, 23) in Judas' *advocacy* of resistance. Otherwise, all that might be construed as advocacy of active revolt would be the remark that they "urged the nation to claim its freedom" or that they "pressed hard for resistance" (*Ant.* 18.4). But Josephus gives no indication that Judas or members of the Fourth Philosophy actually engaged in actions of violence or revolution. He says only that their effect was to fill the nation with "unrest" (*Ant.* 18.9). After the census was carried out, he mentions that its effective advocate, the High Priest Joazar, was overthrown by a popular faction—but he does not connect this with the Fourth Philosophy.

The claim that Judas advocated violent rebellion and led an armed revolt against Rome in 6 C.E. is part and parcel of the modern scholarly misunderstanding of the Zealots as a long-standing revolutionary organization founded by Judas that advocated and practiced violent revolution with increasing success until the massive revolt of 66-70. Thus, not surprisingly, Josephus' harangue against Judas and the Fourth Philosophy, because it is interwoven with his more direct account of the movement, has confused scholars who have misread Josephus through the modern construct of the Zealots. Wherever he can, Josephus blames his people's defeat and destruction less on Roman imperialism than on the Jewish groups who resisted and actually rebelled against Roman rule. Josephus says explicitly in this same passage (18.25) that the folly and troubles that afflicted the nation began when "Gessius Florus, the governor, . . . had driven it to a desperate revolt . . . by his outrageous abuse of power." Even though he does not accuse them of actually engaging in brigand raids and assassinations (18.7), he does blame Judas, Saddok, and the Fourth Philosophy for having "infected the nation with every kind of misery" (18.6). In this passage, which is one of his several explanations of the cause of the Jewish War, Josephus' argument appears to be this: the great teacher Judas and the Pharisee Saddok and their Fourth Philosophy, with their passion for freedom, sowed the seeds of later troubles; following Florus' provocations, those seeds bore fruit in the great brigand raids, the assassination of leading members of the aristocracy, the civil strife, the Roman siege and resultant famine, and finally the destruction of the city. At no point, however, does Josephus imply that the Fourth Philosophy engaged in any of these actions.

Indeed, judging from Josephus' account of the Fourth Philosophy, far from engaging in acts of violence, it appears rather that they were prepared to *suffer* violence and death as a result of their resistance. Their passion for liberty is such that "they shrug off submitting to unusual forms of death and stand firm in the face of torture of relatives and friends, all for refusing to call any man master" (18.23). The passage in 18.5 should also be read in this sense—a passage which also explains how their resistance was rooted in their faith in God's providential care: that "God would eagerly join in promoting the success of their plans, especially if they did not shrink from the slaughter that might come upon them." In this respect Judas, Saddok, and their followers can be seen to stand in the tradition of (scholarly) martyrs to their faith, begun by teacher-sages (Maskilim and others) under Antiochus Epiphanes (Dan. 11:32-35; 12:1-3), and continued by the revered teachers and their disciples who pulled down the Roman eagle from above the temple gate in defiance of Herod.

The Fourth Philosophy would thus appear to be a group composed of, or at least led by, Pharisaic and other teachers of a more activist bent. They formulated a coherent rationale for their resistance, founded on principles they fully shared with their Pharisaic brothers. Although they did not mount

anything like an armed rebellion, they did organize themselves in some way and advocated resistance to Roman taxation. They appear from Josephus' account to have gained a
fair number of partisans, but there is little hint of the particular form that their organization or resistance may have taken
—beyond the vague "unrest" or "noisy stir" they apparently
caused in Judean society in 6 C.E. (*Ant.* 18.9). This passage in
Josephus' *Antiquities* is notoriously difficult to read and
translate. But it is quite clear that the digression or commentary in 18.6-8 on the supposed effects of the Fourth Philosophy refer to subsequent events, largely those connected with
the revolt of 66-70. It is not sound method to read back into
the movement founded by Judas and Saddok the "guerrilla
raids" and "assassinations" carried out later by others. If
anything, once we focus only on what Josephus says about
the Fourth Philosophy itself and its leaders, the stance of the
group would appear to be a nonviolent, if active, resistance
(see *Ant.* 18.23).

As to whether Judas, Saddok and their "party" were suppressed completely or continued to advocate resistance once
the bulk of Jewish society submitted to the tax assessment,
Josephus gives no clear evidence. The report in Acts 5:37 that
Judas was killed and his followers scattered is part of a chron-
ologically confused passage reversing the historical
sequence of Theudas and Judas. It may be that after their
initial agitation against submission to the tax, the group
became, in effect, dormant or went "underground." That at
least some vestige of the Fourth Philosophy continued to
pose a threat to the Roman authorities can be concluded
from the fact that the only action Tiberius Alexander took
that Josephus finds significant enough to mention—other
than his apostasy and the famine that occurred during his
tenure as governor in Judea—was his crucifixion of James
and Simon, the sons of Judas the Galilean (*Ant.* 20.100-3;
J.W. 2.220).

THE SICARII

We first hear of the Sicarii operating in Jerusalem itself in the fifties, i.e., a half century later. The name stems from the weapon they used: "Daggers resembling the scimitars of the Persians in size, but curved and more like the weapons called *sicae* by the Romans" (*Ant.* 20.186). Josephus' reports indicate clearly just how distinctive this group was:

> When they [the social bandits Josephus has just been speaking of] had been cleared from the countryside, a different type of bandit sprang up in Jerusalem, known as *sicarii*. This group murdered people in broad daylight right in the middle of the city. Mixing with the crowds, especially during the festivals, they would conceal small daggers beneath their garments and stealthily stab their opponents. Then, when their victims fell, the murderers simply melted into the outraged crowds, undetected because of the naturalness of their presence. The first to have his throat cut was Jonathan the High Priest, and after him many were murdered daily. (*J.W.* 2.254-56)

At the outset the Sicarii must be distinguished from the scholarly misconception of the "Zealots" on the one hand, and the phenomenon of social banditry on the other. Under the scholarly construct the "Zealots," "bandits" in Josephus' accounts are almost always assumed to refer to Zealots. Thus, Josephus' reports about "a different type of bandit" is understood to mean that the Zealots then turned to agitation in Jerusalem because the Roman governor, Felix, had effectively suppressed their activities in the countryside, and that they were then called *sicarii* because of their new tactics. But of course there was no such movement as the "Zealots" at that time.

Moreover, once we realize that all "bandits" were not "Zealots," we are prepared to read our sources more carefully: Josephus quite explicitly distinguishes this *new type* of banditry from the ordinary banditry which was being suppressed in the countryside. As discussed earlier (chapter 2), ordinary banditry is a rural phenomenon, endemic to many peasant societies. Outlaws live by robbing the wealthy, officials, or landlords, but they usually do not commit murder unless forced into a fight. Further, they are usually well known, not only to the peasants who tend to protect them, but to the governmental officials attempting to capture or kill them. Because of their notoriety, they must retreat to hideouts in which they spend most of their ordinarily brief lives. Josephus' accounts indicate that ordinary Jewish banditry of the time fits this basic pattern. The Sicarii, however, were not rural but urban, operating in the very heart of the city, even in the temple precincts. Their principal activity, moreover, was not armed robbery but murder, or more accurately, political *assassination*. The Sicarii, finally, operated in the most public places, but because of their clandestine manner of assassination, could continue to lead normal public lives, and did not flee like ordinary bandits to mountain strongholds.

Although the aggressive tactics of the Sicarii were utterly different from the defensive posture of resistance assumed by the Fourth Philosophy, there appears to have been some sort of continuity between them. Josephus says nothing of a substantive nature linking the Sicarii with the party founded by Judas and Saddok fifty years earlier. He makes it very clear, however, that there was a direct continuity of leadership between the two groups: from Judas of Galilee, through his sons James and Simon, crucified by Tiberius Alexander about 48, to his son or grandson, the messianic pretender Menahem, leader of the Sicarii at the outbreak of the revolt, and even Eleazar ben Jair, another descendant of Judas who became commander of the remaining Sicarii who sat out the revolt atop Masada. Moreover, Josephus writes or implies that the Sicarii were a continuation of the party founded by Judas in his summary denigrating the revolutionary groups in *J. W.* 7.253-54. Thus, there must have been some continuity between the two groups, however vague it appears in our only source.

Partly on the basis of this apparent continuity, one may reasonably draw two important conclusions regarding the Sicarii's composition and basic religious-political viewpoint. Like the Fourth Philosophy before them, the Sicarii were probably a group of teachers, in membership as well as leadership. Josephus says explicitly that Menahem, son or grandson of Judas of Galilee, and apparently their most important leader at the outbreak of the revolt in 66, was a "teacher" (*J. W.* 2.445). It also seems likely that their resistance against Roman rule was rooted in a coherent ideology similar to that of the Fourth Philosophy (see the four point summary above).

THE NEW STRATEGY OF THE SICARII

What was distinctive and unprecedented about the Sicarii was their new strategy. The aggressive actions of the Sicarii were new phenomena that first appeared under Felix, in the fifties, and are mentioned repeatedly by Josephus.[7] However, why a new group in some continuity with the old one—or a group that had lain dormant for nearly fifty years—should suddenly come to life with unprecedented tactics just at this time is not immediately clear. No direct explanation springs from Josephus' accounts. However, perhaps a brief review of mid-first century socioeconomic turmoil (discussed at the beginning of chapter 2 and in the last sections of chapter 1) can help set the new strategy of the Sicarii in context. Against the background of Herod's lavish spending, there was heavy Jewish *and* Roman taxation, with consequent peasant loss of land; there was also Herod's stocking of the priestly aristocracy with "illegitimate" families and new Herodian gentry; and later, there was direct Roman rule. All of this created tensions that were stretched further by the famine of the forties which yielded more unrest and banditry, as well as increased antagonism between Samaritans and Jews. Finally, the brutally repressive measures, against bandits and the peasantry in general, taken by Cumanus further inflamed a populace who had no peaceful recourse.[8] There were no doubt other important factors in the political-economic situation of which we have no historical record. This brief sketch of the condition of Jewish society in the fifties, however, may enable us to perceive how concerned Jewish intellectuals could have come to the conclusion that their situation was so desperate that it called for a strategy of selective violence against the ruling group.[9]

Perhaps because of their roles as teachers of the people and their heritage of critical awareness of, and resistance to, Roman domination, the Sicarii tended to come to a sharper sense than others of the intolerable situation that had developed. It tends to be just such people in a colonized society who form subversive brotherhoods. Terrorism, moreover, may seem a particularly appropriate tactic for small resistance groups that lack a broader power base among the people. Drawing comparisons from modern colonial situations, nascent liberation movements have often found all ordinary "legitimate" channels of (political) appeal and adjustment denied to them. It is in precisely such a situation that terrorism is likely to occur, for it is the only available means for subject peoples who have decided that their situation is no longer tolerable. For leaders of resistance in such cases, the decision to resort to terrorism is not a choice between violent and nonviolent means, since the latter have been denied to them by the colonial regime. It is rather a choice among violent means. As a liberation leader in modern Algeria explained, "Urban terrorism, like guerrilla warfare, is the only method of expression of a crushed people."[10] And, as experienced in modern history, such a violent response to a situation already dominated by the violence of the establishment can be an effective instrument of social mobilization in cases where the people are generally sympathetic to the purposes of the resistance movement, especially in colonized societies dominated by a foreign empire, and where the subject peoples are unorganized and unable to participate in any political process.

The Jewish intellectuals who formed the Sicarii apparently came to just such a conclusion. It may be useful to carry the comparison with modern liberation movements one step further in order to discern the distinctive strategy of the Sicarii in the ancient Jewish situation. The fundamental strategy of recent anticolonial movements that have employed terrorist tactics has been to convince the government or people of the occupying nation that the costs of maintaining their control by violent repression of the subject people will prove unacceptable, or at least greater than the benefits of continuing their imperial control. Modern liberation movements have been able to create a dramatic "demonstration effect" by means of terrorist acts because of the sensationalist reporting of the modern mass media. The Jewish Zionist organization, Irgun Zvai Leumi (of which Menachem Begin was a leader before he entered "legitimate" political life and eventually became prime minister of Israel, 1977-1984), employed this strategy with considerable success against the British during the 1920s and 1930s.

The strategy of the ancient Sicarii was somewhat different, since they were without the benefit of the modern mass media through which to reach public opinion as well as imperial policymakers in Rome. Their ultimate goal was probably to eliminate Roman rule from Jewish Palestine. But they apparently did not concentrate much direct attention on the Romans themselves. In contrast to the Sicarii, *brigand* groups occasionally preyed on Roman petty officials and supply trains, and the popular messianic movements attacked Roman strongholds and troops as well as Herodian fortresses.[11] But if the Sicarii ever attacked an imperial official or a Roman military object, Josephus certainly says nothing about it. In fact, since the Romans did not maintain a very large or visible military presence in Judea (except to suppress larger disturbances), a strategy focused primarily on the Romans themselves would probably have been inappropriate and ineffective.

The strategy of the Sicarii focused instead on the collaborating Jewish ruling elite: the priestly aristocracy, the Herodian families, and other notables. In the context of Jewish society under the Romans, this must have been the result of rational analysis and calculation. As elsewhere in the empire, the Romans ruled primarily through the upper classes, who collaborated in, and reaped the benefits of, the imperial system. The obvious way to oppose the established system was to attack the collaborators who made it effective. Through terrorist attacks on such persons, the Sicarii could both cause intense anxiety among the ruling circles and demonstrate the vulnerability of the established regime, to both oppressor and oppressed.

Although terrorist actions must be unpredictable and even appear as irrational (in order to have the desired effect), they are usually based in completely rational strategy, calculated in terms of predictable costs and consequences. The Sicarii apparently did not use many of the common tactics of modern terrorist groups, such as sabotage against the occupying military forces or indiscriminate attacks in public places. In all cases mentioned by Josephus, the Sicarii were highly discriminate and always directed their attacks against fellow Jews, not against Roman soldiers or officials. They employed three tactics in particular: (a) selective, symbolic assassinations; (b) more general assassinations along with plundering of the property of the wealthy and powerful; and (c) kidnapping for ransom.

(a) The selective assassinations by the Sicarii seem to have had the greatest impact upon Josephus and probably upon others who lived through those years in Jerusalem. When they have been part of a broader discriminate strategy, assassinations have been carried out for their "demonstration" value, i.e., in order to create wider reverberations among the governing groups or the colonized people or both. Targets are chosen which have the maximum symbolic value, such as those of the established regime or religion. Judging from Josephus' accounts, the Sicarii must have inaugurated their campaign with the assassination of the high priest Jonathan. They attacked *the* symbol of the Jewish "nation" and religion, but a symbol that was then far from a positive one for the masses of people, since the high priest had become a symbol of the aristocracy's collaboration with Roman rule as well as of exploitation of the people.

The Sicarii must have hoped that the effect of the assassination of high priests and others of the ruling elite in Jerusalem would reverberate in two directions at once, i.e., to other members of the ruling circles and to the people at large. To the former, they may have intended the selective assassinations as a punishment for their exploitation and collaboration, as well as a deterrent against future oppression and a warning about further collaboration. The assassinations may well have demonstrated to the pro-Roman aristocracy their own vulnerability and the actual inability of the Romans to protect them. On the other hand, one effect of this tactic was to provoke retaliatory terrorism by the Jewish ruling circles. This tactic would have had some of the same effects on the common people, although from the opposite viewpoint. Nevertheless, they saw their religiopolitical overlords and economic oppressors being dramatically punished and warned. The Sicarii thus demonstrated to the people at large the vulnerability of the imperial system. They may also have forced others, who already had conflicting feelings about the sacred yet exploitative priestly aristocracy, to confront their own ambivalent attitudes. A more practical than symbolic effect was the removal of some of the leadership, whom they themselves perhaps hoped to replace.

(b) Closely related to the selective assassinations was a second tactic, one that extended their strategy into the countryside where the estates of the pro-Roman aristocracy were located: the Sicarii eliminated some of the Jewish gentry and destroyed their property. Thus, as Josephus puts it in another of his polemically exaggerated accounts:[12]

> [The brigand-like elements] . . . urged many to revolt, spurring them on toward freedom and threatening with death those who submitted to Roman rule. . . . Splitting up into armed groups, they ranged over the countryside, killing the powerful rich, plundering their houses, and setting fire to the villages. (*J. W.* 2.264-66; *Ant.* 20.172; see also *J. W.* 7.254)

This less clandestine tactic may have had some of the same purposes as the more symbolic assassinations, i.e., punishment, warnings, deterrence, and demonstration of the vulnerability of the gentry, whether to themselves or to the(ir) peasants. It is conceiveable that, intended or not, such actions may have had the effect of loosening the tenant farmers and landless laborers from their fear and possible loyalty to the "powerful rich" on whom they were almost totally dependent for a livelihood. Some of the peasants may have thus been frightened about cooperation with the pro-Roman landlords and forced into choosing sides. Through this tactic, rather than the more symbolic assassinations, the Sicarii may have been hoping to eliminate the pro-Roman leadership to which they perhaps imagined themselves as the alternative.

(c) The Sicarii employed a third tactic very typical of terrorist groups: kidnapping an important person in order to extort the release of some of their own members who had been taken prisoner. Thus, Josephus notes that at festival time under the governor Albinus (62-64),

> the Sicarii sneaked into the city by night and kidnapped the secretary of the high priest Ananias, and spirited him away in bonds. They then made contact with Ananias and said they would free the secretary into his custody if he would persuade Albinus to release ten of their imprisoned fellows. Having no option, Ananias successfully persuaded Albinus to make the exchange. But this was just the beginning. In various ways the brigands managed to kidnap a string of members of Ananias' household and held them until ransomed for some of their own Sicarii. (*Ant.* 20.208-9)

EFFECTS OF AGITATION BY THE SICARII

It may be well not to overplay or overestimate the effects the Sicarii may have had on the Palestinian situation in the fifties and sixties. Like modern terrorist groups, the Sicarii had limited forces, little mobility, and no stable or extensive base for organizing widespread popular revolt, if such an idea was even entertained. As in our modern experience, actions such as selective assassinations or kidnapping of public officials and the wealthy figures of the establishment constitute harassment rather than an actual revolutionary threat. More-over, we should not allow the old concept of "the Zealots" as an extensive and long-standing organization of national lib-eration to reenter through the back door of the "dagger men." The effects of the campaign by the Sicarii cannot be isolated from, or understood except in relation to, the effects of the many other groups and events of the years leading up to the great revolt. With this cautionary comment, we can turn to Josephus' dramatic portrayal of the effects that the selective clandestine assassinations of high priests and others had on the society.

> The fear of attack was worse than the crimes themselves [dem-onstration effect!], just as in a war when one expects death at any moment. Men watched their enemies from a distance, and not even approaching friends were trusted. But despite their suspicions and precautions they were laid waste, so suddenly did the conspirators strike and skillfully avoid detection. (*J.W.* 2.256-57)

Apparently the Sicarii had provoked great anxiety and fear among the ruling circles, their principal target. They thus contributed to or accelerated the breakdown of the custom-ary framework of social images and assumptions which the people, especially the upper echelons of society, depended on for their sense of security. In its place came vague feelings of insecurity and distrust; anyone could be next. But the effect on the Jewish ruling class went further. Whatever its coherence may have been in earlier times, the ruling elite was now fragmented into individuals, each concerned only with personal safety. Instead of organizing cooperative efforts to suppress the tactics of the Sicarii, the threatened ruling families each collected around them gangs of ruffians. The Sicarii may not have been the only stimulus to this recruitment of goon squads, but the result was a cycle of escalating violence. For the "servants" of the Herodian families and chief priests were not simply bodyguards, but private "storm troopers" for their bosses.

> Ananias had some very unscrupulous servants who, along with some real hoodlums, went to the threshing floors and forcibly seized the tithes of the priests and readily assaulted those who refused to give them up. The high priests were doing the same thing and no one could stop them. So the priests who had long lived on the tithes now died of starvation. (*Ant.* 20.206-7)

By escalating the violence, the ruling families contributed further to the breakdown of the social structure and its assumptions upon which all depended for any semblance of social order. The effects of violence from the aristocracy would likely have been only to provoke the Sicarii and other groups to further agitation.

The attacks on their landlords and ostensible religious-political leaders would have demonstrated to the Jewish populace how vulnerable and replaceable the elite actually was, reinforcing any memories they may have had of the previously successful revolt of the Hasidim and Maccabees. Given the residual ambivalence that the people must have felt about the exploitative priestly aristocracy, the actions by the Sicarii and the counterviolence by the chief priests' goon squads must have affected their "habit of obedience" upon which the high priests and gentry depended for their continuation in power.

Although the Sicarii may have contributed to the loss of respect which the people had for the ruling circles, they apparently did not exercise any informal governing power in opposition to that of the established structures. Certainly at the outbreak of the great revolt they did not command a very extensive following. Rather than contributing toward the mobilization of a broader-based movement, the tactics of the Sicarii appear to have functioned as a safety valve, channeling righteous indignation of seriously concerned intellectuals and relieving the tensions built up by the continuing inaction on a broader front that might well have been simply suicidal and hopeless. On the other hand, the Sicarii may have alienated from their cause some of the more reflective Pharisees (like Josephus and other "leading Pharisees"), by forcing them to confront a polarized situation and to decide which side they would support.

In sum, the overall effect of the Sicarii's actions, combined with banditry or conflicts between Jews and Gentiles, was to help precipitate a "revolutionary situation," especially as it bore on the pro-Roman governing elite. According to Lenin, a revolution is possible only when, among other factors,

> it is impossible for the ruling classes to maintain their rule without any change; when there is a crisis, in one form or another, among the "upper classes," a crisis in the policy of the ruling class, leading to a fissure through which the discontent and indignation of the oppressed classes burst forth. For a revolution to take place, it is usually insufficient for the "lower classes not to want" to live in the old way; it is also necessary for the "upper classes to be unable" to live in the old way.[13]

Lenin could as well have been thinking of the Jewish ruling classes in Palestine in the sixties. The high priestly families, the Herodians, and other notables were not only quarreling among themselves, but were also at odds with both Agrippa II and the Roman procurators, particularly Florus, during whose term the revolt erupted. This extremely unsettled situation and the role of the Sicarii are reflected in a final polemic by Josephus:

The sickness reached epidemic proportions; both private and public life were so infected that everyone tried to outdo each other in sacrilege toward God and injustice toward their neighbors. The people of rank and influence oppressed the masses, and the masses were intent on destroying them in return. The powerful craved tyranny and the masses violence and plunder of the rich. The Sicarii were the first to engage in this lawlessness and barbarity toward their kinsmen. They left no word unspoken, no deed untried, to insult and destroy those whom they plotted against. (J. W. 7.260-62)

THE BRIEF AND LIMITED ROLE OF THE SICARII IN THE JEWISH REVOLT

Although they had apparently tried to promote the over-throw of Roman rule, the Sicarii played an extremely brief and limited role in the actual revolt. Again because of the modern concept of the Zealots, the Sicarii (supposedly identical with the Zealots), and especially Menahem, are often wrongly viewed as having assumed the leadership in the very beginning of the insurrection in Jerusalem. It is appropriate, therefore, to correct some frequent misunderstandings about their actions at the beginning of the revolt.

(1) The Sicarii did not initiate the popular insurrection in Jerusalem. Rebellious activities were already well under way when a number of Sicarii, along with some feebler folk, were able to slip through into the temple during the feast of wood-carrying. They were thereupon recruited by the rebels who had already laid siege to the chief priests and other notables in the upper city (J. W. 2.425; see also 422-24). They were thus among the forces who set fire to the royal palaces and the mansion of Ananias the high priest and then torched the archives which housed the records of debts (J. W. 2.426-27). But these actions were neither initiated nor carried out solely by the Sicarii, however much they accorded with their general program. Any number of the common people would have eagerly done the same thing, as would the ordinary

priests, who had recently been deprived of their rightful income from the tithes by Ananias' gang of ruffians. The Sicarii participated in, but did not necessarily lead, these initial incendiary acts of insurrection against Roman rule and their own ruling circles.

(2) It was apparently not the Sicarii who captured the fortress of Masada from the Roman garrison there (*J.W.* 2.408). A number of "rebels" and "revolutionary" groups were already active during the summer of 66 (2.407). Some of the most ardent among them

> banded together and stormed the fortress at Masada. They captured it by stealth, killed the Roman garrison and replaced it with one of their own. (*J.W.* 2.408)

Nor had the Sicarii been in the habit of attacking the Romans directly. Only somewhat later did Menahem, at the head of a group of Sicarii, proceed to Masada in order to arm his followers and other "brigands" from Herod's old armory at the Dead Sea fortress (*J.W.* 2.433-34). In yet a third incident, numbers of Sicarii, desperately fleeing Jerusalem themselves (see below), captured Masada by treachery, presumably from the rebel garrison already installed there earlier in the summer and presumably still in control after Menahem's raid into the armory (*J.W.* 2.447; 4.400; and 7.297).

(3) Further, Menahem, son or grandson of Judas of Galilee, has been seen as the principal leader of the Jewish revolt from its very outset. However, he was apparently not even the recognized leader of all the Sicarii in their actions at the beginning of the rebellion. Josephus recounts events in which the Sicarii were already active before Menahem entered the city at the head of yet another band of Sicarii. Josephus ordinarily devoted considerable attention to the leaders' roles, as in the cases of Eleazar the temple captain, John of Gischala, Simon bar Giora, or Menahem's (grand)father, Judas of Galilee. Although he may not always be consistent in his composition, it is interesting that he

does not give Menahem the same prominence as other leaders. Hence, perhaps Menahem played no more of a role than Josephus says he did, especially considering the rapidly changing complexion of the insurrection during the summer of 66. The most distinctive thing about Menahem's brief leadership, of course, was his posture as the messianic king (discussed earlier, chapter 3), a stance totally unprecedented in the previous development of the Fourth Philosophy and the Sicarii.

Once they did join the rebels in Jerusalem, the Sicarii played an aggressive role. Their participation was very short-lived, however, since other insurgents quickly turned against them. It was only to be expected that the Sicarii would be among those most eager to capture Ananias, although Josephus only implies that they participated in the killing of the high priest and his brother Ezechias. Their participation in this action would help explain why the temple captain Eleazar, who was the son of Ananias, and his followers now turned against Menahem and the Sicarii. Whatever his alienation from his pro-Roman father and family, Eleazar had undoubtedly built up considerable resentment against those who had previously kidnapped his father's secretary and now (perhaps) had participated in the execution of his father. It may not have been just an accident that it was Eleazar and his followers who now turned some of the heretofore dormant "citizens" of Jerusalem (and perhaps other insurgents) against the "tyrant" (Menahem) and the other Sicarii.

> They planned to attack him in the temple, where he had gone up in pomp to worship, decked with kingly robes and followed by his armed and zealous admirers. Eleazar and his men rushed at him while the rest of the citizens threw stones, thinking that his overthrow would bring the collapse of the whole revolt. Menahem and his supporters held their ground for a while, but when they saw the entire crowd rushing them, they fled in all directions. Those who were caught were slaughtered; those who managed to hide were searched out.

A few escaped by slipping away to Masada, among them Eleazar ben Jair who was related to Menahem and later had absolute control of Masada. Menahem himself fled to Ophlas and
ignominiously hid until caught, dragged out into the open
and put to death through prolonged torture. (*J. W.* 2.444-48)

Thus, a few short weeks after they joined the insurgents in
Jerusalem, the main body of the Sicarii were either killed or
driven out of the city.

The subsequent history of the Sicarii would appear to
involve either a major inconsistency or a dramatic fluctuation
in behavior. After being driven from Jerusalem in the summer of 66, they passively withdrew from the rest of the great
rebellion and retreated to Masada, which ultimately fell to
the Romans.

The "Zealots' last stand" on Masada has become the glori-
fied subject of religionationalist propaganda.[14] It is now
clear, of course, that it was not the Zealots, but the Sicarii,
under the leadership of Eleazar ben Jair, who occupied
Masada. The Sicarii simply sat out the rest of the long war
against the Romans in their secure perch atop Masada. Simon
bar Giora reportedly tried to persuade them back into active
participation in the war. But far from organizing resistance
among the Judean peasantry, as did Simon, the Sicarii
became predators on the countryside around Masada. They
made periodic raids on villages in the area, at one point even
raiding the town of Engeddi ten miles north, in order to
obtain supplies during their prolonged sojourn in the fortress. Numerous recruits joined them, but there is no indication they they were shaped into a fighting force. When the
Romans finally got around to besieging Masada itself in 73, as
part of their "mopping up" operations in Judea, the Sicarii
offered no active resistance (*J. W.* 7.309-14), a striking contrast with the Zealots proper and the forces of Simon bar
Giora at the final siege of Jerusalem. After holding out as
long as possible, the Sicarii finally committed mass suicide
(960 men, women, and children) (*J. W.* 7.320-401).

Following the mass suicide on Masada, however, other Sicarii agitated against Roman rule in Egypt and Cyrene, according to Josephus' report. The pattern of activity is familiar (*J. W.* 7.409-19). In a way reminiscent of the Fourth Philosophy (a way which may be due simply to Josephus' account), they exhorted Jews to view God alone as their master and to assert their liberty. Like the Jerusalem Sicarii in the fifties they assassinated certain Jews of rank. Also familiar is the Jewish elders' turning the people against the Sicarii and killing or driving them out. However, those captured by the Romans held stubbornly to their principles:

> They were subjected to every conceivable form of torture and bodily suffering, all of them contrived for the sole purpose of getting them to affirm Caesar as lord. Not a one of them gave in or was even about to declare it, but everyone maintained their resolve, victorious over coercion. As they endured the tortures and flames, it was as if their bodies felt no pain and their souls actually rejoiced in it. What especially amazed those who saw this were the young children, none of whom could be persuaded to call Caesar lord. (*J. W.* 7.417-19)

The resistance movement led by Jonathan the weaver in Cyrene, on the other hand, appears in Josephus' portrayal less like the Sicarii and more like the popular prophetic movements led by Theudas and "the Egyptian."[15]

Needless to say, it is puzzling that a group that had orchestrated systematic terrorism against collaborating Jewish ruling circles and had joined aggressively in the early actions of the eventual insurrection would suddenly withdraw from the hostilities and sit idly by throughout several years of war against the Romans. One can only speculate as to whether they had abandoned their earlier ideals and program of resistance to alien overlords. Their numbers had been decimated in the Jerusalem massacre led by Eleazar's partisans. They were probably not inclined to rejoin a revolt they could not lead, and found no good opportunity to reassert their leadership. If they had viewed the revolt that finally commenced in

66 as the climactic eschatological holy war, perhaps with Menahem as the messiah, they would clearly have found it necessary to reassess their eschatological anticipations when they were attacked and killed by the very people they expected to lead, and when their anointed king was igno-miniously executed by the unfaithful. Perhaps they inter-preted their rejection by the Jerusalemites as a rejection of God's program of liberation, of which they themselves were the agents. They may therefore have come to the conclusion that the inevitable Roman reconquest was God's punishment for the people's lack of faith and responsiveness to his escha-tological initiative.

THE ZEALOTS

Of all the rebel groups which participated in the revolt against Rome, Josephus harbors the most contempt for the Zealots. In an ascending scale of wickedness and lawless-ness, our principal source ranks the Sicarii as very wicked, the leader John of Gischala and the messianic pretender Simon bar Giora as much worse, the Idumeans simply as mad butchers, and, finally, the Zealots as history's great villains.

> In this [complete lawlessness] the Zealots excelled, a group whose deeds verified its name. They faithfully copied every ruthless deed, and there was no crime on record that they failed to commit. Yet they took their name from the fact that they were zealous for what was right, either ridiculing those injured, brutal types that they were, or regarding the worst evils as good. (J.W. 7.268-70)

It is unclear just why Josephus should hate the Zealots so. But it probably had something to do with why this group was important historically. In military terms they hardly deserve mention. At the beginning of the revolt they did not yet exist, and in the final resistance to the Roman siege they were an insignificant fighting force compared with the followers of John of Gischala and Simon bar Giora. In the middle of the revolt, however, this group, a coalition of peasant-bandits turned Zealots, challenged and rendered ineffective the government of the chief priests and leading Pharisees (including Josephus!) who apparently had been attempting to reach an accommodation with the Romans.

There has been a great deal of confusion about the Zealots because, as mentioned already, modern scholars have so stretched the concept that it has become a catchall for groups which were really very different from each other. As we now focus, finally, on the group which Josephus calls the Zealots, and which he says called itself the Zealots, it would be well first to have a general sense of the sequence of events in which they played a major role, and only then to probe more into explanations of those events.

THE SEQUENCE OF EVENTS INVOLVING THE ZEALOTS

From Josephus' reports, the origin of the Zealots would have to be dated to the winter of 67-68, when the Roman armies were beginning to reconquer Judea. Initially, the revolt had been a success. Rome's first attempt at retaking Jerusalem had ended in a rout of its army. The Romans, moveover, were driven out of much of the countryside in Galilee, as well as in Judea. During the summer and fall of 67, however, they had subdued virtually all Jewish resistance forces in Galilee.[16] With Galilee thus secured, the Roman general Vespasian then turned his attention to Judea, beginning with the northwestern border areas.

> When Titus moved from Gischala to Caesarea, Vespasian marched from Caesarea to Jamnia and Azotus. He subdued and garrisoned these towns, returning with a mass of people who had surrendered under treaty. (*J.W.* 4.130)

As the Roman army moved into northwestern Judea, numbers of Jewish peasants fled before the Roman advance. These fugitive peasants formed bands of brigands (4.134). Seeking a more secure stronghold, a number of the bands converged on Jerusalem, forming a coalition as they entered the city

(4.135). In a second wave, still more bands of brigands from the countryside joined their ranks (4.138). Once in the city, the Zealots took two actions in particular which proved threatening to the high priestly government then still in control of the city. They attacked certain Herodian nobles still in the city with whom they had "ancient quarrels," and accused them of betraying the city into the hands of the Romans (4.140-46). They proceeded to elect, by lot, commoners to high priestly offices, even installing a crude villager as the high priest, actions interpreted as a bid to place themselves in power. Alarmed at these actions, the high priestly leaders decided to organize an attack on the Zealots (4.147-57).

High priests such as Ananus and Jesus son of Gamala finally generated enough concern among the Jerusalemites to organize a fighting force (4.158-95). Attacking the Zealots, Ananus and his men drove them into the temple courtyard and then forced them to take refuge in the inner court (4.197-204). Now imprisoned in the temple, in effect, the Zealots appealed to allies from the villages and towns of Idumea (the district south of Jerusalem and Judea) to rescue them (4.224-32). The Idumeans managed to enter the city, despite the tight security forces posted by Ananus, liberated the Zealots from the inner court of the temple, and killed Ananus and Jesus son of Gamala, among others. The Zealots and Idumeans together then purged more of the young nobles, before most of the Idumeans withdrew from the city (4.233-53).

Having effective control of the city, the Zealots then conducted a third wave of purges, including persons formerly in positions of power as well as more of the nobility (4.254-365). Within the collective leadership of the group, however, tensions were developing. Most of the Zealots refused to submit to the dominant authority of the ambitious John of Gischala. Failing to take command of the whole, John then broke away from the main body with his own followers (4.389-96). Meanwhile, the messianic movement headed by Simon bar Giora was expanding its numbers and influence throughout the Judean and Idumean countryside not already under Roman control (4.503-13). The Zealots, expecting that Simon bar Giora might eventually come to challenge their regime in Jerusalem, attempted to block his movement in Judea (4.514-57). Within the city itself, John of Gischala once again became allied with the Zealots when part of his army mutinied (4.566-70).

In the spring of 69, the Idumeans still in the city eventually conspired with the high priests and Jerusalemites to invite Simon bar Giora into the city as their "liberator" from the Zealots and John (4.571-76). With his now vast following, Simon commanded the strongest fighting force in the city by far. He forced the Zealots back into the temple again (4.577-84). The Zealots once more split into two factions, the collective leadership again refusing to follow the dominating leadership of John. For a time there was a three-way battle raging, with the main body of the Zealots in the inner court of the temple above, John of Gischala and his followers in the temple courtyard in between, and Simon bar Giora in control of most of the rest of the city (5.1-12). John, by trickery on the feast of unleavened bread (Passover), forced a reunion of the main body of Zealots with his own followers, under his sole command (5.67-106).

With the Roman siege now well in place, the rival groups in the city finally began to focus their energies on resisting the Romans instead of struggling with each other. Because they were much smaller in numbers (2,400) than those under the command of John (6,000) and Simon (10,000 plus 5,000 Idumeans), and perhaps because they did not produce a single dominant leader, the Zealots were relatively insignificant as a fighting force during the rest of the prolonged resistance to the Roman siege (*J. W.* 5.248-374). Yet they fought courageously to the end alongside the other, rival peasant revolutionary groups against the overwhelming military might of the Romans.

ZEALOT ORIGINS:
A PRODUCT OF THE ROMAN RECONQUEST OF JUDEA

In two successive passages Josephus indicates that the Zealots originated as a coalition of brigand groups entering Jerusalem from the countryside in late 67.

> When at last the chiefs of the scattered brigand bands had had
> enough of raiding the countryside, they joined forces, form-
> ing a single pack of thugs, and infiltrated Jerusalem. . . .
> (J.W. 4.135)

The brigands, moreover, arrived in more than one wave.

> Fresh brigands from the countryside slipped into the city and
> joined the more formidable gang within, missing no opportu-
> nity for heinous crime. . . . (J.W. 4.138)

In an awkward insertion, Josephus does "connect" this new
upsurge of banditry with the Roman advance into northwest
Judea. But he appears to obscure the relationship rather than
explain it, since his description of civil strife reflects more of
Thucydides' famous observation on sedition (III.81-84) than
it does the situation in Judea in the fall of 67. We might be
led to dismiss his portrayal of the proto-Zealots as a "pack of
thugs" as simply a pejorative epithet, were it not for his
description of a similar state of affairs elsewhere in Judea the
following summer (J.W. 4.406-9),[17] a passage clearly describing banditry and its sudden rise to epidemic proportions.
Again, however, Josephus simply blames the brigands and
offers no explanation for the upsurge of banditry itself.

However, other sections of his description of the Roman
reconquest may shed some light on the origins of epidemic
banditry which produced the groups called the Zealots. Thus
we read about typical Roman procedure in the reconquest of
Gerasa and its surrounding villages:

> Annius [the commanding officer] took the town by assault,
> killed a thousand of the young men—all those who had not
> escaped, made prisoners of women and children, and
> allowed his soldiers to plunder the property. Finally, he set

fire to the houses and marched against the surrounding villages. Those who were able-bodied fled, the weak perished, and all that was left went up in flames. (*J.W.* 4.488-89)

Gerasa was not an isolated incident in the war. Judging from a number of similar accounts in Josephus, Vespasian and his officers carried out a systematic "scorched-earth" policy in district after district, razing the villages, slaughtering peasants by the tens of thousands, selling thousands of others into slavery, and putting in charge either his own soldiers or the Jewish gentry who had surrendered their town.[18]

Yet another passage from Josephus provides a telling illustration of how the Jewish peasantry reacted to the Roman advance. The location is Gadara (on the east bank of Jordan), but one can imagine similar panic among the peasantry in other areas as the Roman forces proceeded on their "search and destroy" operations. The Romans took the town without much struggle, since the local elite secretly capitulated, "partly from a longing for peace and partly to protect their property, since Gadara had many wealthy residents" (*J.W.* 4.414). The rebellious elements fled for their lives.

Vespasian sent Placidus with 500 cavalry and 3000 infantry to go after those who had fled from Gadara. . . . When the fugitives suddenly caught sight of the pursuing cavalry, they swarmed into a village called Bethennabris before any battle got started. . . . Placidus led an attack, and after a spirited battle that lasted until evening, he captured the wall and the entire village. The non-combatants were slaughtered wholesale, while the more able-bodied fled. The soldiers ransacked the houses and then torched the village. Those who fled, meanwhile, stirred up the countryside. By exaggerating their own disaster and saying that the entire Roman army was advancing against them, they drove everyone out in fear, and with the whole multitude fled for Jericho, the one remaining city strong enough to encourage the hope of survival in view of its large population. Placidus, relying on his cavalry and made bold by his previous successes, pursued them all the way to the Jordan, killing all he could catch. . . . Their path through the countryside was a long trail of carnage, and the Jordan . . . and Dead Sea were filled with dead bodies. . . . Placidus, taking advantage of his success, launched attacks against the small towns and villages in the neighborhood. Taking Abila, Julias, Besimoth, and all the others as far as the Dead Sea, he established in each of them the most suitable deserters. . . . (*J.W.* 4.419-20, 429-33, 437-39)

Along with the systematic slaughter and devastation on an immense scale, two further aspects of these Roman practices are notable with regard to the escalation of banditry. Those who deserted to the Roman victors, generally the wealthy gentry or local officials, were placed in charge. As for the peasantry, those who did not flee were simply killed. To cite another example, when Vespasian and his troops came to Jericho,

the mass of the population, anticipating their approach, had fled to the hill country opposite Jerusalem, but the many left behind were put to death. (*J.W.* 4.451)

That is, by simply killing all those who did not flee, the Romans in effect *created* the phenomenon of dispossessed fugitives forced to plunder their own former territories now in the hands of the pro-Roman factions. These brigands now had virtually no alternative but to fight against the Roman advance.

In the face of Roman military might, however, even brigand bands, which normally would have continued their operations in the remoter regions of the countryside, were inclined to flee to the large towns or to the city of Jerusalem for refuge.

A complete pattern of Roman conquest and Jewish peasant reaction can thus be discerned from these descriptions of Josephus. The Romans relentlessly pursued the peasants and devastated their villages. The peasants had no alternative but to fight (and inevitably be killed) or to flee. Their panicky flight had a snowballing effect on other peasant villages. Once they had fled, it was impossible for them to return to their villages and towns, which had either been destroyed or were now in the hands of their wealthy enemies who had deserted to the Romans. Many fled to the nearest fortress-city or town-stronghold, such as Jericho. Such were the circumstances in which large-scale brigand groups formed, "smaller than an army, but bigger than an armed gang. . . ." The brigand groups formed and operated in areas which the Romans had not yet completely "pacified." But as the Roman forces advanced farther into Judea, the brigand bands were eventually forced to seek refuge in the fortress-city of Jerusalem itself.

Ironic as it may seem, Roman practices produced the very groups that continued and prolonged the war. That is, the methods used by the Roman forces in reconquering Jewish Palestine created the conditions which gave rise to epidemic banditry and escalating peasant revolt, precisely what they were trying to suppress. In particular, the brigands which came together in Jerusalem were a direct outgrowth of the Roman reconquest of northwestern Judea.

ZEALOT ATTACKS ON THE HERODIAN NOBILITY

When the bands of brigands coalesced in Jerusalem to form the Zealots, Josephus laments that they no longer

> restricted their audacity to raids and highway robberies. They now went so far as to commit murder, not just at night or secretly or on the chance passerby, but openly, in broad daylight, and starting with the most distinguished citizens. They first seized and imprisoned Antipas, a man of royal descent and among the most powerful in the city so that he was entrusted with the public treasury. Next came Levias, one of the nobles, and Syphas son of Aregetes, both of royal blood, then the others of high reputation. (J.W. 4.139-41)

That is, the Zealots began attacking members of the ruling aristocracy, especially the Herodian nobles. Ordinarily in traditional agrarian societies, the peasantry will patiently suffer under the burdens which God—and their overlords—

have assigned them. Very occasionally, however, when sparked by something unusual, they will go on a wild rampage, destroying the symbols of luxury and privilege and exercising a violence on their lords nearly equal to what they have been suffering so long themselves.[19] The Zealots' actions in Jerusalem were no sudden, irrational peasant rampage. Nor were their purges of the nobility a passing passion. They were deliberate in both the persons purged and in the procedures followed. The first action came soon after their entry into the city. A second wave of purges was carried out together with the Idumeans after they had rescued the Zealots from their virtual imprisonment in the temple by the high priests and city people (*J. W.* 4.325-27). Then a third phase came after most of the Idumeans had left the city (*J. W.* 4.357)

The Zealot purges were part of an overall pattern of popular attacks on the ruling aristocracy throughout the revolt. At the very beginning of the revolt, those who cut off the temple sacrifices for Rome, along with other rebels, attacked the high priestly aristocracy and Herodian nobles, besieged them in the royal palaces, and executed those whom they captured, such as the high priest, Ananias, and his brother Ezechias (*J. W.* 2.430-41). Then, after the Zealots began their attacks on the royalists, the Idumeans attacked and killed the high priestly leaders Ananus and Jesus, while both John of Gischala and Simon bar Giora conducted purges of the priestly aristocracy and other wealthy and powerful individuals (*J. W.* 5.440-41). The Zealots in particular appear to have focused their attacks on the Herodian nobility. Only in connection with the third wave of trials does Josephus mention that they attacked other aristocratic leaders or officers, such as Gorion son of Joseph and Niger the Perean.

The Zealots also observed certain procedures in their purges. For the trial of Zacharias son of Baris, for example, they attempted to use the Sanhedrin, the great council of the nation, as the court. However, the aristocratic members were not very cooperative, according to Josephus. Moreover, they did not merely execute their prisoners summarily, but attempted to persuade them to convert to the popular cause. As Josephus puts it, "They arrested and imprisoned the young nobles, postponing their execution in the hope that some would come over to their side" (*J. W.* 4.327).

The roots of the Zealots' (and others') attacks on the ruling aristocracy are not difficult to find, whether in Josephus' narrative or in the social conditions (discussed earlier at the end of chapter 1, and the beginning of chapter 2). Josephus mentions two principal reasons for the Zealots' purges of the ruling elite. One was the intense class conflict which permeated Jewish society at the time and was now erupting in revolt. Josephus gives this motive a superficial cast the first time he mentions it:

> They had decided to liquidate Zacharias son of Baris, one of the most distinguished citizens. . . . Since he was rich, they could hope both to plunder his property and to get rid of a powerful and dangerous opponent. (*J. W.* 4.335)

Later he more clearly indicates just how deeply rooted this class conflict really was. The Zealots moved against "those with whom any had ancient quarrels. . . . And none escaped except those whose humble birth or fate made them utterly insignificant" (*J. W.* 4.364-65). Josephus gives no specifics as to what those "ancient quarrels" may have been. However, it is not difficult for us to speculate intelligently about the general structure of political-economic relationships in which the Herodian nobility would have been the focus of popular hostility, and Josephus happens to inform us of one particular quarrel which some may have had with Herodian families. Generally, the Herodian nobles were some of the largest landholders in the society. Numbers of peasants may have been indebted to them. As for particular quarrels, in which some of the "weaker" Jewish people may have been the victims of the power of the noble families, Josephus took note that the Herodians, as well as the powerful high priestly families, engaged in predatory behavior against the people in the years preceding the revolt:

Costobar and Saul [brothers] assembled some vicious gangs
on their own. They were of royal descent and were well
regarded due to family connections with Agrippa [II], but they
were lawless and quick to plunder the property of those who
could not defend themselves. (*Ant.* 20.214)

The Zealots, no matter how much their struggle was against
the alien Roman oppressors, were first fighting a class war
against their own Jewish nobility.

The second reason for the Zealots' attack on the royalists
was their belief that the nobles were betraying the city to the
Romans. For example, in the case of Zacharias already mentioned, they accused him of "betraying the state to the
Romans and of sending an offer of treason to Vespasian"
(*J.W.* 4.336). Josephus, in *War*, claims that this charge is
utterly unjustified. When the Zealots "butchered their prisoners, they justified their outrageous crime with an equally
outrageous lie by arguing that their victims had approached
the Romans about surrendering Jerusalem and had been
killed as traitors to the freedom of the people" (*J.W.* 4.146).
In fact, however, Josephus is at pains throughout this part of
his history to insist that this charge by the Zealots was utterly
without foundation. He makes John of Gischala, who had
supposedly befriended the High Priest Ananus and other
aristocratic leaders, report to the Zealots that "Ananus had
persuaded the Jerusalemites (*dēmos*) to request that Vespasian come at once and take over the city." But he then insists
that John is telling "an embroidered tale" and is libeling
Ananus and his friends (*J.W.* 4.218, 224, 226). Moreover, he
has Ananus claim that "we are now at war with Rome" in his
speech rousing the Jerusalemites (*dēmos*) against the Zealots (*J.W.* 4.177). He also makes the other high priestly
spokesperson, Jesus, refute the charge that the aristocracy
was about to betray the city (*J.W.* 4.245-68). This pattern of
denial or refutation continues with Zacharias and a renegade
Zealot (*J.W.* 4.338, 347).

The aristocracy, however, had no credibility whatever with
the common people. According to Josephus' own narrative

of the events, regardless of what he had various speakers say, the Zealots were not the only ones who distrusted the ruling groups. Their allies, the Idumeans, also largely a peasant force, did not for a moment believe the high priests' protests of innocence and called their bluff with deeds as well as with words: "Standing over their dead bodies, they ridiculed Ananus for his devotion to the citizenry and Jesus for his speech delivered from the wall" (*J. W.* 4.314-16; 278-81).

Furthermore, Josephus' insistence on the aristocracy's innocence here is incredible to anyone who has read his apologetic autobiography or even *Jewish War* with a critical eye. No matter how he attempts to obscure it at points in the *War* narratives, Josephus nevertheless at several other points reveals the real intention of the Jewish ruling groups, namely, to reach accommodation with the Romans.

In *War,* for example, Josephus' encomium on Ananus as a moderate aristocrat attempting to mediate a settlement with Rome rings truer than his protests that he is a faithful head of the revolutionary government. "He made peace his supreme objective" (*J. W.* 4.320). Josephus clearly implies that even while pretending to prepare for war, he was attempting to arrange terms of surrender (for "he knew that Roman power was invincible" [*J. W.* 4.320]). The eminent and wealthy "citizens" who constituted the high priestly government's principal support in the city also wanted to surrender or to escape to the Roman lines. Many "citizens" "fled from their countrymen to take refuge with foreigners, finding in the Roman camp the safety which they despaired of finding among their own people" (*J. W.* 4.397).[20]

The aristocracy, moreover, knew that they would receive a warm reception from the Romans. It was not simply that Vespasian and Titus welcomed deserters as a source of intelligence on the squabbles and weaknesses of the Jewish rebel forces. A long-standing Roman policy for imperial rule was alliance with the native aristocracy of major cities; this policy is presupposed in Ananus' speech to the citizen body (*J. W.* 4.181). Therefore, when the wealthy and powerful Jewish elements surrendered, the Romans set them up as garrisons in district towns, sent them to the country for a peaceful respite from the war, and even restored their property.[21] In stark contrast to the rebels and even the noninsurrectionary peasantry, the aristocracy and "citizens" had powerful incentives to surrender or desert.

Josephus explicitly confirms this strategy of the Jewish aristocracy in his apologetic *Life*. When the revolt erupted in the summer of 66, he and other leading men of Jerusalem, the high priests and leading Pharisees, were alarmed to see people in arms. "Since we were powerless to stop the revolutionaries and in such obvious and imminent danger, we professed to agree with their views" (*Life* 21-22, 28). They then proceeded to set themselves up at the head of the nation, precisely in order to control the rebellious impulses until a settlement could be arranged with the Romans (see further, e.g., *Life* 73, 77-80). Indeed, this moderating strategy of the aristocracy seemed to be working satisfactorily, if slowly, until the emergence of the Zealots in Jerusalem in the winter of 67-68.

The Jewish peasantry, of course, was not unacquainted with the ways in which Rome governed, nor ignorant of the interests and inclinations of its own aristocracy. As Josephus points out, the wealthy and powerful men of Gadara had secretly, "unseen by the rebels, sent a delegation to Vespasian with an offer of surrender" (*J. W.* 4.414). Small wonder then that the Zealots and Idumeans suspected the aristocracy of negotiating a secret settlement with the Romans and betraying their battle for liberty. Indeed, in the case of Antipas, one of the first of the Herodians whom the Zealots brought to trial, there was a well-known record of such betrayal. This Antipas, whom the Zealots found in charge of all the public funds when they entered the city in the fall of 67, had been a member of the delegation sent by the Jerusalem ruling group to Agrippa II in the summer of 66, asking him to send troops to suppress the nascent rebellion (*J.W.* 2.418-19). As the Jewish people generally must have been aware, royalists such as Antipas occupied the same position and had the same interests in the imperial system as did the priestly aristocracy. Thus, not only was the Zealots' charge that the Herodian nobility were betraying the city to the Romans highly credible, it was almost certainly true.

THE ZEALOTS' ELECTION OF NEW HIGH PRIESTS: AN EGALITARIAN THEOCRACY

A great deal has been made of the fact that the Zealots were located in the temple during much of their activity in Jerusalem. In fact, this has become a principal basis for arguments that the Zealots were primarily a Jerusalem priestly group, in leadership if not in membership.[22] Zealots, moreover, were supposedly filled with *zeal* for the temple as well as for the Torah.

The Zealots' presence in the temple, however, was largely a function of circumstance. Most of the people in the movement were from outside Jerusalem, having no homes and probably few relatives or friends in the city. For such outsiders the outer court of the temple provided about the only large public space in which large numbers of people could congregate. More decisive for the Zealots' location in the temple was the fact that they were driven there in an attack by the high priests and the city people. Josephus says clearly that they initially withdrew into the temple because they feared an attack instigated by Ananus, the leading high priest, and sought "refuge from an outbreak of violence by the city-people" (*J.W.* 4.151). Indeed, once he was able to recruit a sufficient fighting force from the city people, Ananus did lead an attack on the Zealots, and drove them to take refuge in the inner court of the temple, bar the gates, and post a heavy security force. Thus, in one sense the Zealots did hold the temple fortress, "the strongest place in the city" (*J.W.* 4.173). On the other hand, "having revolted in the

cause of freedom, they were now imprisoned in the temple"
(*J. W.* 4.229). The priestly aristocracy was horrified that "the
scum and trash of the whole countryside" "should now
freely roam around our holy place" (*J. W.* 4.241, 183). The
high priests, of course, had not given them much choice in
the matter. Over a year later, when Simon bar Giora entered
the city, the Zealots were again forced to take refuge in the
inner court of the temple. In the interim, however, when
they had effective control of the city themselves, they were
located here and there around the city, and were no more
headquartered in the temple than any other group. Thus we
should not make too much of their supposed zeal for the
temple and motivation to carry out a "cleansing" of the temple or a "purification of the cult."

Yet Josephus indicates that the Zealots took a keen interest in the officers of the temple. Indeed, one of the two main
actions they took upon entering the city was to hold an
election of new high priests. Josephus is aghast:

> The brigands became so rabid that they took upon themselves
> the election of the high priests. Setting aside the families
> which in regular succession had always supplied them, they
> appointed obscure and low-born persons, to gain partners in
> sacrilege; for those who found themselves in the highest
> office without deserving it were inevitably subservient to
> those who had put them there. Furthermore, they sparked
> dissension among the people in authority by various tricks
> and fabricated stories, turning the squabbles of those who
> should have stopped them to their own advantage. Then,
> when they had had their fill of wrongs against the people,
> they directed their insolence to the Deity and invaded the
> sanctuary with polluted feet.
>
> The Jerusalemites were now on the verge of revolt, urged
> on by Ananus, the most senior of the chief priests and a man
> of exceedingly good judgment who might have saved the city
> if he had escaped the hands of the conspirators. They made
> the temple of God their stronghold and a place of refuge from
> upheavals of the citizenry, and the sanctuary became the
> center of their tyranny. There was irony in these atrocities,

more distressing than the actions themselves. To test the fear of the people and prove their own strength, they tried to choose the high priests by lot, despite the fact that the succession was hereditary, as we have said. Their pretext for this undertaking was based on ancient custom. They said that in days of old the high priesthood had been determined by lot. But in reality this was a reversal of the established practice and a means of consolidating their power by arbitrary appointments.

Thus they sent for one of the high priestly clans called Eniachin and cast lots for a high priest. The luck of the throw clearly demonstrated their depravity. His name was Phanni son of Samuel from the village of Aphthia. He was hardly descended from high priests and such a clown that he did not even know what the high priesthood meant. In any case, they dragged him in from the countryside and, like an actor on the stage, dressed him for the part, robing him in the sacred vestments and teaching him what was required for the occasion. (*J. W.* 4.147-56)

This passage has usually been understood to mean that the Zealots elected a new high priest, the head officiant in the temple. Perhaps this is because the most memorable part of the passage is the scandalous scene of a crude priest from a peasant village suddenly being thrust into all the pomp and ceremony of the august office. The passage, however, says much more than that. To understand what the Zealots may have been doing, and why it provoked an attack on them, two things in particular must be kept in mind. One is that in ancient traditional societies, and certainly in ancient Jewish society, there was little or no difference between religion and politics or even economics. It is extremely difficult to distinguish these dimensions even analytically. The popular messiahs and prophets discussed in chapters 3 and 4 were religiopolitical figures. Paying taxes to Caesar was a religious offense as well as an economic burden for Jewish people. The temple was not just a religious institution, but also an economic and political one. It was the center of national life in every respect. The second thing to note is that Josephus uses the plural, "high priests," more than once in this passage, not the singular, as if he were discussing only *the* officiating high priest. The Zealots are apparently selecting lowborn folk not simply for the top office, but for the several offices at the head of the temple apparatus. In modern terms, this would be described as electing a new or an alternative *government,* for the high priests as officers of the temple were also the heads of the government. As Josephus explained in another context, "After the death of [the Hasmonean] kings, the form of government became an aristocracy, and the high priests were entrusted with the leadership of the nation" (*Ant.* 20.251). Thus, the Zealots were less interested in the purification of the temple rituals and the cultic roles of the priesthood than in the key priestly roles as the nominal leaders of the theocratic government. Indeed, Josephus twice suggests in the quoted passage that this was the Zealots' motivation in electing new high priests. Since the new occupants of these offices would be beholden to those who conferred it (*J. W.* 4.149), the elections would thus be a device to bring themselves into power (*J. W.* 4.154).

A closer look at three other features of Josephus' report may give us a more precise sense of what the Zealots may have been attempting in their new elections for high priestly offices. First, the Zealots were "setting aside the families which in regular succession had always supplied them," and were appointing the high priests by lot, although "the succession was hereditary." The peasant-brigand-Zealots, however, had a longer memory and a greater respect for tradition than Josephus cares to admit. The Zealots had the sacred traditions, indeed the scriptural traditions, on their side. The ruling priestly aristocracy were the ones who were illegitimate, and the result of an abrogation of the traditional customs. Herod had displaced the hereditary Hasmonean dynasty of high priests and, by elevating men from families loyal to himself, had created a new priestly aristocracy. But even the heroic Hasmoneans were illegitimate upstarts who had maneuvered themselves into office by arrangement with

the Seleucid court officials, thus replacing the true hereditary Zadokite line which had been in office since the return
from exile. The Zealots knew that the occupant of the high
priest's office was by ancient tradition a legitimate Zadokite.
They also knew that there were still some true Zadokite
families around, even if they were now simple villagers. Thus
they summoned one of the "high priestly clans" named
Eniachin/Jachim. Josephus makes "election by lot" and
"hereditary succession" appear as mutually exclusive alternatives. This, however, is because he is presupposing
the hereditary hierarchical position of the established (but
illegitimate) high priestly families. The Zealots are clearly
against hierarchical power and privilege. But they are restoring, not abrogating, the true traditional principle of hereditary succession.

Second, the Zealots appealed to "ancient custom," assert-
ing that in the old days the "high priesthood had been determined by lot." What this "ancient custom" may have been is
a puzzle to us if what we are looking for is a precedent for the
selection of *the* presiding high priest by lot. However, if the
ancient custom pertained to the selection for the high
priestly offices generally, then some passages in 1 Chroni-
cles may be relevant. Supposedly, at the time of David, the
twenty-four courses (divisions) of priests were originally
organized by lot, and the duties of both the musicians and
the gatekeepers were to be determined by lot.[23] The Zealots
may have had in mind just such an "ancient custom," by
which the various duties and responsibilities of the officers
of the temple-government were determined by lot. Acts 1:26
may provide an interesting parallel from the early church:
they cast lots to determine who would replace Judas among
the twelve disciples.

Third, selection of officers by lot was simultaneously a
theocratic and a democratic or egalitarian (i.e., nonhierarchical) principle. Selecting leaders by lot was the ancient
Israelite method by which God, the true ruler of society, was

understood to make the choice. According to ancient covenantal traditions, no one individual or family was to gain
undue power over others. All were to live together in just
social-economic-political relationships, as protected by the
covenantal principles to which all had pledged allegiance.
The choice by lot of the first popular king, Saul, provides a
good illustration of how the principle of selection by lot was
used both to have the true king, God, make the choice, and
to protect the egalitarian political relationships within the
society. First the tribe, then the family were chosen by lot.
Indeed, early Israel must have provided an abundance of
traditions of how *theocracy,* the direct rule of God, operated
in an egalitarian manner. In more recent memory, in the
early stages of the Maccabean revolt, the Hasidim and others
had probably operated in a democratic-charismatic fashion
before the Hasmoneans reimposed a hierarchy. The memories of earlier times, when hierarchy and privilege had been
overthrown and a more democratic theocracy had flourished,
may well have informed the Zealots' actions. In opposing a
hierarchical order, however, the Zealots were not abandoning the *hierocratic* forms, i.e., the rule of God through
governance by priests, headed in this case by officers from
legitimate Zadokite families. They were rather implementing a nonhierarchical principle of equality, in which a simple
uneducated village priest could be chosen as *the* officiating
high priest (in effect, the head of state!). The parables of
Jesus, along with his other sayings, indicate that the Jewish
peasantry entertained ideals of a (restored) egalitarian theocracy (the kingdom of God)—inasmuch as it was members
of the peasantry who not only heard such sayings, but also
preserved and transmitted them.[24] The Zealots, however,
were now implementing such ideas.

The pattern of leadership among the Zealots is further
evidence of the democratic character of the movement. The
messianic movements, the prophetic movements, and the
other principal fighting groups in Jerusalem in 68-70 were all
headed by individual charismatic leaders or strongmen. By

contrast, the Zealots appear to have had a collective leadership. In their very origins, of course, they were a coalition of brigand groups headed respectively by brigand-chiefs. Throughout their history apparently no individual strongman emerged to head the group. In his narrative of the struggles with the priestly aristocracy, Josephus always refers to the Zealots as a collective, without mentioning any particular leader. When Josephus does mention particular leaders at a few points, he always refers to more than one.[25] When, at several points early in book 5, he uses the phrase "those around Eleazar," he does so to distinguish the main body of Zealots from those Zealots and others who remained under John of Gischala's command in the struggle for control of the city between three rival groups. But Eleazar is not indicated as the sole leader of the group.

The most telling evidence for the group's leadership comes in his portrayal of the break between John of Gischala and the main body of the Zealots:

> John was now bent on one-man rule and despised sharing honor with his peers. He gradually built up a following of the more villainous types and broke with the coalition. Repeatedly disregarding the decisions of the others and issuing his own orders like a tyrant, it was clear that he was seeking to rule alone. . . . A large group of those who resisted this move left him, partly motivated by envy and a reluctance to be ruled by a former equal, but mainly put off by fear of a single ruler. . . . Everyone preferred war, with all its miseries, to throwing away freedom and dying like a slave. (*J. W.* 4.389-94)

Assuming that Josephus' narrative here is not a complete fabrication and represents valid information that reached him by way of a report of their enemies, we find a highly distinctive commitment to collective leadership among the group. The Zealots were apparently accustomed to reaching decisions collectively. After John joined the group, friction developed with his more singular and ambitious style of leadership. It was only much later, during the final stages of the Roman siege, when their numbers had dwindled under repeated attack and intergroup conflict, that the Zealots proper were reluctantly forced to accept John's leadership (see *J.W.* 4.98-105). From the time of its formation and throughout the period in which it played a primary if not dominant role in Jerusalem, the Zealot group practiced collective decision-making apparently out of the strong egalitarian sense within the group.

With regard to leadership, finally, it would be well to correct a possible misconception about the Zealots. Much has been made, in recent studies, of the priestly character of the Zealot leadership.[26] As we have noted, however, one of the principal pieces of evidence adduced for this, their location in the temple, can hardly be used in this way. The other argument for the priestly character of the Zealot leadership and membership also collapses, since it is based on a false presupposition (still somewhat dependent on the old scholarly concept of "the Zealots"): that the Zealots proper are the continuation of the group led by Eleazar son of Simon, in the fall of 66, and even have connections with the followers of Eleazar son of Ananias, who started the revolt in Jerusalem in the summer of 66. The former was indeed a priest, and the latter was temple captain. However, there is simply no evidence for continuity between the followers of either Eleazar in 66 and the Zealots proper. Conjectures about such continuities can hardly be given precedence over the explicit statement of Josephus that the Zealots formed as a coalition of brigand groups in the winter of 67-68. Throughout his accounts of the Zealots' actions generally and his references to their leaders in particular, moreover, the only time Josephus mentions anything about priests is in connection with Eleazar son of Simon and Zachariah son of Amphicalleus. That is not much of a basis for claiming that the group was primarily priestly in leadership.

THE HIGH PRIESTS' ASSAULT ON THE ZEALOTS

The high priestly leaders in the city, alarmed at the Zealots' growing influence and anxious about the erosion of their own authority, organized a massive attack on the "brigands." It is understandable that the priestly aristocracy felt threatened by the two main Zealot actions: the purges of the Herodians and the formation of an alternative (democratic) government. On the other hand, there is no indication that the Zealots had attacked the high priestly leaders themselves. Nor had they made an attempt to take over the city by force. Judging from their inability to hold their own against the attack led by the high priest Ananus, the Zealots would hardly have had the fighting strength to attempt such a takeover.

The people of Jerusalem, moreover, do not appear to have been unusually concerned about the Zealots' presence in the city. Judging from Josephus' reports, the Zealots communicated with the city people. There were even public discussions involving interaction between the Zealots and some government officials (*J.W.* 4.150). Prior to the high priests' incitement of the city people against the group, there is nothing to indicate that the Jerusalemites had taken any significant action to oppose the Zealots.

The elite of the high priestly government traditionally had the support of the people of Jerusalem for effecting their policies and decisions in the rest of society. As a result, they would understandably expect such support. Besides the high priestly families and leading Pharisees, the most prominent Jerusalemites would have been the wealthy landowners who had the same basic interests as the priestly aristocracy. Moreover, most of the other city people were dependent for their livelihood on the temple, directly or indirectly, given its economic and religious-political centrality in the society as a whole.[27] The high priests Ananus and Jesus (and their colleagues in the government), therefore, alarmed at the Zealots' actions in the city, naturally turned to the city people for assistance in getting rid of the Zealot threat to their authority.

The high priestly government, however, apparently found it necessary to mount a major effort to incite the city people against the Zealots. They worked both through public assemblies and private visits. That they had to cajole the city people behind the scenes and "upbraid the people because of their apathy" indicates both that the aristocracy were a good deal more alarmed than the people and that the city people were hardly unanimous in their opposition to the Zealots, or even necessarily against them at all. Josephus has helped to obscure this situation by his portrayal of the "city-people" or "Jerusalemites" in *Jewish War*. He almost always portrays *the* "citizen-body" (*dēmos*) or "citizens" or "crowd" as a collective body unanimous, as it were, in opposing the rebellion against Rome and following the lead of the high priests. Almost certainly the "city-people" he is referring to were the moderate faction, including those who opposed hostilities from the beginning and those who finally deserted the besieged city and went over to the Romans. As Josephus' reports of desertions and attempted desertions indicate, this faction included the wealthier "citizens" whose property the Romans restored (as distinct from the "non-citizens" of the city who were simply killed or enslaved). Josephus' attempt to give the impression that the whole citizen-body was in favor of peace, however, cannot hide the fact that numbers of Jerusalemites, including priests and even the temple captain Eleazar were "revolutionaries." Similarly, there must have been Jerusalemites with yet other attitudes toward the revolt, whether ambivalent or shifting according to the circumstances. Thus also, the Zealots may have had some impact on the situation in their interaction with the Jerusalem populace. Josephus indicates as much when he notes that "they sparked dissension among the people in authority by various tricks and fabricated stories, turning the squabbles of those who should have stopped them to their own advantage" (*J.W.* 4.150). It is thus hardly surprising that the leaders of the ruling aristocracy had difficulty in arousing the city people to take action against the Zealots.

Indeed, the unsettling effects the Zealots may have been having on certain segments of the population and their apparently successful erosion of the authority of the ruling officials (who were now driven to bickering among themselves) may have been factors adding to the alarm of the high priests. They were losing their ability to hold the city people in check. The presence and influence of the Zealots in the city, in fact, must have been affecting the high priestly government's ability to pursue its strategy of negotiating a settlement with the Romans. Their strategy of pretending to prepare defenses against Roman reconquest while attempting to hold the lid on the revolt and to negotiate with the Romans had been successful for over a year. Now the Zealots threatened to block the implementation of their strategy, perhaps just as they were anticipating a settlement with the Romans, who were taking a break in the campaign of reconquest during the winter of 67-68. The preceding paragraphs are somewhat speculative, but they may provide an explanation for why the high priestly leadership in Jerusalem worked so vigorously in organizing an attack on the Zealots.

The high priestly leaders were finally able to recruit a sufficient number of aroused city people into a fighting force. Ananus and his men attacked the Zealots, drove them first into the temple courtyard, then forced them to take refuge in the inner court, where they held them prisoner. The aristocracy, however, had not anticipated the solidarity with the Zealots of the non-Jerusalemites, the rural population of their society. Thousands of men from the Idumean villages and towns, responding to the Zealots' appeal to rescue them, marched on Jerusalem. The Idumeans freed the Zealots from the inner court of the temple and eventually killed the high priestly leaders Ananus and Jesus after taking control of the city. When most of the Idumeans finally departed, the Zealots were left in control of the city.

For the period during which the Zealots held control of the city, Josephus provides very little information. He does mention in passing that they were located here and there about the city (*J.W.* 4.567-70). It may be indicative of the Zealots' discipline that he mentions no general retaliation against the city people who attacked them, something we might well have expected. Moreover, although the Zealots continued their purges of the nobility, no mention is made of any general attack on the remaining high priestly leaders. Indeed, it is at a point after they had been attacked by Ananus and his men and had gained control of the city with the Idumeans that Josephus mentions their postponing the execution of the young nobles "in the hope that some would come over to their side." It would appear from these fragments of information that the Zealots, far from acting like vengeful fanatics, were operating in a disciplined manner, and that they had some longer-range social-revolutionary goals which their lords and city people could embrace and become loyal to once they were made plain to them. When the remaining high priests, in collaboration with some of the Idumeans and perhaps the city people, brought Simon bar Giora into the city as their "liberator," the Zealots were again on the defensive, effectively besieged in the inner court of the temple.

The principal historical significance of the Zealots, in the context of the revolt as a whole, was to block the high priestly strategy of negotiating an accommodation with the Romans, thus providing an interlude during which other popular groups could come together in the countryside and mobilize for continuing resistance to the reconquest by the Romans.

The actual historical group called the Zealots was thus very different from the synthetic modern (mis)conception of the same name. Historically, it is totally inappropriate to use the Zealots as a foil (of advocacy of violent rebellion against

Rome) for interpretation of Jesus (as a prophet of nonviolence). Far from having agitated for rebellion until they finally touched it off, the Zealots as a group were themselves a product of the vicious Roman suppression of a revolt long since under way. Only when the devastating advance of the Roman legions left no alternatives but flight and resistance did these peasants from northwestern Judea form brigand bands which, once they took refuge in Jerusalem, emerged as an organized coalition. The Zealots, moreover, were not a "sect" or "philosophy." The Zealots proper were a totally separate phenomenon, historically, from the Fourth Philosophy mentioned by Josephus as active over sixty years earlier. Moreover, not even the Fourth Philosophy, led by a "teacher" and a Pharisee, advocated armed revolt, but rather resistance to payment of the Roman tribute, and a willingness to suffer as a consequence of one's resistance. Probably not even the Sicarii advocated armed rebellion against the Romans. Very likely they, like other sages and teachers, were well aware of the military might of Rome and knew how suicidal such a rebellion might be. The Sicarii, rather, carried out a calculated strategy of selective assassination against the Jewish high priests who were collaborating in Roman rule. Besides being neither a party nor a philosophy, the Zealots were also not primarily a priestly group. But as peasants who knew very well the sacred traditions of their society, once they reached Jerusalem, then in a "revolutionary situation," they did attempt to set up an alternative government more in accord with those traditions.

NOTES

1. See M. Hengel, *Die Zeloten* (Leiden: Brill, 1961), as an example of the synthetic misunderstanding of Josephus' texts.
2. See *J.W.* 2.163; compare DSS, 1QM 1:9-11; 12:7-9.
3. See Dan. 11:34-35; 12:1-3; 1 Enoch 47:2; 2 Macc. 6:12-31; 7:9.
4. 1 Macc. 7:12-18.

5. The Greek word here (*epanastasis*) translated as "demonstration" is usually understood to mean "insurrection," "revolt," or "uprising" (see, for example, *A Complete Concordance to Flavius Josephus,* vol. 2, ed. K. H. Rengstorf [Leiden: Brill, 1975], 135, or H. St. J. Thackeray's translation ["insurrection"] in the LCL). Josephus' use of *epanastasis* is a good example of his tendentious writing, since he does not describe an "insurrection" in the text which follows. What he does describe is a demonstration or civil disobedience against the action of Herod in putting up the golden eagle. The parallel account in *Ant.* does not employ *epanastasis.*

6. See M. Hengel, *Was Jesus a Revolutionist?* (Philadelphia: Fortress, 1971), 10-13, 32.

7. See *J.W.* 2.254-57, 264-65; *Ant.* 20.163-65, 187-88.

8. See *J.W.* 2.230-31, 245-46; *Ant.* 20.116-17, 134-36.

9. See T. H. Greene, *Comparative Revolutionary Movements* (Englewood Cliffs: Prentice-Hall, 1974), 77-79; H. E. Price, "The Strategy and Tactics of Revolutionary Terrorism," *Comparative Studies in Society and History* 19 (1977): 52-65; T. P. Thornton, "Terror as a Weapon of Political Agitation," in *Internal War,* ed. H. Eckstein (New York: Free, 1964), 71-99 [see the important critique by L. Stone, "Theories of Revolution," *World Politics* 18 (1966): 161, 175]; B. Crozier, *The Rebels: A Study of Post-War Insurrections* (Boston: Beacon, 1960), 159; M. C. Hutchinson, "The Concept of Revolutionary Terrorism," *Journal of Conflict Resolution* 16 (1971): 385, 388. These are standard studies of the phenomenon of terrorism.

10. Amar Ouzegane, *Le meilleur combat* (Paris: Julliard, 1962), 257.

11. *J.W.* 2.55-65, 228; *Ant.* 17.271-85; 20.113.

12. It is clearly about the Sicarii, as is evident from the duplication in *Ant.* 20.187-88.

13. V. I. Lenin, "The Collapse of the Second International" [1915], *Collected Works,* vol. 21 (Moscow: Progress, 1964), 213, quoted in R. Moss, *The War for the Cities* (New York: Coward, McCann & Geoghegan, 1972), 64-65.

14. E.g., Y. Yadin, *Masada: Herod's Fortress and the Zealots' Last Stand* (New York: Random, 1966). On the other hand, see R. A. Horsley, "The Sicarii: Ancient Jewish Terrorists," *JR* 59 (1979): 455, n. 62-63.

15. *J.W.* 7.437-40; see also *Ant.* 20.97-98, 169-71; *J.W.* 2.261-63.
16. It was in the aftermath of the Roman reconquest of Jotapata that Josephus himself deserted to the enemy, after persuading the rest of his colleagues to form a suicide pact. Of the group, he alone remained alive.
17. The passage is quoted on p. 82.
18. E.g., *J.W.* 4.443-51; 4.551-54. On Roman practices of slaughter and enslavement, see, for example, E. N. Luttwak, *The Grand Strategy of the Roman Empire* (Baltimore: Johns Hopkins, 1976), 21, 25-26, 32-33, 41-42, 46-47; R. Syme, "The Northern Frontiers under Augustus," *Cambridge Ancient History,* vol. 10, *The Augustan Empire, 44 B.C.-A.D. 70,* ed. S. A. Cook et al. (Cambridge: Cambridge University, 1963), 344-45, 348, 376.
19. See E. LeRoy Ladurie, *The Carnival of Romans* (New York: G. Braziller, 1980), chap. 8; J. Blum, *Lord and Peasant in Russia* (Princeton: Princeton University, 1961), 554-60.
20. See also *J.W.* 4.27-30, 53; 6.113-14.
21. See *J.W.* 4.438, 444, 629; 5.421-22; 6.113-15.
22. See, for example, D. Rhoads, *Israel in Revolution: 6-74 C.E.* (Philadelphia: Fortress, 1976), 97-110; G. Baumbach, "Die Zeloten: ihre geschichtliche und religionspolitische Bedeutung," *Bibel und Liturgie* 41 (1968): 8; M. Stern, "The Zealots," in *Encyclopedia Judaica,* suppl. vol., 1972, ed. C. Roth et al. (Jerusalem: Keter, 1974), 143-44, and "Sicarii and Zealots," in *World History of the Jewish People,* 1st ser., vol. 8, ed. M. Avi-Yonah (New Brunswick: Rutgers University, 1977), 296-97.
23. 1 Chron. 24:1-6; 25:8; 26:13.
24. E.g., Mt. 22:1-14//Lk. 14:15-24; Lk. 6:20-26; Mk. 10:23-31; see also E. Schüssler-Fiorenza, *In Memory of Her: A Feminist Theological Reconstruction of Christian Origins* (New York: Crossroad, 1983), 140-53.
25. *J.W.* 4.225; 5.56; 5.248-50.
26. See n. 22.
27. See J. Jeremias, *Jerusalem in the Time of Jesus* (Philadelphia: Fortress, 1969/1975).

CONCLUSION

A Typology of Popular Movements and Their Implications

Standard portrayals of first-century Jewish Palestine, the context of Jesus' career, tend to be somewhat simplistic and overly intellectualized. Much of the secondary literature in New Testament studies and Jewish history tends to focus primarily on the four principal "philosophies" or parties of the Jews: Sadducees, Pharisees, Essenes, and Zealots. Moreover, the secondary literature has emphasized *ideas* at the expense of other features because of the strong interest in Jewish messianic expectations which Christians believed were fulfilled in Jesus, and because of the keen interest in the Pharisaic origins of rabbinic teachings. This interest in expectations and ideas necessarily leads to the study of groups that left literary remains, thus reinforcing focus on groups such as the Pharisees and Essenes. However, the dramatic increase in our knowledge about the Essenes through the discovery of the Dead Sea Scrolls has only served to highlight how little we actually know about the Pharisees and Sadducees. Furthermore, we are beginning to recognize that we know far less than we thought about Jewish messianic expectations. The actual situation in Jewish Palestine, of course, was both more complex and more concrete than the standard portrayals allowed. In addition to the four "philosophies" among the literate, there were a number of other

244

social movements. These other movements were composed basically of peasants. It is thus important to recognize both the concrete reality and the specific diversity of these movements in developing a new understanding of the social history of Jewish Palestine.

Fortunately, the way toward a clearer recognition of the social realities of first-century Jewish Palestine has been made possible by the demise of the Zealots concept. The supposedly long-standing, organized, religiously motivated movement of national resistance to Roman domination has functioned both as a foil for interpretation of Jesus and as an explanation for the origins of the Jewish revolt against Rome. Once we recognize that no such movement of national liberation existed during the first century C.E., it is possible to begin to observe, and to pursue the implications of, the extreme diversity of forms of social unrest among Palestinian Jews at the time.

Perhaps the first step in moving toward a focus on the diversity of movements is to recognize that the differences between these movements did not constitute the primary conflict in the society. The fundamental conflict in Jewish Palestine was between the Jewish ruling groups and the Romans on the one side and the Jewish peasantry on the other. In this respect, Jesus shared the same basic concerns as the (other) popular leaders and movements. The Fourth Philosophy, the Sicarii, and probably most of the Pharisees among the literate groups, furthermore, in all likelihood shared these concerns of the common people as well, with certain variations. Thus, the discernment that all of the popular groups and leaders were rooted in, and responding to, the same general social situation and shared common concerns should then make it possible to place their differences in proper perspective.

The moving force toward change in the social situation almost always came from popular agitation of some sort. Short range and *ad hoc* forms of unrest such as angry urban mobs in Jerusalem, protest demonstrations, and peasant strikes arose from time to time. Most dramatic and historic in its effect was the spontaneous but long-lasting and wide-spread popular revolt of 66–70. Standard historical accounts of the period often mention these protests and the massive revolt, i.e., the phenomena which stand at both ends of a spectrum of social unrest. What remains almost unexamined are the many movements and leaders in the middle of that spectrum. These leaders or movements lasted anywhere from a few weeks to several years, and all of them assumed one or another distinctive social form, discernible through even the limited sources available to us.

The most elementary form of these popular movements was social banditry. Some of those who were forced off their land by economic pressures, or who came into political trouble with the ruling groups, banded together into "self-help" groups. They lived by plundering Roman baggage trains or by raiding border areas. Although the bandits remained in contact with villagers, who at times risked severe consequences to protect them, the Roman governors generally succeeded in their campaigns to suppress them. There is evidence of such bands of brigands from before Herod's rise to power right on through mid-first century C.E. Following the disastrous famine in the late forties, Jewish banditry escalated to epidemic proportions, and became a major factor at the outbreak of the Jewish revolt.

Much broader in scope and more serious in implications for Jewish society were the popular messianic movements. Following the death of Herod in 4 B.C.E., in the middle of the Jewish revolt, and then again sixty years after that, large numbers of Jewish peasants gathered around a charismatic leader whom they acclaimed as king. Under such elected (or, traditionally, "anointed") leaders they asserted their independence in armed rebellion. Depending on how quickly the Roman forces were able to reassert imperial control, these kings and their movements were able to govern their own territories for a few months or even for a few years.

Parallel, in some ways, to the messianic movements were the several prophetic movements which occurred around mid-first century C.E. "Prophets" inspired large groups of their followers to leave homes and fields to join in divinely led new actions of liberation from alien rule. Each of these prophetic movements was apparently inspired by some vision of an eschatological act of deliverance modeled after one of the great historical acts of salvation. These movements, usually ended by swift and deadly Roman military action, were much shorter-lived than the messianic movements.

Besides these prophets who led movements, there were also prophets who delivered oracles, of judgment or salvation. In a number of respects these oracular prophets appear similar to the classical oracular prophets of biblical tradition, such as Amos or Jeremiah. Although the Roman officials did not take such ecstatic rustics too seriously, they were clearly threatening to the Jewish ruling groups, who either persecuted or executed them.

The Zealots proper, the group actually called by that name, far from being a long-standing resistance organization, was merely one among several groups from among the Judean or Idumean peasantry which emerged in the middle of the great revolt and continued the armed resistance against the Roman legions. The Zealots were simply the first group to enter Jerusalem, but were quickly followed by others which were far more important in the final but ultimately futile resistance to the Roman siege of the holy city. Having formed as a coalition of brigand groups from the Judean countryside, the Zealots attempted to set up an alternative government in Jerusalem. After surviving an attack led by the high priestly junta which had controlled Jerusalem since the fall of 66, the Zealots themselves controlled the city for a brief interlude before Simon bar Giora and his sizable messianic movement entered the city and drove them back into their temple refuge.

There is no historical relationship whatever between the
Zealots proper and the Fourth Philosophy and the Sicarii,
two groups which have been included in the synthetic modern scholarly concept of "the Zealots." The Fourth Philosophy, founded by the teacher Judas of Galilee and the
Pharisee Saddok, was apparently an activist wing of Pharisees
and other intellectuals. Whereas other teachers and sages
also believed that God was the Jews' true and only Lord and
master, however, Judas and company were prepared actively
to oppose alien rule. Insisting that the Roman tribute would
constitute servitude to Caesar, they organized to resist the
census which accompanied the imposition of direct Roman
rule in Judea in 6 c.e. Thereafter we hear nothing more of
them.

The Sicarii, or "dagger men," emerged as a group in the
fifties c.e. The teachers who formed the group, apparently
concerned for the liberty of the Jewish people and perhaps
despairing over the increasingly oppressive circumstances
and the intransigence of both Jewish aristocracy and Roman
officials, concluded that the situation called for a desperate
and unprecedented new strategy. They thus inaugurated a
program of assassination and kidnapping against key, symbolic figures of the Jewish ruling circles who were collaborating with Roman rule. Then, after joining other groups who
were battling against Jewish aristocratic leaders and Roman
troops in Jerusalem at the outset of the great revolt in the
summer of 66, they withdrew from the hostilities when their
fellow Jewish insurgents turned on them—and sat out the
rest of the revolt atop Masada.

Each of these types of leaders and movements is distinctive in its characteristics. Some of the types of movements are
found in other societies and historical periods as well as in
ancient Jewish society. Thus, among intellectuals such as
teachers and lower clergy, groups organized to resist colonial rule are well known, especially in the twentieth century,
e.g., in Africa and the Middle East. Some of these groups
even engaged in a systematic campaign of terrorism against

their alien rulers. Cross-cultural analogies are also plentiful for the banditry and insurrectionary groups among the Jewish peasantry. Social banditry is found in most traditional agrarian societies, particularly when times are difficult for the peasantry. The mobilization of large forces of peasants to assert their independence of oppressive lords and alien rulers, particularly in circumstances which threaten the peasants' ability to continue their traditional way of life, is also now a familiar historical phenomenon, whether from sixteenth-century Germany, eighteenth-century France and Russia, or twentieth-century Mexico and China.

On the other hand, the rustic oracular prophets and both the popular messianic movements and the popular prophetic movements were all unique to ancient Jewish society, as there are no close parallels in other societies. In these cases the particular social forms were decisively influenced by distinctive traditions in ancient Israelite-Jewish culture. The sacred traditions included stories, apparently familiar to the common people as well as to the literate strata, of prophets such as Moses, Joshua, and Elijah or popularly anointed kings such as David leading their followers in resistance to domestic or foreign domination. In the case of oracular prophets, it appears that the phenomenon may simply never have completely died out, from the classical figures of Amos, Micah, or Jeremiah, through the rustics in hairy mantles in postexilic times, to the appearance of figures such as Jesus son of Hananiah in the first century c.e. The appearance of groups or leaders of these types required a certain sophistication of historical memory and social organization among the Jewish peasantry. For a popular movement to have taken the explicit form of a prophetic movement instead of a riot, or of a messianic movement instead of uncoordinated brigand bands, required a memory of a particular historical tradition, of the ancient prophetic movements or of the prototypical messianic movements, and the application of the remembered paradigm to the new situation.

All of these various types of movements occurred during a period of Jewish history in which an apocalyptic spirit was apparently widespread, at least in times of tension and conflict. The evidence for our sense that there was a mood of imminent eschatological expectation in the society generally comes mostly from apocalyptic literature and the Christian Gospels. For a possible apocalyptic spirit among the popular movements and leaders, however, we have little direct evidence, largely because our principal source, Josephus, avoids distinctive Palestinian Jewish imagery and ideas. Nevertheless, in a few cases the apocalyptic perspective and motivation can be observed or deduced. John the Baptist apparently preached an imminent eschatological judgment. Some of the other oracular prophets, particularly those at the time of the Jewish revolt, proclaimed an imminent deliverance, for example, by means of the heavenly armies, imagery well known from contemporary apocalyptic literature. The type of movement most clearly caught up in an apocalyptic frame of mind was that of the popular prophetic movement. These prophets and their followers conceived of the solution to their intolerable situation in terms of a new, eschatological enactment of one of the great historical acts of deliverance. Convinced of the imminence of divine action, they abandoned their homes to participate in the anticipated deliverance. We have no corresponding evidence for the possible eschatological orientation or heightened anticipatory mood in any of the other groups. We can only surmise that the popular messianic movements were motivated by an eager yearning for deliverance (as well as by pent-up frustration at the intolerable conditions). Both the epidemic banditry and the Sicarii, moveover, would appear to have been caught up in a heightened anticipation of liberation at the beginning of the Jewish revolt.

Closely related to the possible eschatological orientation of the popular Jewish leaders and movements would have been their degree of critical sociopolitical awareness. As in other societies, banditry in Jewish Palestine was likely "prepolitical," a serious but nonrevolutionary protest. Jewish brigand bands apparently lacked a conscious political understanding of what was wrong with the social situation and an idea of how to alleviate it. Nothing indicates that they had any idea of, or took any action toward, bringing about change in the social order. Historically, although Jewish banditry certainly evoked repression by the authorities, it also functioned to maintain certain actual and symbolic checks on oppression by Roman and Jewish ruling groups. The popular prophetic movements were also probably "pre-political" in the sense of lacking a conscious understanding of the social-economic forces affecting the intolerable situation of the people. Yet the historical prototypes of liberation on which they patterned their action included rather distinctive images of political domination. In contrast with mere banditry, moreover, the prophetic movements were fired by a hope, if not an actual program, for the liberated character of their society. More than any of the other movements or leaders, the consciousness and actions of the popular prophets and their movements were directly informed by the religious-political traditions of historical deliverance. Thus, like the Qumranites, they may well have expected the new exodus and gift of land to be followed by renewal of the covenantal society.

In comparison with the prophetic movements, the oracular prophets and the messianic movements were more politically aware. The oracular prophets seem to have taken the concrete political power situation into account, whether consciously or subconsciously. They did not hesitate to deliver sharp pronouncements of judgment. Yet they did not take individual or collective action which would inevitably have provoked the threatened ruling groups to send out the troops. More than the prophetic movements, and far more than banditry, the messianic movements possessed a clear political awareness. They were more cognizant of the concrete political situation than were the prophetic movements: they at least knew that self-defense was necessary. In contrast with both the prophetic movements and banditry, moreover, the popular kings and their followers not only took direct political action to claim control of their own lives and territories, they also took measures to restore just social-economic relations, such as the liberation of (debt-) slaves. In their eagerness to overthrow the reign of injustice, however, these kings and their followers obviously had no sense of the overwhelming military might of the Roman empire and of the inevitability of Roman reconquest of the land.

In comparison with all of these popular groups, the Sicarii possessed, and were motivated by, a high degree of political awareness. Whereas the other groups were spontaneous movements composed largely of peasants, the Sicarii were led by intellectuals who reflectively and deliberately formulated a long-range strategy. They were hardly "primitive rebels" like the brigand groups with which they have often been confused. Rather they pursued a strategy deliberately calculated to deal with their situation. They were not able, and perhaps did not attempt, to build a social-political base among the peasantry or common people of Jerusalem. When the widespread revolt finally erupted, they appeared to be somewhat isolated, from popular groups on the one side and the Jerusalemites on the other. Finally, of course, in contrast with the largely peasant groups who carried resistance against Rome to the bitter end, the Sicarii simply withdrew to Masada, where they became another chapter in the history of martyrs to the radical faith in the one true Lord of history. Perhaps they did this because they knew resistance was ultimately futile.

The Zealots proper, finally, although they originated as a spontaneous response to Roman reconquest of Judea in 67–68, also pursued a conscious political strategy. They brought members of the (to them) oppressive ruling groups to justice. They countered the political strategy of the high priestly group still in control in Jerusalem, and implemented a more egalitarian theocracy, with commoners selected by lot for the high offices and themselves observing collective decision-making. Although their numbers were small in comparison with the other popular groups which continued the resistance to Rome, the historical significance of the Zealots derives from the conscious political actions they took in Jerusalem. That is, they successfully challenged and blocked the strategy of the high priestly government still in control in Jerusalem in 67–68. They thus provided time for other popular groups such as the Idumeans and Simon bar Giora's movement to mobilize in the countryside and to continue popular attempts to preserve their recently regained liberty.

Because it has been such an important issue in the historically ill-founded and misleading "Jesus and the Zealots" debate, we should give at least some attention to the matter of violent versus nonviolent action on the part of these movements. Clearly the issue is far more complex than that often posed between Jesus as the teacher of nonviolence and a resistance movement as practitioners of violence. The social level or stratum and the situation in which violent or nonviolent behavior occurs are important factors which have not often been considered. Action by the ruling groups was almost always violent, manifest in the very conditions which gave rise to the various kinds of movements. The Romans conquered and continued their control by violent means, including intimidation by terror. Herod maintained security by means of repressive violence. The high priests preyed violently upon and tortured their own people. At the middle, literate stratum of society, nonviolence, or rather calculated nonaction, characterized most of the Pharisees, at least from Herodian times onward. With this the calculated terrorism by the Sicarii stands in stark contrast, especially considering that, as teachers, and perhaps the continuation of the Fourth Philosophy, the Sicarii may have shared some of the basic religious-political principles with many Pharisees. At the popular level we find little or no calculation, but spontaneous action, violent or nonviolent depending on the occasion and the movement. The nonviolent prophetic movements were clearly responses to an anticipated divine transformation of the intolerable situation. The brigands' violent action was a matter of simple survival when, in effect, there was no alternative means of survival. The popular messianic movements were apparently spontaneous attempts to seize an opportunity of claiming their own independence with arms against the establishment's attempts to reassert control by violent reconquest.

Although a more adequate exploration would require far more extended discussion, we can at least touch on the implications of the various types of popular leaders and movements for both the origins of the great Jewish revolt of 66-70 and the career of Jesus and origins of the church.

It is clear that the Jewish revolt was not the result of any long-standing resistance movement agitating for decades until finally touching off a more widespread national insurrection against the Romans. Indeed, the Zealots proper, far from being a principal cause of the revolt, were themselves a product of the Roman reconquest once the revolt was well under way. The social-historical situation leading up to the outbreak of popular rebellion in 66 was complex and the "causes" of the revolt multiple. Most of the popular movements examined above, however, were not so much contributing causes as symptoms of the more causative conditions.

The most important dimensions of the complex situation leading toward the revolt were probably the deteriorating economic conditions of the peasantry and the disintegrating social structure, at both the village and the society-wide levels. The prolonged drought and serious famine in the late forties, for example, exacerbated the already difficult conditions. Banditry, especially as it increased in scope from midcentury onward, was one very dramatic and revealing symptom of the economic deterioration and social disintegration. Thus it would be rather superficial analysis to conclude that even widespread banditry was a cause of the revolt. Of course, widespread banditry combined with sharply renewed repressive measures by the Roman forces may have contributed to the increasing social disintegration in the years immediately preceding the revolt, and already existing bandit groups provided experienced fighters for the popular armies once the revolt broke out. The popular prophets of both types, similarly, are symptoms of the deteriorating state of affairs. Moreover, whether it be in the sense of foreboding in the oracles of Jesus son of Hananiah or in the desperate search for renewed divine deliverance in the actual movements, these prophetic phenomena provide revealing indicators that something was seriously wrong in the social-economic order of society. The messianic movement gathered around Simon bar Giora, furthermore, like the similarly spontaneous movements in 4 B.C.E., was the form which the popular uprising took in the countryside, and not a cause of the revolt which had erupted long since.

The only group which might have contributed actively to the outbreak of the revolt was the Sicarii, a group led by intellectuals and not a peasant movement. The terrorist acts of the Sicarii may have provoked the ruling groups to become even more tightly repressive in their anxiety, thus contributing to the general deterioration of the social order. Not the popular groups, however, but the ruling groups would appear to have been contributing factors to the outbreak of the revolt. Even though he is writing with the Romans in mind, Josephus himself places considerable blame on the Roman governors in the years preceding the revolt. In particular Josephus declares explicitly that the governor Gessius Florus (64-66) provoked the desperate rebellion by his arrogant and provocative actions (*Ant.* 18. 1-25). Similarly, in this same passage and elsewhere, Josephus himself views the predatory behavior by the high priestly families and the Herodians as a serious contribution to the disintegration of the social order. The popular movements must be seen not as causes of the revolt, but rather as either symptoms or signals of deteriorating social conditions, or as one form (messianic movement) which the popular uprising assumed once it broke out.

The popular leaders and movements, finally, may have certain implications for our understanding of Jesus of Nazareth and the early Church. Because it has been presupposed and embodied in so much secondary literature in New Testament and theological studies, it will continue to be important to push the old "Zealots" concept out of our minds, that is, to avoid falling into the old discussions of "Jesus and the Zealots." It may help to remind ourselves that the Zealots proper did not originate as a group until almost forty years after the career of Jesus, i.e., until the gospel traditions had taken shape and until almost the time when the first Gospel, Mark, was written (usually dated in the sixties or seventies). Some of the other movements, however, may be useful for our understanding of Jesus.

Study of Jewish social banditry may shed some light on the way in which Jesus was arrested (as if a brigand, Mk. 14:48) and on the crucifixion scene, in which Jesus was crucified with two brigands (not thieves, Mk. 15:27). More importantly, the occurrence of banditry illustrates the disintegrating social conditions in which Jesus' words and actions would have found a resonant response.

The frequent occurrence of popular groups with the particular social forms of messianic and prophetic movements has far more significance for the study of Jesus and early Palestinian Christianity. As noted above, there is little evidence for Jewish *expectations* of a messiah or a prophet. This makes all the more significant the occurrence and actual social forms of popular movements gathered, respectively, around a popularly recognized king or prophet. These social forms must have been familiar precisely in villages such as those from which Jesus and his first followers came. Of course, some of the significant facets of Jesus are so different from the characteristic features of the popular kings and their movements that it is not surprising to find that the social

form of popular kingship is not prominent in gospel traditions about Jesus' activity in Galilee. To be sure, there is also
no opposition to such a form in the gospel traditions, except
for the (late) sayings in the "Synoptic Apocalypse" in Mk. 13
(see esp. Mk. 13:5-6, 21-22) and the report in Jn. 6:15. The
popular kings and their movements do give us some comparative materials for pondering the significance of Jesus'
actions once he turns toward Jerusalem, the reasons behind
the inscription on the cross (king of the Jews), and the reasons for Jesus quickly receiving the designation "Christ"
following the crucifixion and resurrection.

The two types of popular prophets clearly provide the
most potentially fruitful comparative materials for exploration of aspects of Jesus' career. Judging from the earliest
strata of the Christian gospel traditions, Jesus displays more
similarities to these prophetic figures than to the popular
kings. For example, Jesus' lament over Jerusalem (Lk. 13:34-
35 par) and other woes sound quite similar to the oracle of
doom pronounced by Jesus son of Hananiah. In a general
way, gospel traditions consistently associate Jesus and John
the Baptist, the latter clearly an oracular prophet. Behind the
various apologetic stances of the evangelists with regard to
John the Baptist lies the possibility that Jesus and his followers historically had roots in the activity and proclamation of
the Baptist. Furthermore, the parallels between Jesus and the
traditions about Elijah and Elisha have often been noted,
both in terms of a prophet who makes pronouncements and
in terms of one who forms a movement by calling followers
(with both aspects being reinforced by the parallel of heal-
ing miracles). There is a special twist in a final example:
some of the *sayings* of Jesus are similar in their typological
pattern to the *actions* of the prophetic movements. That is,
the historical-eschatological typology seen in the new exodus or new conquest led by popular action prophets is evident in certain sayings of Jesus with the pattern of "as it was
in the days of old . . . so now will it be. . . ."

Perhaps precisely to head off any reversion to the misleading discussions of "Jesus and the Zealots," we should also
note the ways in which the resistance groups led by teachers
and sages may provide useful comparative material. As noted
above, the Fourth Philosophy, since it apparently did not
engage in armed revolt, cannot be used as a foil for Jesus'
(supposed) teaching of nonviolence. However, the more
precise issue of tribute to Caesar, which Judas and his colleagues brought to a head in 6 c.e. remained a prominent
one, as can be seen in Jesus' controversy with the Pharisees
and Herodians in Jerusalem (Mk. 12:13-17). Lest the false
foil of "the Zealots" be allowed to slip back in through the
"dagger men," it is important again to remind ourselves that
this activist group of intellectuals, the Sicarii, did not
become active until twenty-five or thirty years after the death
of Jesus. Moreover, the tactics of the Sicarii are such a distinctive aberration from anything in any other group we know of
throughout this whole period, that it hardly seems appropriate to elevate it into one of the principal foils for interpretation of Jesus.

The Zealots proper, who emerged as a group nearly forty
years after Jesus' career, may provide a useful comparison for
some aspects of early Palestinian Christianity, if not for Jesus
himself. In an extreme emergency situation in Jerusalem in
68, the Zealots attempted to set up an egalitarian social-
political-religious order among their number. The early Palestinian followers of Jesus, of course, had been doing something similar to this for over a generation by then, only in
more normal circumstances in towns and villages. Insofar as
the renewal of covenantal community by the followers of
Jesus may have been initiated by Jesus himself, then the
Galilean peasant leader Jesus of Nazareth would have given
earlier expression to a current of religious-social renewal of
sacred Jewish covenantal traditions, which finds similar
expression among Judean peasants in a later situation of
crisis. Violent reimposition of the *pax Romana,* of course,
simply ended both the Zealots' utopian social experiment in

Jerusalem and the longer-lived communities of Jesus' followers in Palestine. This also meant that little survived of the concrete movement started by Jesus in Palestinian Jewish society and that the Christian church developed out of other communities which by then had become well established outside of Jewish Palestine.

ROMAN EMPERORS	HIGH PRIESTS	OFFICIAL RULERS & PROCURATORS IN PALESTINE			BANDITS	MESSIAHS	PROPHETS
Augustus (30 BCE-14 CE)	Joazar son of Boethus (4 BCE) Eleazar son of Boethus (4-? BCE) Jesus son of See(?) Ananus son of Sethi (6-15 CE)	Herod the Great (37-4 BCE) Herod Archelaus *Ethnarch of Judea* (4 BCE-6 CE) Coponius (6-9 CE) Marcus Ambibulus (9-12 CE)	Herod Philip *Tetrarch of Iturea* (4 BCE-34 CE)	Herod Antipas *Tetrarch of Galilee* (4 BCE-39 CE)	Hezekiah (c. 47-38 BCE)	Judas son of Hezekiah [Ezekias] (c. 4 BCE) Simon (c. 4 BCE) Athronges (c. 4-2? BCE)	
Tiberius (14-37 CE)	Ismael son of Phiabi (15-16 CE) Eleazar son of Ananus (16-17 CE) Simon son of Camithus (17-18 CE) Joseph Caiaphas (18-36 CE) Jonathan son of Ananus (36-37 CE)	Annius Rufus (12-15 CE) Valerius Gratus (15-26 CE) Pontius Pilate (26-36 CE) Marcellus (36-37 CE)	[Iturea, Batanea, Trachonitus and Auranitis attached to Province of Syria (34-41 CE)]		Galilean Cave Brigands (30s CE)		John the Baptist (late 20s CE) The "Samaritan" (c. 26-36 CE)
Gaius Caligula (37-41 CE)	Theophilus son of Ananus (37-? CE)	Marullus (37-41 CE)		Herod Agrippa I (40 CE)	Eleazar ben Dinai (30s-50s CE)		
Claudius (41-54 CE)	Simon Cantheras son of Boethus (41-? CE) Matthias son of Ananus (41-44 CE) Elionaeus son of Cantherus (44?-46? CE)	Herod Agrippa I (41-44 CE) Fadus (44-46 CE)			Tholomaus (early 40s CE)		Theudas (c. 45 CE)

High Priests	Procurators	Rebel Leaders	Prophetic Figures
Joseph son of Camei (46-48 CE)	Tiberius Alexander (46-48 CE)		
Ananias son of Nedebaeus (c. 47-59 CE)	Ventidius Cumanus (48-52 CE)		
	Felix (52-60 CE)		The "Egyptian" (c. 56 CE)
Ismael son of Phiabi (59-61 CE)	Porcius Festus (60-62 CE)	Jesus son of Sapphias (60s CE)	
Joseph Cabi son of Simon (61-62 CE)			Jesus son of Hananiah (62-69 CE)
Ananus son of Ananus (62 CE)	Albinus (62-64 CE)		
Jesus son of Damnaeus (62-63 CE)			
Jesus son of Gamaliel (63-64 CE)	Gessius Florus (64-66 CE)		
Matthias son of Theophilus (65-?)		John of Gischala (66-? CE)	
		Menahem son of Judas the Galilean (c. 66 CE)	
Phanni son of Samuel (68-70 CE)	Zealot Coalition (68-69 CE)	Simon bar Giora (68-70 CE)	
	Simon bar Giora (69-70 CE)		
		Bar Kochba (132-135 CE)	

Emperors:

Nero (54-68 CE)

Galba (68-69 CE)
Otho (69 CE)
Vitellius (69 CE)
Vespasian (69-79 CE)

Titus (79-81 CE)
Domitian (81-96 CE)
Nerva (96-98 CE)
Trajan (98-117 CE)
Hadrian (117-135 CE)

PALESTINE IN THE FIRST CENTURY C.E.

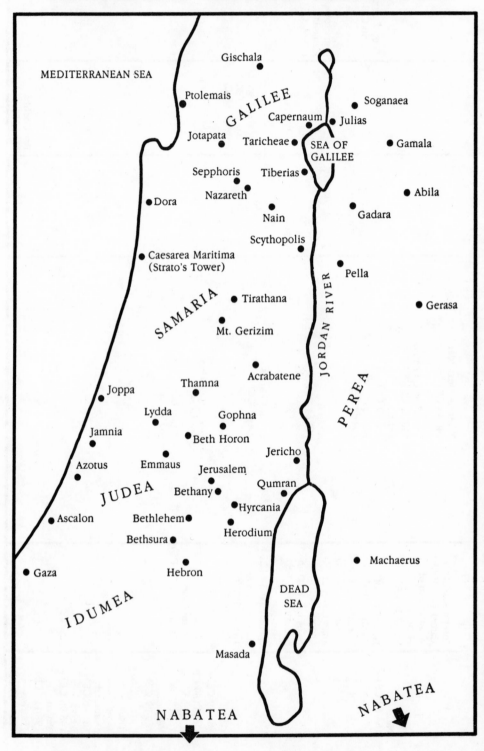

Index of Citations

Hebrew Scriptures

Other Greek and Latin Authors

Rabbinic Literature

Dead Sea Scrolls

Index of Modern Authors